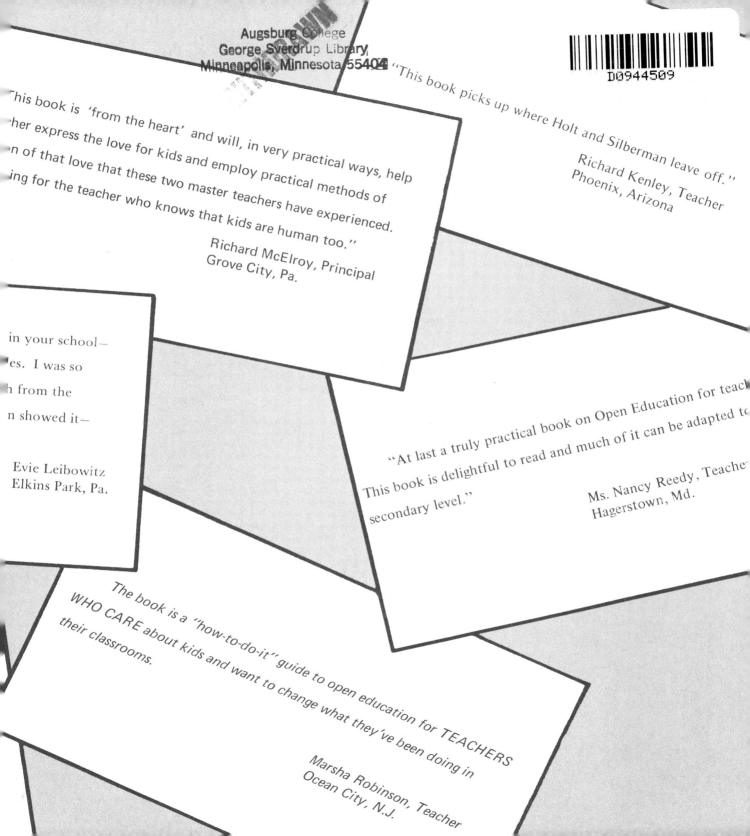

"This book is 'from the heart' and will, in very practical ways, help
...her express the love for kids and employ practical methods of
...n of that love that these two master teachers have experienced.
...ing for the teacher who knows that kids are human too."

Richard McElroy, Principal
Grove City, Pa.

"This book picks up where Holt and Silberman leave off."

Richard Kenley, Teacher
Phoenix, Arizona

in your school—
...es. I was so
...h from the
...n showed it—

Evie Leibowitz
Elkins Park, Pa.

"At last a truly practical book on Open Education for teach...
This book is delightful to read and much of it can be adapted t...
secondary level."

Ms. Nancy Reedy, Teache...
Hagerstown, Md.

The book is a "how-to-do-it" guide to open education for TEACHERS
WHO CARE about kids and want to change what they've been doing in
their classrooms.

Marsha Robinson, Teacher
Ocean City, N.J.

John pflum / anita hanks waterman

the new **open education:**
A PROGRAM FOR COMBINING THE
BASICS WITH ALTERNATIVE METHODS

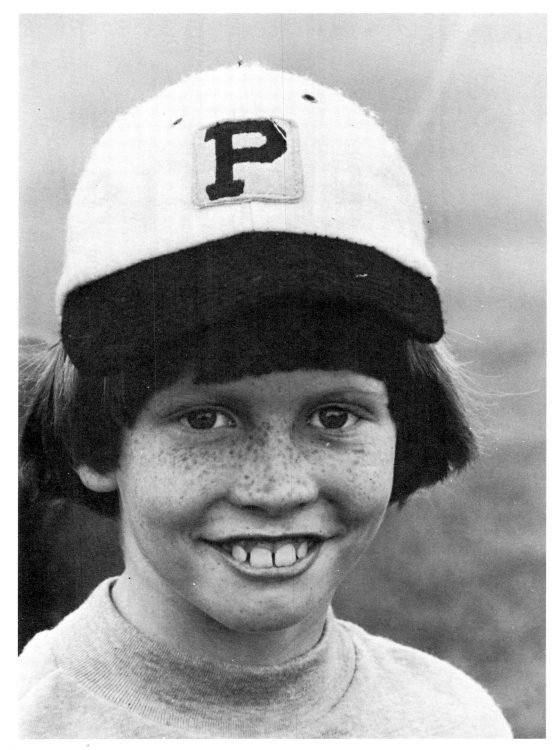

Each child is unique.

"Freedom with Responsibility"

the new OPen education:

A PROGRAM FOR COMBINING THE BASICS WITH ALTERNATIVE METHODS

John pflum / anita hanks waterman

Photos by RON BOWMAN
College Photographer, Millersville State College, Pennsylvania

ACROPOLIS BOOKS FOR Contemporary EDUCATION

PUBLISHED BY **ACROPOLIS BOOKS LTD.** • WASHINGTON, D.C. 20009

THE ACROPOLIS CONTEMPORARY EDUCATION SERIES

ACKNOWLEDGMENTS

Grateful acknowledgment is made to the people below for permission to reprint their materials. Without their contributions, this book could not have been written.

Frederick County School District, Frederick, Md., and especially Nancy Watkins, Alonzo Peters, Neil Shipman, Edward Hallock, Kyle Pritts, Nancy Hendricks, Oliver Crouse, Richard Van Tries, Richard Petre, Iris Zimmerman, Jean Stine, Jeanette Tuck, Patricia Brown, Ann Kupferberg, Marjorie Reid, Delmar Rippeon, Nancy Greenwood, Sandra Wiebel, Audrey Baumgardner, Dawn Stine, Florence Thackston for the Leveled Communication Skills Sequence and Accompanying Evaluation Instruments (pp. 229-348).

Mary Ann Heltshe, Millersville State College, Millersville, Pa., for the Sample Report Letter (pp. 193-194).

Tompkins B. Smith, Assistant Superintendent of Schools, Lancaster City School District, Lancaster, Pa., for the Sample Report Card (pp. 196-198).

Judi Sheer, Millersville State College, for What is Team Teaching? (pp.65-66).

Karen Herceg, Millersville State College, for Sample Learning Station (pp. 151-158, 400-407).

Lori Reynolds, Tom Wee, and Kristen Meier, Elizabeth Jenkins School, Millersville, Pa., for Sample Learning Stations (pp. 408-409).

Marjorie Hammond, Fort Frye Elementary School, Beverly, Ohio, for Leveled Mathematics Skill Sequence (pp. 349-352).

Grace Karsnitz, Annville Cleona School District, Annville, Pa., for Topical Social Studies Skills Sequence (pp. 380-385).

Diane Kyle, Millersville State College, for Sample Packet (pp. 124-135, 391-399).

Ira Light, Open Space Coordinator, Millersville State College, for List of Kits and Materials (pp. 225-228).

Fred Goudy, Millersville State College, for Cartoons for Learning Station (p. 152).

Graduate Class, Millersville State College, for Wild and Wacky Ideas for Creative Writing (pp. 40, 224).

Ron Bowman, Photographer, Millersville State College, for all photographs in this book.

Reprinted in 1975.

© *Copyright 1974 by John Pflum and Anita Hanks Waterman*

Library of Congress Catalog Number 74-3468
Standard Book No. 87491-392-6

Printed in the United States of America by
Colortone Press Creative Graphics, Inc.
Washington, D.C. 20009

ACROPOLIS BOOKS LTD.
Colortone Building, 2400 17th St., N.W.
Washington, D.C. 20009

```
Library of Congress Cataloging in Publication Data

Pflum, John, 1934-
   Open education:  for me?

   Bibliography:  p.
   1.  Open plan schools.  I.  Waterman, Anita Hanks,
1938-    joint author.  II.  Title.
LB1029.06P45      372.1'3            74-3468
ISBN 0-87491-396-9
```

Dedicated to forward-thinking,

unselfish, cooperative educators

everywhere—who care—but most especially

to Ray, Gwen, Judi, Audrey,

Yvonne, Mary Ann, and Alice.

Open Education is caring.

FOREWORD

To parents, teachers, administrators, and school board members everywhere:

We all agree schools must change to meet the challenging demands of our society, but, some of us, because of tradition, caution, or fright have decided to move slowly.

This book is *not* a dream to think about until the year 2074.

It is a NOW book, a practical, how-to-do-it guide for change that can be brought about here and now in one classroom or in a whole school. For this reason it is written in a practical, how-to-do-it, informal style, as if the authors were talking with you rather than lecturing at you.

It *does not* suggest that a child do "his own thing" from morning until afternoon.

It *does* suggest that the child should *play a role* in deciding what he ought to do.

It *does not* suggest that everyone do the same thing at the same time.

It *does* suggest that we try to meet each child's individual needs.

It *does not* suggest having no schedule and a laissez-faire attitude.

It *does* suggest a flexible schedule, providing opportunities for children to make choices and decisions, and giving children chances to assume responsibility for their own behavior and learning.

The book *does not* tell you how to have an open program *only if* you're in a shiny new $3,000,000 open-space school.

It *does* tell you how to begin in your self-contained classroom; it encourages you to begin team-teaching, and to consider a non-graded, continuous-progress program.

You will *not* find elaborate, sophisticated, research-oriented chapters on the rationale for an open concept school.

It *does* assume that you believe in opening up education and it does tell you in easy-to-understand language how to use techniques such as learning stations and contracts.

The book *was not* written by people who have not been in an elementary classroom for twenty-five years.

It *was* written by people with a totally professional background in elementary education—people who are actually working in an open concept school. One is the director of the school and the other is the former team leader of the intermediate unit of the school; both were directly involved in changing the school from self-contained classroom units to an open concept program.

The book was written because we, the authors, feel a genuine concern for the children in today's classrooms. We know most teachers care about children, but for one reason or another, they've been teaching content, not children. Some have known the system was wrong, but now teachers everywhere are beginning to realize that the students in their classrooms are human beings, and deserve to be treated as such.

Our plea is to humanize education. We want to show you that by opening up your minds and your hearts, you can open up education, care for and meet the needs of individual children, and still teach the children.

We have looked into the future, and we see children mapping out their entire programs, working on subject matter that interests them at their rate, and adhering to no formal schedule. But we know the steps to reach this goal must be carefully taken. We must know where we're going and minimize the possibility of error. Our educational system is not ready for this concept on a broad scale *YET;* parents aren't, administrators aren't, teachers aren't, and kids aren't.

The steps we've outlined in this book are only a beginning but if we change just some of the things we do, we will have advanced one level. Then, only a level beyond will be truly individualized instruction, which strangely enough, has been listed as one of education's immediate goals *for the past hundred years.*

Contents

Chapters

*In the paperback edition pp. 219-410 have been published separately as a Teaching Materials Kit for individual classroom use. Part Two is available from the publisher, Acropolis Books Ltd., 2400 17th Street, N.W., Washington, D.C. 20009, at $5.95 per copy.

PART ONE

CHAPTER I

A Ray
of Sunshine

EACH OF US in our lifetime, at one time or another, encounters something that gives us a special kind of feeling—that creates in us an unqualified excitement about life and our place in it.

The open concept in education has done this for us. It has brought meaning to our professional existence and it has given us new hope for our educational system and for our society.

Why get so excited over something new? New things are just fads! They come, go and recycle. The new "gimmicks" fit this description. But, from our point of view, the open concept is here to stay—here to stay because it provides a milieu out of which can come an implementation of those things we hold dear in this country. It provides an opportunity for human concern to span the fissures of our society and embody itself in the one

place it can recreate itself and chain react—our schools. It is, in effect, a ray of hope, a ray of sunshine in our future.

School is the one place in our society where we get all the children together. This is the one place where we have a chance to reach enough people to effect change on a broad scale. This is "where it's at"; the open concept in education is "where it's at." You can be a part of this movement. You can help get it all together, so, don't miss out, join us in leaving your mark. Join us in making the world a better place for children and for us.

"How?" you ask. We'll begin by beginning at the beginning. The beginning is Chapter I of this book. It is the only chapter that discusses philosophy or rationale in general terms. The rest of the book is devoted to specifics that tell you how. Chapter I, we feel, helps you to understand the why for the how, and the how makes more sense when you know why, right? Well, anyhow, here we go.

In talking with 7,000 teachers in the past three years, we've developed an approach to the rationale for open education that makes sense to us. We've decided to use that approach here.

The chapter is organized to deal with the following topics:

- The Problem of Meaning

- Trust

- Decision Making

- Responsibility and Freedom

- Punishment

- Socialization

- Self-concept

THE PROBLEM OF MEANING

Perhaps it is justifiable to begin this discussion of open concept education by attempting to relate the open concept to life. A basic concern of every human being is the problem of life's meaning. What is life and what is our role in life? What does it mean to each of us? These are broad-based philosophical questions. We certainly will not

attempt to answer them, but we will attempt to discuss the school and its role in helping each of us to find our own answers.

We are the product of the total of our experiences. One experience almost all of us in this country have in common is a school experience. School has been a part of each of our lives. It will be a part of each child's life. It must have some influence on the lifestyle of the people it touches. Since the school is an inevitable part of our life, it must play a role in helping us to arrive at some conclusions to the problem of life's meaning.

The open concept suggests this is a responsibility of the school and should be provided for in the structure of our programs. When an examination is made we find much that is being done in the name of scholarship and education aimed at influencing our children. There is no denying that learning is good. We should encourage scholarly pursuit and research; we should acquaint the young with our cultural heritage. It certainly is commendable that we attempt to help people use the methods of science to influence their thinking about current problems. However, it is difficult to deny that the students' undertakings are often rather empty. There is much that is meaningless along the academic road from the nursery school to the doctorate degree. Much of what goes on consists of scholarly motions—motions 15 lacking the vital spark of personal concern. The search for meaning in life is not a search for either abstract or concrete knowledge; it is a distinctly personal search. It raises the basic question, "What really counts for me?"

Existence as a human being in relationship to other human beings is a real concern to every individual. Each person asks, "Who am I?" Each must seek the answer to this question for himself. Hopefully each of us will develop an attitude of self-respect, which in turn will enable us to demonstrate a genuine concern for others.

This is where the open concept of education can come into play in terms of our lives. It is a concept which attempts to help each of us arrive at a point of self-respect and understanding that enables us to demonstrate a genuine concern for others. It gives each of us a chance to know ourselves, and our relationship to others, well enough so that we can begin to arrive at some conclusions about our problem of meaning. It does this through design, not chance. It puts us on the spot in terms of finding ways to meet the goals of an educational system that alludes to love, concern, respect, and individuality for every human being.

There is something wrong when we state goals that allude to these qualities and we engage in behavior that has the opposite effect.

The open concept in education suggests that we need to get our goals and our behavior together. We have got to help people reach some conclusions about the problem of meaning in their lives. It is only through solving that problem that people can turn their attention to the broader problem of man's relation to man.

TRUST

Trust is either directly stated or implied in the philosophies that guide our educational efforts. The implication of trust as it is alluded to in our schools is that we want children to be trusted to learn to accept the responsibility for their own behavior and learning.

We not only write about these ideas, but we also verbalize them, and yet our behavior shouts out to the children, "We don't trust you."

Two tragic examples of this come too easily to mind—one is the 10 o'clock syndrome in our elementary schools. Ten o'clock is bathroom time. If you're a child, you line up and go. You line up at 10 o'clock and go to the "john," then you go out to play, then you get a drink of water and return to your seat. Inevitably the water goes to work and someone asks to go. We've heard teachers say, "Is it necessary?" and have even heard them say "Wiggle," or "You were just there," or whatever.

16

The tragic part is that we establish this procedure because we don't trust them to go to the bathroom alone. All the wonderful reasons in the world still don't mask the reality—lack of trust.

Will they learn trust in such a setting? We doubt it. Do they know why they must march in line? Whether they say it or not, we believe they know.

Why can't we trust them? We know we can trust possibly 22 of them if we've got 25. Why, at least, can't these 22 go when they've got to? Take those three by the hand and march them to the bathroom, but trust the others. In fact, start out trusting them all and then march those who prove they can't be trusted. Do we teach trust and responsibility when we behave like this? No, we're teaching just the opposite of what we want to teach.

Another example that points out the carry-over of our efforts is found in the high school. There are 2,000 students in a high school and all 2,000, in order to get into the hall, must have one of those pink slips commonly referred to as a hall pass. Again when we examine why hall passes are used, we find there are possibly 200 people we can't trust, so everyone has to have a pass.

We've heard the cries of "What else are we going to do?" We'd suggest looking for another solution, or at least admitting the real reasons for the one we've chosen.

What we've identified are examples of a cross-purpose in terms of our goals and our behavior. Why can't we be consistent? If we believe that trust is a worthy objective to pursue in our educational system, then let's pursue it. If we can't, then let's change the goal to suit our behavior.

But changing our goals is unthinkable, to us. Our goals for education in this society are beautiful. We believe that if anything should be changed, it must be our behavior, and our behavior then must be consistent with our goals. (We feel the vibrations—you're going to try to let your students go to the bathroom when they have to. Good for you—that's step one!)

DECISION MAKING

One of the vital concerns in our society is developing the ability to make decisions. This ability should be fostered in our school programs. Decision making is an aspect of our classrooms that has a powerful impact on our children. The structure of decision making in our classrooms needs to be more flexible, and needs to be designed to provide opportunities for the child to make some decisions.

However, when we examine the structure of decision making in the classroom we find some startling data. The interaction analysis studies Flanders*

*Ned A. Flanders, *Interaction Analysis in the Classroom*, Rev. Ed. (Ann Arbor: Univ. of Michigan, 1966).
Edmund J. Amidon, Interaction Analysis: Recent Development, Paper—A.E.R.A., February, 1966.

and Amidon conducted, and the replications of these studies, produced the same set of data. This data substantiates that teachers in the classroom talk two-thirds of the time. The two-thirds of the time they are talking, they are lecturing, giving directions, or criticizing. Well, if that's what's going on, at best, the children could only play a one-third role in the decision making of the classroom. Who's making the decisions when the teacher is talking two-thirds of the time? The answer is obvious. And what about that one-third of the time that's left? If we take a look at that time—we find that about 13 percent of it is quiet time. We need quiet time in our classrooms. Children need time to think and work in a quiet way, no one can knock quiet time. But where do the children get involved in the interaction? Just where can they begin to interact verbally?

About 10 percent of the time the teacher and child are involved in questions and answers. At last the child finally gets a chance to open his mouth. But what do we find? Upon examination of the questions, we discover that we're asking questions with presupposed answers. We ask, "What are the causes of the Civil War?" and a child says, "states' rights," and we say, "No, that's not what *I'm* looking for. Who knows what *I'm* looking for?" And another child puts his hand up and says, "slavery," and the teacher says, "Yes, that's what *I'm* looking for!" But what are *we* looking for? What's wrong with "states' rights" as an answer to that question, if a child can justify that answer? Do teachers give children a chance to justify their answers? We don't think so, because when we look at the analysis of teacher interaction in the classroom, we find an awfully high percentage of questions being asked with obvious or predetermined answers. Is decision making allowed in that kind of setting? We don't believe it is. And so we have a child who plays only a 5 or 10 percent role in what's happening in the classroom in terms of making decisions. The evidence suggests that is what happens in most classrooms, and we also believe that the implications of this in any one year of the child's life aren't really very foreboding. A child can overcome one year, but how about thirteen years of that? How about a thirteen year life-style of having all the decisions made for you? We believe that has implications for an adult, because we don't think you can demonstrate decision making at age eighteen if you've never had a chance to learn the process. And if you do learn later, it's awfully tough.

Why go to school? There are other things that schools exist for besides reading, writing, and arithmetic. If the structure of decision making in the classroom is developed so that the child continuously has a greater role in decision making, perhaps this too would have implications for his adult life. We need to begin offering the children choices. Why not at age four? And why not structure the choices based on the child's ability to deal with them, so that we may have one nine year old choosing from six options and another nine year old choosing from two options, and maybe a couple of nine year olds who haven't learned to choose from two yet. So we make that decision for them but we keep giving them more chances. What we are trying to say is let's move the decision making ratio from 90-10 to 50-50. Let's at least try to structure decision making opportunities for the children so that when they encounter opportunities to make decisions in life, they at least have some familiarity with the process.

RESPONSIBILITY

It is difficult to discuss decision making without some attempt to relate that ability to the acceptance of responsibility. We suggest that rather than consider the atmosphere of an open school as one of freedom, we ought to consider it as one of responsibility. The child's ability to make reasonable decisions about his intellectual progress and his personal behavior standards is an important thing, and it ought to be constantly assessed. We can only assess the child's ability to accept responsibility by providing opportunities for him to be respon-

sible. We do not do this when we march the kids in line through halls, when we leave monitors to write down the names of talkers, and when we tell how many of what kind are to be done in which way. We need to plan and structure opportunities for learning to deal with responsibility in our schools.

But how does a child make decisions about his personal behavior standards if he has never had a chance to set any? We must offer varied kinds of opportunities and evaluate them as we go along. We have to give the child opportunities to demonstrate responsibility—not only for his learning but for his behavior. Thus, when you go into an open school, what may appear to be confusion on the part of the children and disorganization on the part of the teacher may in fact be the structure of responsibility as it pertains to each child.

People may say, "That's a beautiful excuse for what you're doing," but it's not an excuse. No one is making excuses. We want each child to learn to be responsible for himself. And he doesn't do that without the opportunity to fail. When he fails we tell him about it. When he fails we help him to learn to succeed and we don't take away all the chances. We give him another chance.

But when a child demonstrates continued inability to accept responsibility, *then* we assume it for him, and   19 structure the setting for *that* child. We don't take it away from everybody when we only need to take it away from a few.

We're not abdicating our responsibility as teachers. We think we'd be abdicating our responsibility if we suggested that every child is the same and every child should do the same thing at the same time in the same way.

As teachers we need to provide for each child in terms of *his* needs.

PUNISHMENT

We have to begin to distinguish between punishment for misbehavior and punishment for lack of intellect. There are many incidents in schools where children receive verbal or physical abuse because of inability to provide correct responses.

There's the example of Mary. Mary was six years old and in a first grade classroom. Her teacher was a well-meaning person who said Mary was going to learn "C-A-T" one day. Therefore she spent a lot of time during that day with Mary, and Mary said, "car" and "can" and "rat"—and everything except "cat." And the teacher got more and more frustrated as the day wore on. Finally at the end of the day, she pulled Mary aside and worked with her. Then at 2:58 Mary said "CAT!" The teacher told Mary how

beautiful that was and how excited she was because Mary finally learned "cat." And so Mary went home, she went home feeling good because of what had happened in school.

The difficulty began when Mary came back the next day. The teacher hadn't erased "cat" off the board, and her first greeting was, "Good Morning, Mary, what's the word?" And Mary said "car." The teacher gave her a stare that said, "Do you realize how much time I spent with you yesterday? Do you think I have nothing else to do but spend time with you trying to teach you things? Then you come in and don't even remember them? What's the matter with you?" All the while she was telling Mary she was dumb because Mary didn't know the word was "cat." We submit that if Mary had known it was cat she would have said "cat." She loved her teacher and wanted to please her. She wanted to derive some pleasure or reward for pleasing her teacher, but her teacher didn't give her a chance. She punished her for being stupid. Now if that happened to Mary over and over and over, Mary would have no choice but to end up with a badly damaged self-concept. She'd know what it feels like to be a child who thinks she's no good. A lot of us haven't known that feeling, and a lot of us don't mean to inflict that feeling on children. The teacher in question was well-meaning and thought she was helping, but she was destroying. Teachers don't want

20

to destroy. Our goals say help, but our behavior says destroy.

We plead again, why can't we get our goals and our behavior together—to help and not destroy? If Mary punched someone in the mouth, she deserved to be disciplined. If she jabbed a pencil in someone's back, she deserved to be disciplined. We think behaviorally she can understand, unless she's emotionally disturbed, that hurting other people is wrong. And we think we can use discipline to that end if we have to. But we should certainly never make a human being feel less than a human being. And certainly never in a situation she cannot understand. Mary cannot understand why she should be "hollered at" for not knowing something she really doesn't know. And it's not fair to punish her for not knowing.

We should teach for not knowing—not punish for not knowing. Punishing for ignorance can be a powerful force and it can affect the children's attitudes about us and about school. It's absolutely unreasonable to ask human beings to perform acts which they are incapable of performing, so we ought to recognize and accept mistakes of an intellectual nature without infringing upon the child's self-respect. We can still demand excellence in performance as befits the child's potential and not reflect antagonism toward the child. On the other hand the process of socialization requires that standards of personal behavior be established. Although we try to use positive approaches to deal with failure concerning behavior standards, it would seem that discipline may fit better into this area than into the intellectual area. In a situation where injury to another child might result from a particular behavior, discipline is an acceptable procedure. At least let's get them separated. At least let's get discipline where it belongs.

SOCIALIZATION

One of the fringe benefits of open concept education which comes about through the non-graded structure occurs in the social realm—that of developing insight into and understanding of oneself in relation to others. A child in such a setting has an opportunity to experience what it feels like to be the oldest and the youngest in the group. A five year old who has been helped by an eight, nine, or ten year old is certainly going to be prepared and willing to help a younger child as he grows older. Certainly he will be more prepared than a five year old who was isolated in the kindergarten room with no opportunity to encounter older children except at the bus stop and on the playground. This is the socialization process we've been talking about in this country for a long time. We've talked about every human being respecting the rights of every other human being. Yet in our schools children are grouped together by age. We believe this is a tremendous disadvantage to the children. One wonders how we can further the socialization process when we encourage the fifth grade to beat the sixth in softball, when one room competes against the other in clothes drives for the needy, and separatism is encouraged by rewarding the class with the most parents joining the parents organization. How can we talk about bringing people together when we structure situations that forbid it?

Certainly open education alone can't assure learning about interpersonal relationships. It does, however, at least provide a setting where varied interests can meet. Our program development also provides an opportunity to structure activities that give children chances to get together.

Let's have multi-age groups and let children experience what it's like to be the oldest and the youngest in the group. Let them feel the sequential change of status that takes place as they live in a nongraded group for three years. Let's see what that does for them. There is no other way that a child can feel the impact of being six, seven and eight except in a setting where he can be six, seven and eight. We believe the child's perspective changes over those three years. We should be involved in helping him to see and understand this change. This can't help but give him some percep-

tion of his relationship to the other children. With guidance the children will develop empathy and broaden their frame of reference as human beings. This aspect of the open concept, then, should help us develop a better frame of reference for ourselves in relation to other human beings.

SELF-CONCEPT

One final area we must consider in this section is the development of the child's self-concept. We recognize the relationship that exists between a child's concept of self and his intellectual development. There is no question that a child must feel good about himself in order to reach his potential. We are, in effect, trying to get each child to maximize achievement in relationship to his ability. Those with outstanding intellect can explore without restrictions, and they ought to be encouraged and challenged to do so. Those with limited ability ought to be encouraged to achieve as much as possible, and success and reinforcement should be emphasized for those children.

But what does that all mean? Basically what it means is that the child who doesn't have average or better academic ability will also live in this world. And his chances for success should be measured in his terms, not measured by a teacher's or anybody else's. These chances are related to his understanding of his abilities and his acceptance of his limitations and his strengths. What chance does a child who can't read have in this world? If he feels good about himself, we think he'll find a way to be successful, in his terms, accepting his weaknesses. We've got to send every child out of school thinking that he's a good human being, that he can contribute to this society, and that he can give of himself to others. We don't think at that point that it makes much difference how bright he is.

At this point it will be worthwhile to reconsider some of the things we've said and summarize the philosophy of the open concept. We've tried to say that the open education concept basically is a concept of human concern, of human love, of human understanding—a concept in which the teacher demonstrates these behaviors to children. It's saying that children are human beings and that we should treat them as human beings, recognizing their frailties and recognizing our own, but trying to develop a real life setting. This setting should, as close as possible, equate what happens to the child after he leaves the school with what he encounters in school. Since school and society are related, school ought to prepare the child for society, not only intellectually but socially and emotionally. Perhaps we do that best by helping him to understand himself, to learn to accept responsibility for his own behavior, and to learn something about decision making as it applies to his own life.

The preceding ideas lend themselves to the development of a definition of open concept education which we shall use to conclude this chapter.

Open concept education is education for children in the U.S.A. It is an approach to learning that is totally consistent with the ideals espoused in our democracy for every citizen. It considers all aspects of the child's development important enough to be approached at an individual level. Learning should be need-based, and teaching should be guided by diagnosis. Open concept education considers the affective areas of development to be equally as important as the cognitive and psychomotor. It is education founded on the notion of love, respect, and concern for the dignity of each and every human being. It is a ray of sunshine. It is education for children in a democracy, for yesterday, for today, and for tomorrow.

We know that there will be criticism of these statements because they are too simple. We think we can say it in a different way. We could use bigger words, and jargonize it, but we think we ought to try to say it as simply as possible. We're talking about a concept of love—giving and receiving love. Perhaps this is an idealistic dream, but 23 what are philosophies if they are not dreams? And what good are philosophies if they are not idealistic?

We should reach for the stars for every child, and have every child reaching for the stars with a feeling that he will never stop reaching, so he can learn the joys of living and the joys of loving.

Thus we end up with an educational system whose goals and behaviors are consistent with those of the society which they endeavor to foster—an educational system for our Democracy.

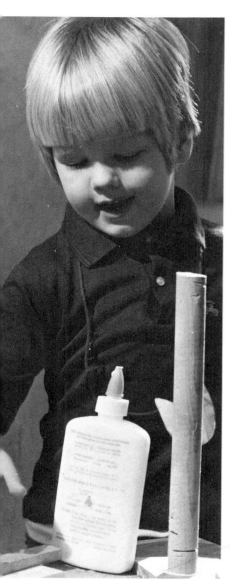

Children learn to make decisions with help and guidance.

CHAPTER II

Further Comments Concerning Responsibility, Self-concept and Decision Making and Their Relationship to the Classroom Setting

2

WE DISCUSSED THE above concepts or terms in Chapter I as part of the philosophy or rationale for the open concept. Perhaps we should try to relate them more to the classroom setting and children. We've chosen to begin with the basic question of why they are important considerations in the schools and in life.

When we look at our society closely we find continuous opportunity for individual choice. We choose where we live, where we work, and where we play. We choose what we wear, what we eat, what we ride in, or walk on. In fact, we choose as adults those things that we want, or wish we had. And wishing enters into our decision-making, forcing us to couch our choices in terms of our ability to pay the price for our wants. It also forces us to consider the effect our wants have on other people, especially those close to us. If, in fact, we live a life of rea-

sonable and practical choice, then it should behoove society to provide us with an opportunity to learn about making choices. If the above is rationale enough for developing the ability to make choices, then we need to suggest ways that the classroom can be structured to affect this ability. We must begin in our classroom a planned program for developing the ability to make decisions, a program that will insure carry-over to life beyond the school setting. We must, therefore, begin by asking what inconsistencies in decision making are apparent in our classrooms?

Primarily we lack an organizational structure which encourages the child to be involved in decision making. Perhaps this is due also to our adult perception of our role as teachers. We believe we are to teach, to instruct, to tell, and we behave exactly that way. We feel it is our responsibility

25

to be decision makers, and we have corrupted that responsibility to the point of impinging on the child's self-respect. We make decisions for children knowing full well that they are capable of deciding themselves. We make decisions for them in terms of the time allotted to tasks. We give a worksheet and a half hour to complete it. Two-thirds of our class is finished before the one half hour is up, and their "choice" is to be quiet and wait for the others. We make decisions for them in terms of tasks. Each child must do the whole page—whether he needs it or not. We make decisions in terms of content, the way to sit, stand, walk, when to talk, move, jump, how to stand, wait or play. We direct, direct, direct.

We use curriculum as an excuse for directing their thoughts, and we use behavior standards as an excuse for directing their behavior. We have organized ourselves into a principal-teacher-pupil syndrome where one tells the other what to do and each waits for his signal to jump. It threatens us to acknowledge the reality of our situation and thus we say on one hand, "No one tells *me* what to do"—and on the other "I agree with what you say, but my principal would never let me do that!"

When we begin to listen to ourselves we have no choice but to get frustrated, defensive, or just plain mad. Isn't it time we began to listen to our-selves—to question ourselves—to look at our goals and our behavior—isn't it time we took stock and changed what we do? We can begin with a simple question—How can I give my students more chances to make decisions in my classroom?

There are many things we can do in our schools within the present organization and many more within the organization we hope to have. There is one danger, though: we must be aware that the children we work with are not yet used to making decisions. Therefore, initially, they are going to be poor at decision making and make poor decisions. Our easiest, and primary reaction could very well be to say, "I knew it wouldn't work." We hope you can avoid that trap and begin decision-making opportunities in a reasonable way designed to provide success. We will discuss in later chapters the teaching strategies that offer decision-making opportunities to children in your classroom, both academic and behavioral.

One final point concerning decision making—it is never too late to begin providing opportunities for learning decision-making techniques, but if we begin early in the child's life it will be easier for him to make carefully calculated decision making a part of his life style. Specifically, then, what are the components of decision-making ability that we must plan for and teach?

1. Recognition of choice—Perhaps the first aspect of decision making which must be considered is that of recognition of choice. We believe it is necessary to help children to become aware of the fact that in most situations there is some choice. An individual who is always given chocolate ice cream may lose, or never attain, the awareness that there is vanilla ice cream. He may not even know that a choice exists. Therefore we must develop strategies that put him in a position to ask, "What are the choices?" There may only be one, but asking the question at least puts him in the position of knowing that there is only one.

2. Evaluation of implications of choices—This aspect of decision making comes logically after the recognition of the alternatives. In this stage the child must decide what will be the result of each choice. He must examine the choices in light of the desired result and the cost to him.

3. Making the decision—The third step obviously is making the choice and following through on it. This step then helps the child to realize the effectiveness with which he handled steps one and two.

4. Evaluation—Thus he arrives at step four and decides whether he's made a reasonable decision or a poor one.

Of course these steps are not obvious to the decision maker at first. *He should learn to use them without thinking about them.* They should become automatic. It is important, however, that the teachers, at least understand the steps involved in the decision-making process. We can then design activities and situations to reinforce each step and lead the child to use all the steps.

Another aspect of the open concept mentioned in Chapter I was self-concept. It is easy to see the relationship between decision making and self-concept. As a child makes decisions and is satisfied with them, he reinforces his self-concept since the decisions he makes are his. Most of us are aware of the satisfaction we derive from making a decision that pleases us. Of course self-concept extends beyond decision making. It is basically how we view ourselves in terms of others and in terms of our role in society. It is seeing ourselves capable of contributing to society. It is knowing the limitations of our ability to contribute, and performing confidently within these limits. It is recognizing society's need for us. It is that feeling that says I am good, I am productive, I am ME.

We do many things in our classroom that affect self-concept. Some of these we plan but most of them we don't intend at all. In fact, we perform many well-meaning acts in the name of self-concept that have an effect opposite to our purpose. We have watched many children being "chewed out" because they fail to know an answer the teacher wants. One cannot help but wonder if the teacher who is castigating six year old Mary, who can't recognize the word CAT, is really aware of what she's doing to Mary. In her well-meaning way the teacher is contributing to the demise of Mary's self-concept. Mary can't be expected to understand that the teacher doesn't mean that she's dumb, even though she makes her feel that way.

We affect self-concept in the way we look at, respond to, and feel about the people around us. In our position as teachers this is particularly true. We begin with a captive audience who love, respect and trust us. We inadvertently break down this love, respect and trust by disregarding the child's role as a human being. We punish, we ridicule, we hurt. We are amazed at the strength of the love, respect and trust the children have for us, because in spite of us they persist in caring about us. They accept our inconsiderateness, and thrive on snatches of concern.

We must learn to use the force of love, respect and trust to our advantage. We must capitalize on the latent energies of these feelings and help them to grow, first in terms of the child himself (self-concept) and then in terms of his concern for others. A two thousand year old message keeps coming to mind. "Love thy neighbor, as thyself." The key is "thyself." Can we really give more of ourselves when we love, respect, and trust ourselves? We believe we can. We believe it certainly deserves emphasis in our school programs.

To be "put down" by a teacher that a child cares about can have tremendous impact on the child's concept of self. He can then become submissive, aggressive, or withdrawn. Since the child must do things within the context and standard which we establish and thus is sometimes in a position where he can't win, we must be particularly sensitive.

We affect self-concept with the reward system we use in the classroom. We rave over Billy's answers and grunt to Tommy's. We smile when Mary answers, and frown when Barbara answers. When we continually show our preferences for one answer over another, one behavior over another and, yes, one child over another (both verbally and non-verbally), it's the "another" child whose self-concept suffers. We know we can't help liking some children better than others. The children know they like some teachers better than others, and they're willing to accept this and live with it as long as there is some fairness in our treatment. They accept it as long as the standards for one are the same as the standards for all.

The implication of this for our classroom is very clear. Try to be fair—all the children ask is that you try—and in trying you will succeed. We affect the self-concepts of the children in our classrooms. If we accept this fact, we will become more aware of the behaviors we demonstrate which affect this very important aspect of the child's life. What chance does Billy have for success, on his terms, unless he feels good about himself? He can't read very well, he can't write very well, he can't do math very well. He must know what he can do well and believe in his ability to do it. Only then can he find a place in our society where he can be a "success," a success to himself as an individual and a human being.

Thus we arrive at the concepts of responsibility and freedom. It seems that decision-making ability is related to self-concept development and these in turn are related to the development of responsibility, and responsibility must be related to freedom. The ability to make decisions thus implies the acceptance of the responsibility for the decision. Acceptance of the responsibility for the decision is related to the ego strength of the individual to accept the consequences of the decision— good or bad.

We must then provide opportunities for children to be responsible for their decisions not only as they relate to behavior but as they relate to intellectual development. It is therefore important that we couch freedom in its proper perspective, that is, as it relates to responsibility. It is not license, and it cannot be license, because that would result in reinforcement of a lack of responsibility. Freedom implies the responsibility to act in a responsible way in terms of ourselves and other human beings. It extends from the rights of others to the belongings of others. It implies that a child who has been given the responsibility of going to the media center (library) alone to perform a task will go to the library, perform the task as well as he is able, and return to the classroom. He will do this "unsnoopervised," but supervised in terms of your trust, and your respect for his ability to supervise himself. This is the process of developing in the child the freedom to become responsible.

One of the most frequently heard criticisms of the open education concept is that there is no discipline, and that there is too much freedom. This is, in our viewpoint, most unjust. Why do we fail to realize that freedom and responsibility are interrelated? Why do we expect children to immediately demonstrate responsible behavior when they are freed? Why do we not accept our responsibility as teachers and provide opportunities for children to learn responsible use of freedom?

We not only need to provide opportunities for learning these behaviors but also we need to be patient in repeatedly offering opportunities to learn. Some of the children are going to fail in their acceptance of responsibility. We can not fail in our responsibility to "give them another chance." Thus we must be patient, and more importantly we must know what we are intending to do.

This leads to a final comment about the terms discussed in this chapter. If children develop the ability to make decisions, and demonstrate an understanding of responsible freedom, they may use these behaviors in developing a positive concept of self. If we leave the development of these skills to chance, however, we gravely err. They must be a planned part of our program. In later chapters we will discuss how the development of skill in these areas can be planned and executed as an integral part of the learning process.

There is a need for structure underlying any open program.

3

Organizing and Scheduling for an Open Concept Program

PROBABLY THE AREA of greatest concern to the self-contained classroom teacher, as pertains to the open educational concept, is the question of organization and scheduling. At least this is the question we are most often asked. An understanding of one's role in the program is important in easing apprehension. In order to apply the philosophy and implement the teaching strategies suggested in this book, you simply need to know *where* you're supposed to be, *when* you're supposed to be there, *what* you're supposed to do and *with what children* you are to do it. Thus we've chosen to deal very early in the book with the basic question of how to organize and schedule the program.

It appears as though schools can accept the basic notion of a primary unit and an intermediate unit. At least

this is what we suggest to begin with. This approach can reduce administrative problems connected with a large school population and bring to bear the advantage of smallness within bigness. For example: a large elementary school with three kindergartens, three first grades, three second grades, three third grades, three fourth grades, three fifth grades and three sixth grades can be organized into three kindergartens, three primary units and three intermediate units. Assuming a ratio of 25 students per teacher, we thus have three primary groups, each consisting of 75 children ages six, seven and eight with three teachers. Thus we have a nongraded, multi-age, team-teaching approach to each of three primary units.

Each of the teams of teachers should have a team leader, thus there are three primary team leaders.

31

TEAM APPROACH TO ORGANIZATION

Kindergarten #1:
1 teacher
25 five year olds

Kindergarten #2:
1 teacher
25 five year olds

Kindergarten #3:
1 teacher
25 five year olds

Units A, B, and C—Primary Teams—
Each would consist of:

3 teachers including 1 team leader
25 six year olds (first grade)
25 seven year olds (second grade)
25 eight year olds (third grade)

Units D, E, F—Intermediate Teams—
Each would consist of:

3 teachers including 1 team leader
25 nine year olds (fourth grade)
25 ten year olds (fifth grade)
25 eleven year olds (sixth grade)

The intermediate teams would be organized the same way—three teams of 75 children ages nine, ten, and eleven, each with three teachers, one of whom would be designated team leader.

Why do we suggest teams of three teachers and 75 children? There are several reasons, each important in its own way:

1. We would like to make it possible for each team member to feel some attachment, some relationship, some closeness to each child in the group. Beyond 75 this becomes increasingly difficult even though the children will work with the team for three years.

Part of the rationale for the team approach involves the opportunity to know each child's strengths and weaknesses and to have the expertise available to help with these. Therefore the three year span with three teachers, and consideration of practical economical matters leave this approach as a reasonable one. Teams of six to eight teachers with 150 to 200 children create problems in management of both children and adults that are greater than the returns derived from such an organizational pattern.

2. It seems that the larger the group of adults on the team the more difficult the team is to control, organize and harmonize. In an open concept where "openness" is the byword, we adults must demonstrate it with each other if we want the children to believe it and practice it, or the children never really learn it. We believe at least, initially, it is easier for three people to learn openness with each other than for six people to do so.

3. There is still something to be said for group identity, and this size group offers wide but manageable opportunities for children to choose friends, to learn about others, to feel largeness and smallness, to sense and explore

their place, and still be identifiable by the teachers. AND BESIDES

4. IT WORKS!

It is easy to see then that, large school or small school, the organization remains basically the same. In the large school it reduces, as in the example, the number of units from 21 to nine. This is not only administratively easier to control but in terms of scheduling of special teachers and special areas is much more manageable. (A detailed discussion of special teachers may be found in chapter VI.)

One advantage of this organizational pattern deals with the curriculum. If your district insists on adhering strictly to the curriculum, it is then possible for the team leaders to cooperate with one another in exercising the necessary control. The team leaders can coordinate the development of content for each of their units. They can cycle the content through the units enabling all the materials available for a certain topic to be used intensively by a single unit. That is, one group can be studying Indians, while another works on insects, while another looks at the community. This approach not only organizes and correlates the use of materials, but enables the teams to share planned units of work. It provides for communication among the teams, while still allowing autonomy within each team. A continuous progress curriculum should also be devel-oped and implemented in each unit. This would control the children's skill development and provide opportunities for teachers to develop a range of topics as befits the children's interest which could eventually replace the curriculum guide. The chapter on Skill Sequences will discuss this in more detail.

The obvious next question (if you haven't asked it yet, we thought we'd anticipate you) is what do we do with those 75 children. We will attempt to answer that with a model scheduling and grouping arrangement. However, please remember, our model can be adapted to suit your program.

Let's talk about grouping. As you begin the program, we believe it makes sense to group the children in math and communication skills in a manner as follows:

Communication Skills: We would suggest an appropriate diagnosis of the children's reading level be given. The results of such a test would then be used to group the 75 children into three groups—a "top" group of about 30, a "middle group" of about 30, and a "low" group of about 15. (Please excuse the "top," "middle," and "low" terminology but we can't think of anything else except "good" and we don't like that at all.) We know that you're thinking—"homogeneous grouping." Yes and no—and why? Well, yes and no because! Because we know that teaching the skills of reading is ideally best accomplished in a setting as close to one-to-one as possible (an example is remedial reading programs). However, if we can't reduce the number of children (don't count on the pill, because all we do then is hire fewer teachers), then in the skill areas we'd better do some diagnosis and get children together with minimal differences in ability. We should try to use heterogeneous grouping for everything but skill lessons.

Well, back to the "top," "middle," and "low" groups. We now have three groups and three teachers. AHA! you guessed it—each teacher takes one group. We know you're still going to have to regroup within your group, but when you read the chapters on individualizing your program, contracts, packets, learning centers and skill sequences, we think you'll feel better about it. At least reserve judgment until then. Remember, this is a cook book, and you've just put in the flour. We've got a lot of ingredients, mixing and patience to add yet, so hang on.

We've now got three communication *skill* groups and three teachers, each of whom is responsible for one of the groups. When do you work with them? Now we're into scheduling. We think you need about two hours each day— say 9-11 A.M. (Before you scream, re-read the last part of the preceding paragraph, please!)

Isn't it amazing how the morning is almost gone. Here it is 11 o'clock— and what do you do next? We'd suggest math. Let's organize it the same way, a math test for diagnosis, divide into three groups, each teacher take one, and let's work with math until lunch time. (If we made you hungry and if you want a snack go ahead—we'll continue when you get back. Feel better?—well, let's go on.)

A word of caution about math. We'll have to do some unit regrouping and retesting because of children's varying abilities in the different topics of math. We'll discuss this in detail later, but some of the areas we must deal with separately are addition and subtraction of whole numbers, multiplication and division of whole numbers, addition and subtraction of fractions, multiplication and division of fractions, addition and subtraction of decimals, multiplication and division of decimals, multiplication and division of decimals, numeration, money, and time and measurement.

So you see there can be flexibility of grouping built into the math program. In the communication skill program, we have to work for it. You will be surprised as you work through the program at the opportunities available for you to help each other and put some flexibility into your grouping, but be patient at first.

Well, now we've got social studies and science left and in the schedule we're developing that leaves the afternoon. There are two ways to begin—both social studies and science each afternoon or alternate social studies and science units. We favor the latter approach especially when the techniques suggested later are superimposed on the unit. Thus you begin with all seventy-five children working on the same unit for the whole afternoon until the unit is completed. You can use large groups, small groups, and individual techniques in the approach to the unit. We know it sounds "scary," but it works and we'll show you how.

There are a couple of things to consider, though. One is the content, the other is the responsibility for the organization of the content. We can't forget the children will be in this program for three years, thus we must cycle our content over a three year period. This makes our curriculum guides obsolete and forces us to use a sequence of skills in order to assure skill development and record-keeping, regardless of the topic. In terms of the responsibility for organization, if teacher A plans, organizes and supervises the implementation of the first unit, while that unit is in progress, teacher B can be working on the second unit, and teacher C on the third. (Do you think you'll be able to stand being organized that far ahead? Well, not at first!)

Now what have we got? An organization and a schedule! That wasn't too difficult, was it? Repeat it? Well, o.k. How's this?

9–11	Communication Skills
11–12	Math
12–1	Mmmmmm (Lunch)
1–3	Social Studies or Science
1–3:30	(if you have a long day)

"Ouch" not 4:00 (Negotiate!)

There are a couple of ideas to consider beyond this basic beginning notion of organization. We'd like to briefly discuss those, however, we think the basic schedule involving large blocks of time ought to be adhered to regardless of the approach you take in terms of organization.

Schools have evolved into various grade level designs. If you're in one that does not have K-6 it is probably K-5, K-4, K-3, 1-3, or 4-6, or some other one. We'd like to suggest some organizational options for these:

K-5: This organization can result in any of the following options—

K-1-2	a primary unit
3-4-5	an intermediate unit
	or
K	separate
1-2	primary
3-4-5	intermediate

35

K-4:	K-1-2	primary			1-2-3	primary
	3-4	intermediate				
		or				
	K	separate				
	1-2	primary				
	3-4	intermediate			1-3:	1-3	primary

K-3:	K-1	early primary I	or what-	4-6:	4-6	intermediate
	2-3	primary II	ever			
			titles			
			you can			
			think of.			
		or				
	K	separate				

4-6: 4-6   intermediate

What about specials and planning time? In order to get a little mystery and suspense into the plot, we're not going to answer that yet (it's in a later chapter).

Individualized instruction can be one to one, one to ten, or one to fifty.

CHAPTER IV

The Program in Communication Skills, Math, Science and Social Studies

IN THE LAST chapter we suggested ways to organize the children and schedule the day, and you were saying to yourself, "That's easy to say, but what am I going to do with those kids for two hours in communication skills. Well we thought you'd ask, and here's an answer.

THE COMMUNICATION SKILL PROGRAM

The intent here is to describe in detail the structure of an individualized communication skills program. We'd like to emphasize structure, since we feel that the individualized programs that have failed, have failed as a result of lack of structure. Our plan is a flexible one. It provides structure that the child can understand, flexibility for the teacher to implement, and options for both. There are ten aspects of the communication skill program we'd like to discuss. We feel all ten are needed

to comprise a complete program. Let's begin!

1. *Limits in terms of time and effort.* In plain English that means a specified number of pages to be completed in a specified period of time. Let's say 200 pages for one week. The child can understand this, that's primary, and the teacher can control it. Where does choice come in? Well, the child decides what 200 pages he will read. Can he do that? Of course. Do you need to be completely familiar with what he reads? Of course not. What about the child who only reads *The Hardy Boys?* Well, if he's ten or eleven that's not so bad, it's better he reads and enjoys it, than is forced to and hates it. Anyhow that same boy whose interest in *The Hardy Boys* is insatiable at age eleven at fourteen or fifteen will have switched to *Playboy* and if that's not a broad interest switch, what is?

If you feel you can't give up your basal reader, it can fit in. Just designate that twelve of the 200 pages must be the basal reading story. That still gives the child 188 pages to pick for his own. Did you ever stop and think about how many children are sitting in our classroom reading a basal reading story a week, twelve pages, when they should be reading 1200! The injustice of this is that we have bright children being successful, beating the system with little or no effort, and we owe these kids more.

2. *Related activities,* limited again in terms of time and amount—let's say three for this week.

The activities should be related to some of the pages the child has read for the week. An efficient way to handle this is to provide a broad list of related activities from which the child can choose; the first page of one has been included for you. (See Fig. 1.) The complete list is included in part 2 of this book. We can't give the child hundreds to choose from but we can still exert controls and give him some choice. How? Well, tell him he can choose his three from numbers 5, 6, 9, 12, 28, 33, 42 or 51. This way he's still structured into the program, choosing what he reads and what he does with what he reads.

What about the basal? We thought you'd remember that. Just ask him to do one of the optional activities

(numbers 5, 6, 9, 12, 22, 28, 33, 42 and 51) relating to the story and the other two with other things he's read.

3. *Creative and functional writing.* You guessed it, limits in terms of time and amount—three this week. We need to provide a list of creative writing topics to get started (Fig. 2). (We know you can expand this list without much effort—but it's a start.) This one was written by a graduate class of teachers, Millersville State College, Millersville, Pa. Handle it the same as the related activities. Choose from numbers 5, 6, 9, 12, 15, 18, 21, 14 and 27. He'll pick the three he wants, or pick two and make one up—there are lots of variations, but when you begin, be specific and control the options.

For those of you who believe in motivating creative writing, then get the kids together and set up a motivation lesson. Give them some options and let them write. This approach can be combined with the list of options or used exclusively. Either way we have to give them a chance to write.

A word about this part of the program. Creative writing is a beautiful way to get feedback about spelling, handwriting, vocabulary, usage, punctuation, capitalization, sentence structure and attitudes. However we can blow the whole thing with our little red pencils—SO keep those red pencils in the drawer! Don't put any red marks on

FIGURE 1

ACTIVITIES FOR INDIVIDUALIZED READING

1. Describe the main character(s).
   a. What he looks like.
   b. What is he like, is he real or not?
   c. What do you think of him? Why?

2. Describe the setting.
   a. Time
   b. Place

3. Draw a series of cartoons showing the plot of the story.

4. Draw a picture or map of the place in which the story took place (setting). Label to show what happened in each place.

5. Why did the author write the book or story? Pick one point below as the reason and write a paragraph or two about it.
   a. To share an experience
   b. To give information
   c. To give an opinion

6. Describe the most exciting part of the story.

7. Describe the most beautiful part of the story, the most humorous, the saddest.

8. Could this be a true story? Why or why not? Give your reasons in paragraph form.

9. Make a poster to advertise a book you liked very much.

10. Write an original story, using the main characters from the book.

11. Write an original story using the same setting as the book.

12. Write another ending for the story.

13. Write a biography of the author of the book. Include a list of the other books written by the same author.

14. Write a short summary of the story.

15. Write a review of the book telling why you liked or disliked it; give good reasons for your views.

16. Why did you choose this book? Give your answer in paragraph form.

17. After reading two or more biographies, write a biography of yourself.

18. List the events of the story in order of time.

19. Make a book jacket and write a blurb to accompany it.

FIGURE 2

WILD AND WACKY IDEAS FOR CREATIVE WRITING

1. How would you feel if it rained ice cream?
2. How would it feel to live in a walnut shell?
3. What is Excedrin Headache #56?
4. What if everyone wrote backwards?
5. Spray on clothes.
6. What would you do with another hand?
7. If I were a germ!
8. Design a new person.
9. The day the fleezle schoofeed!
10. How would you like to have gills?
11. What would it feel like to be an umbrella?
12. Would you like to be swallowed? If so, by whom or what?
13. What would you do if someone sat on you?
14. Where is the freeazort in your car?
15. The day the rain fell up.
16. Who put glue in the toothpaste?
17. The dog who lost his bark!
18. What kind of sandwich would you like to be?
19. Who tied knots in my pajamas?
20. How did you feel the day you opened the door and found a six foot pink rabbit?
21. What would you do if you were shut up in a box by yourself for three days?
22. How would it feel to be a bouncing ball?
23. What do ants think about?
24. A day without gravity!
25. How would you wash an elephant in your bath tub?
26. How did the leopard get his spots?
27. The adventures of a turtle on his way to New York City!
28. What would you do if it snowed purple?
29. Who is McDoogle?
30. What would you do if you didn't have to go to bed every night?
31. What is in a magician's hat?
32. Describe a day of living without water.
33. Exchange places with your parents for a day.
34. How would you feel if you were a dog about to be hit?
35. What would you do for recreation if you lived underground?
36. Whose wacky idea was this?
37. What is over the hill behind your house?
38. What would happen if some people had no gravity?
39. What would you do if you didn't have to go to school every day?
40. Pretend a rich old woman died and left you with $1,000,000 to take care of her cat. What would you do?
41. Where do freckles come from?
42. How big is the largest person?
43. What would you do if your bed caved in?
44. Where does the white go when the snow melts?
45. How would it feel to be the sun?

these papers. Read these products of the child's imagination and take from them everything you can get—but deal with it in another context. Those four kids who hand in creative writing without periods, won't gain anything from your criticism of their ignorance. Take those four and teach them a lesson on punctuation in another setting without alluding to their creative writings. Then give them the worksheet with twenty sentences to punctuate and watch them get eighteen of them, then pat yourself on the back, and wonder why their next creative writings are devoid of periods. They haven't learned it until they use it in their creative writings, so try again, until it shows up in their everyday efforts. Then they've learned it.

The directed or functional part of this aspect of the program can and should be corrected. It's where we deal with friendly letters, business letters, thank you notes and things of this nature. We can give two creative writings and one functional writing as an example of a week's limit.

4. *Spelling.* (We heard that!) Yes, we've got to build it into our program, either with a text or a kit or something, but we've got to do it. One approach is to devise an individualized spelling list from words misspelled on the creative writings. We can develop topical lists related to areas of study as another approach. (Some people suggest we pray as the best approach, and since we earlier brought up the controversy of "the pill," we won't add to our problems.) The only addition that we can make to what you already know about spelling is that the structure of the program should require some limit in terms of time and amount, and we shouldn't avoid it. (Spelling, we mean.) The Economy Co. offers a buddy system spelling kit which is great. It's called, Continuous Progress Spelling. (See Part II, "List of Kits and Materials.")

5. *Handwriting.* (Here we go again!) It's a good thing this book is printed or you'd have some perfectly justifiable remarks to make about us talking to you about handwriting. Well, here goes anyhow.

We've got to have a program of some type that provides an opportunity for the child to learn to write with some semblance of legibility. We don't believe our renowned handwriting programs with their round, round ready's do this. (We can feel the sting of that rebuttal.) Do *you* hold your pencil that way? Does anyone? What we suggest is that you use the creative writings and other papers that the children turn in to determine just who needs handwriting instruction and who doesn't. Who doesn't? (We thought you'd react to that.) There are children in our upper—(oops) intermediate—programs who write legibly and easily. They need very little in the   41 way of writing instruction except reinforcement. So reinforce them. Now, those guys whose writing you can't read, what do you do with them? (Since you're already praying for spelling, what's left—panic?)

We need to set up a systematized program of instruction to keep the child working on it. We'd suggest simplifying the structure of handwriting to the point of straight lines and curves, developing models for the child to use, helping him understand the structure of the models, patience, and H O P E. (Boy, some of us just don't make it in this writing game, do we?) Oh! you thought we forgot about the child who has to learn cursive from manuscript, well we didn't, we just thought we'd save it. Do you know that we've (the system not us) decided that everyone is ready to do this at the same time. How about that! Anyhow if we could be a little flexible about when we make the transition (like, when the child asks for it), maybe we'd have more success with the transition. Another thing, why do we ridicule children for using manuscript after they've learned how to use cursive? No one's proven that it's faster or better to use cursive, and anyway what about personal choice? (Thank you, manuscript writers. We can hear the cheers, and anyway everyone deserves a "plug" now and then.)

We wonder if we've made the point: include handwriting in the skill pro-

gram, try to systematize it, shoot for legibility, and try to make it fun. And by the way, "good luck."

6. *Listening.* Listening? Even if we talk two-thirds of the time (which we do), a child needs to develop some skill in this area. Our first inclination is to think, "Yes, that's right. Those children who can't read too well need to learn to listen." That's true, but there's also a group of average and bright children who could profit from the development of some listening skills. Remember when you were in college and you were sitting in that room taking that test. You looked at question number six and thought, this guy is throwing us a curve, he never mentioned that. Well, he did mention that, only you were intently taking notes about number five and never heard it. Wouldn't it have helped you to be able to listen more and write less? Anyway when we ramble on two-thirds of the time, are we teaching listening specifically aimed at the development of listening skills? Organize these activities and include them in the program. Read some stories to the children, short stories, that begin and end in the time allotted. We know some of you will cringe and maybe slam this book down on the table, but we see little value in reading a chapter a day of a book. First of all, it's too long on the same topic, and we always forget a day or two, and you'd be amazed at how many never get finished (or are finished before

they start). Let them listen to cassettes. Read a short story and ask them questions about it. Read a *Reader's Digest* skill builder type story and let them work on the answers to the related questions. (Don't grade them, please.) The child can check his own and keep a record of his successes. Plan some listening experiences for the child and help take him beyond hearing.

7. *Speaking.* We heard that, we're not kidding, and we know how much they talk. But the only organized program of speaking seems to be that day that you dress up, shiver and shake, stand behind the lectern and describe how you hang wallpaper. That's speaking? Yuk! Perhaps this part of the communication skill program would be enhanced if we'd permit some talking in our schools. We've got such a priority on "quiet," though, it's difficult to imagine this happening, because the child has to "sneak in" most of the talking he's able to do in school. We can't talk in the halls, in the bathroom, in the classroom, in the lunchroom, anywhere. We've sat in classrooms and recorded the word "quiet" fifty times in a one hour lesson. Did you ever stop to think that the one ability we use when we get out of school is the ability to speak. Is it any wonder that after 13 years of being quiet, it has to come out.

Like listening, we need to provide opportunities in our program for talking, discussing, reacting, time to look at what we say and how we say it, and what it might mean. It goes on around us all the time, and we just let it develop. We try to structure every other aspect of the child's life. Why don't we try to bring some structure to a program directed toward speaking.

8. *Kits.* We've all got them in our building or our classrooms. Many of them are beautiful aids to learning, so let's use them. Remember they are not a program in themselves, but as a part of a program, they can be very effective, broaden your effectiveness and stimulate interest. Use them, but don't abuse them. Part two of this book contains a list of kits including brief descriptions and prices.

9. *Skills.* Here's another part of the program that we've had a tendency to overdo, or over teach, or overreact to, or over something. It is important to deal with phonetic and structural analysis, the structure of language, vocabulary development, study skills and comprehension; there is no question about this. It's the "how" that bothers us. What has been needed is a systematized approach to skill development. Learning sequences make this possible. We will discuss these in detail in the chapter on continuous progress. For now it is imperative that skill development be a part of the communication skills program. Initially it is probably best, in your classroom, in terms of management, to start two

43

or three groups at different places in the skill sequence. Work these groups through the skill sequence by scheduling small group instruction sessions and including work with the skill in their program. Teach only those kids who need each skill. Your workbook will fit into the skills program, but be flexible in its use. Those basals don't have to be followed story by story to be effective. Use the stories when it makes sense to integrate the workbook into your skills program.

10. Last, but not least—*speed*. This aspect of the program is certainly not for everyone, but many children at the intermediate level can profit from some attention to it. It's simply a matter of the child practicing speed reading techniques and checking his progress two or three times weekly. We've seen eleven year olds go from 250 words per minute to 650 words per minute with comprehension in a school year. Give it some thought. One way is to begin with a double column page. put a red line down the middle of each column (it's o.k. to mark your books this way, we said so), and ask the child to practice reading down the column keeping his eyes on the red line. He can do this on his own. When he feels comfortable with this, switch to a single page of material, put the line down the middle and watch him go. That's a way to practice.

To get his speed—he should read for three minutes, stop—count the num-ber of words in one line, count the number of lines, multiply these two and divide by three. (For mathemaphobics just read for one minute and count the words.)

To check comprehension, tell the child that for one of every three exercises he does, he should (after he's figured his speed) try to write down what he remembers about his reading and compare it with what he's read.

One caution. They need to be aware that they read different materials at different speeds, so we don't just have one reading speed but several. When he records his result he should categorize it somehow, like—*fun, work* and *ugh*—and record the speeds with a categorical code.

Well, those are the ten parts of a communication skill program as we see it. (We heard that.) We didn't forget oral reading, in fact we feel it deserves special mention.

We've been in classrooms where children as young as seven read the same story six times so that everybody got a turn. We've tabulated frequency of error for some of these "lessons" and it increases as the story is repeated. We've asked teachers why they've done this. Inevitably the answer comes back "because I wanted to hear how well they read." So, always being alert, we've come back with, "and how well did Joey read?" You should see the expression and stammering this question evokes. "Well, uh, what do you mean?" You said you wanted to see how well the children read, we're interested in knowing what mistakes Joey made. "I'm not sure." "How about Lisa?" "I don't remember," etc.

Simply stated, we believe that we should have reasons for asking children to read orally and those reasons should justify our approach. If a teacher is interested in using oral reading to give her feedback about a child's reading then she should deal directly with that child on a one to one basis, and she should record what she discovers in a continuing way.

But when do you have time? It takes only a minute to listen to a child read a few sentences or a paragraph, to note his errors and move on. (It really works—try it.) Having some children on contracts makes it possible.

For what other reasons do we ask children to read orally. To take a turn in social studies? (Well, we'll hit that one later.) To read with expression? Certainly justifiable, but have you heard this one. . . .

Teacher says to Billy, "Read that sentence with expression." Billy reads, "The - boy - went - to - the - store - to - get - a - pre (present) - for - his - sister." "Now Billy, that's not the way that should sound. Read it again and this time read it like you mean it." So Billy reads it exactly the same way, and teacher (a little exasperated) says, "No, Billy this way." She reads the sentence with beautiful expression and says, "Now Billy you try it" and he does it exactly as he's told and teacher says, "Very good, Billy, that's the way you should read it." Billy smiles to himself and teacher is pleased with herself. Which one of them knows what happened? We bet on Billy. The teacher reinforces the notion of "do as I say." Billy mimics and everyone is happy. Really? Billy doesn't read with expression until he reads with expression motivated from within. Let's stop kidding ourselves that when children mimic us they're learning what we want them to learn.

What about oral reading: Have a reason and use an approach befitting the reason.

We've gone through ten components of a communication skill program—we'll repeat them here to put them together. We have to talk about how to keep records, how to establish standards for the child's work, and how to implement this program.

1. Number of pages
2. Related activities
3. Creative and functional writing
4. Spelling
5. Handwriting
6. Listening
7. Speaking

8. Kits
9. Skills
10. Speed

Now that we've discussed the major areas of concern in a communication skills program, you're asking yourself how do you keep records for this and where do you start. WHOA! you're asking the questions faster than we can answer them. Let us try and then let's see what questions you have left. Now, record keeping. Since most children from age seven are capable of keeping most of the records, let them. Here's how. The children need a notebook or something that they can keep for awhile—at least a marking period. They should date a page for the week covered. They should then write down the titles of their readings and the number of pages. That's all, not the publisher and copyright.

They should next record the number of the related activities they did, if they are from the list, and if they made them up they should describe them.

Third, they should record the numbers of the creative writing topics if they are from the list and if the topics are original they should describe them.

There are already means available with the kits for record keeping, so use those. You'll have to devise a way to keep spelling records.

Handwriting you'll see a lot of.

If you do listening exercises the child should record his results. Speaking will take care of itself. They'll have to keep records of any speed reading exercises they do. This leaves the skill area. If the children do worksheets and check them, they should keep track of the scores. If you integrate your basal workbook into the program, it will help with record keeping. The more records the child keeps himself, the more time you will have to work with the program. And as you'll find out in chapter 9 a contract can become your record-keeping system.

Now we'll talk about grades. If you're locked into a system where you must give grades, this program will increase the number of grades you will have "four fold." You can grade the related activities and the skill sheets. If you assign these in groups of three, there's six grades right there each week. That ought to satisfy any parent. Where do you start? Well, if you organize your program as suggested in chapter 3, start with the "top" group. If you're going to try it in your self-contained classroom, start with your "top" group. The reasons for this are simple—you're more likely to be successful with them. You have to learn to manage the program, so do it in the easiest way possible, and that's with the students who are most likely to be able to handle it.

Now for that big question you've been trying to ask and we've gone past— How do you handle checking-out all the children's work? First of all check-out is the time that you go over what the child has done. This is a time-consuming process as it must be done one to one. Since it is discussed in detail in the chapter on contracts, briefly, it can be handled in one of two ways. You can check-out every-one on Friday. Most people don't like this idea but some do. You can cycle the check-outs; that is, if you have a class of 25, five students would work on a Monday to Monday cycle, five on a Tuesday to Tuesday, etc. This way you only need to check-out five a day—believe us, that's a manageable number!

We'd suggest you begin with the "top" group, setting the same limits in terms of time and amount of work for each child. As the program progresses and your management skills improve, the children will then begin to spread out and set their own limits in terms of their ability. Some will increase their limits, some will reduce them, and some will be comfortable with the original limits.

One of the things you must remem-ber to do is to schedule times for spelling instruction, handwriting in-struction and skill teaching. These should be group lessons and everyone could be in the group who needs that skill, if you're in a self-contained class. If you're team-teaching (as in chapter V) then it could be one-half of any of your groups. Aim toward getting

the children into only the skill lessons they need. There will be more on this in the chapter on skill sequences. But keep it in mind now as something to work toward. Having children on con-tracts, however, will help you manage it.

Some cautions should be considered. First of all, we must apply standards to the children's work. They must be standards related to each child, but simply stated, so we don't accept poorer work than any student is capa-ble of performing. Secondly, there will be some students who cannot func-tion without your constant attention. Their movement should be restricted to an area of your description and only expanded as their ability to be responsible increases. Third, give it time.

We know this program will work in your classroom. As you get into it, we're sure you will see the potential it holds for modification and expan-sion. At that point it's your program, and don't hesitate to modify it and change it. We know you'll be im-pressed with the students' attitudes as they develop and expand the pro-gram for themselves.

One possible thing to try when you really feel confident is a long-term project superimposed over the con-tract. For example, the child could pick a topic, such as, "cats." The first week of the project, he or she 47 could develop a bibliography about cats.

The second week of the project the student could narrow the bibliography to manageable size and begin reading and taking notes. The third week he or she could continue to read and take notes. The fourth week organize the notes in logical order and at the end of five or six weeks the child will have written a paper about cats. Other long-term projects can be models, murals, time lines, songs, dances, plays, learning centers, or packets. This will work with many students, especially in an area of interest. It gives depth to their program and improves their skills in many areas.

If this seems like a lot to swallow at one time, remember it's a total program of communication skills. Why don't you sit back, relax, or take a break and get a snack. When you come back we're going to talk about the math program. Yes, the math program—thought that would move you!

MATHEMATICS

Mathematics presents some unique problems. Many of us feel very shaky about the whole idea of teaching this subject. Well, fear not, we shall help you!

If we organize as suggested in chapter III, we've got three math groups. The question then becomes what do I do with mine? Well, we've got math texts and need the security they offer. How-

ever, we should use them with flexibility. In a nongraded program we need a math sequence to follow. We would suggest some caution in adopting or developing a math sequence. We feel that diagnosis is most easily adapted to the program of math. Therefore, we should begin the program relating to a sequence by diagnosing the child's placement on the sequence. Since there are two basic types of sequences we will offer approaches for both.

The first type of sequence is developed in terms of levels. This type permits the development of level tests for placement. This type of sequence generally includes all aspects of the math program in each level; that is, level seven will probably include skills in set theory, numeration, addition and subtraction of whole numbers, multiplication and division of whole numbers, decimals, fractions, geometry, measurement and special math topics. Thus as you work through level seven with a child or a group of children you must deal with a broad spectrum of skills.

One problem with this type of sequence is the assumption the teacher makes that a child in level seven has developed equal ability in each of the aforementioned aspects of math. This is a dangerous assumption and should result in further diagnostic testing within the level. It is easy to see that management of such a sequence could theoretically be hampered by cross leveling of skill development in various areas, and could become horrendous in terms of record-keeping. Of course keeping the child in level seven will prevent this.

In terms of teaching we can take the top group and work with one half of them as a group in level seven and the other half as a group in level six. We are saying that the math program will involve small group instruction in presentation of skill areas, and individual practice with the skill areas. In the individual area we can use skill tapes, programmed texts, and worksheets correlated with the skill sequence to provide practice, extension and enrichment.

In practice we meet with the top group, pretest for a skill—let's say, two column addition with regrouping. We bring the children who performed poorly together and teach the skill, and give them practice exercises to do through tapes or worksheets. But what about the children who perform well on the diagnostic test? Well, initially they could, perhaps, work on their communication skills contract until you get to them. Once you're operating, they can be fullfilling an obligation in math on the same terms as communication skills; that is, a limit in terms of the amount of work and time they have to complete it. They can work through the skill sequence on their own using the book, tapes and skill sheets corresponding to the sequence. They can check these themselves and report to you when their score falls below a certain level, say 90 percent.

Again you start with a group basically in the same place, and they will begin to individualize themselves. They are going to need skill lessons as they come across new concepts. Some of these lessons are presented very well through skill tapes, movies, or by other children. Try some of these and get in on the skill only when their methods fail. You know there are some students who will have to have every skill presented by you, but don't let this slow up the progress of the others.

If you don't want them to get too far ahead of you on the sequences, you can let them go so far and then offer enrichment choices such as a history of numeration systems, or history of measurement, calculating devices old and new, numbers in other bases, developing their own number systems or math games. There are lots of ways they can go that you can manage and that they will find productive.

The second kind of math sequence is developed sequentially in each area. Thus set theory is sequenced totally and separately, numeration is sequenced totally and separately. The same is true for each of the other areas such as addition and subtraction of whole numbers, multiplication and 49 division of whole numbers, fractions-addition and subtraction, fractions-multiplication and division, decimals-addition and subtraction, decimals-multiplication and division, geometry, measurement, and special topics such as Roman numerals, percentage, and probability. In a self-contained classroom, a suggested organization to begin with might be to allocate a period of time to each of these topics. A placement test would put the child somewhere on the sequence, let's say numeration. You then can divide the class into three groups according to their scores on the test. Thus you will have a "top," "middle," and "low" group all dealing with numeration. It will be necessary to make a decision concerning the amount of time to be spent on this topic. You should spend that amount of time and then go on to another sequence, pretest it, and group the children. Once you begin this approach and record where the children are when you finish a sequence, you will be able to return to any sequence at any time, move back a couple of skills and pick the child up where he is.

An approach with this second type of sequence in a nongraded setting is to have each teacher on the team responsible for two or three sequences for all the children. Thus Teacher A might be responsible for numeration, addition and subtraction of whole numbers, and geometry. Teacher B would have three topics and Teacher C would have three. Teacher A would then have one-third of the students in numeration to pretest and work with, Teacher B would have one-third of the children to work with in multiplication and division of whole numbers, and Teacher C one-third of the group in measurement. This requires a record keeping system that identifies which areas the child has worked in. It also requires that a time limit decision be made, for example, two weeks, to be spent by each teacher on his topic. One way to handle the movement of the children is to designate them as groups A, B and C. Start group A in the first sequence or area, B in the second, and C in the third and rotate the groups through the sequence at the time period decided upon.

It is possible at this point (after you've got the program and the children organized) to begin some contract work in math. The contract should be developed with the same criterion as the communication skills program, that is, limits in terms of time and amount. Due to the nature of available math materials we can include the following:

1. The Text—we can contract for a certain number of pages in the text. This means the child can skip through the book doing all the pages related to a certain skill that he is able to contract for.

2. Tapes—a variety of math skill tapes are available for use in our programs.

We can contract a specified number of tapes related to a topic.

3. Workbooks—many math workbooks are also available and we can contract these the same as we do the text book.

4. Math Kits—we can include math kit assignments in the contract. The SRA kits are good.

5. Games—there is a variety of math games available that can be used to reinforce the necessary skills. These can be included in the contract and add fun to it.

6. Supplementary—in this part of the contract we can include assignments related to special interests the student might have in math such as math history.

We end up with a six dimension contract that certainly can be designed to meet the child's need. Using a contract and small group skill lessons enables the child who is not scheduled in the skill session at a particular time to move along and engage himself productively. This gives you time to teach small groups and check on individuals' progress.

If able, the children should keep their own records in this program also, checking their own papers when they are able, or taking them to checkers until they are able to check their own. Their records need to show the page numbers, skill tape number, skill from the skill sequence, kit skill, game, workbook page, and supplementary activity. Check-out is simplified in that you only need to check the scores for the activities they've done. These give you direction in organizing small groups for instruction. We would again suggest beginning this approach with the top group. This will give a chance to learn how to manage the program. We think you'll be pleased with the results, as children will be moving at their own pace. They will reach a point where they will be able to follow the sequence and develop their own contracts to meet the skills in the sequence. When this happens you're going to pat yourself on the back and you'll deserve it.

Well, there's your math program. All you need to do is assess the materials you've got, and decide where you're going to start—so "go get 'em!" Overwhelmed? It can do that to you, but take heart, what we've suggested so far works, but you don't need to do it all at once. Besides, all we've got left to discuss is social studies and science. You need another break? O.K., take it, and when you're ready we're going to discuss social studies and science.

Couldn't wait to get back? We knew it. It's almost as exciting as a mystery, isn't it?

SOCIAL STUDIES AND SCIENCE

If you recall in chapter III, social studies and science are scheduled for the afternoons. We've tried having both in the same afternoon, i.e., two units running concurrently, and we've tried alternating units, i.e., social studies for four weeks, science for three then social studies, etc. We prefer the latter approach. The real impact of the open concept begins to be demonstrated in these afternoon units. The total group should work on the same topic. Thus you will have 75 students and three teachers dealing with a unit on Mexico. One of the teachers will have preplanned the whole unit and will have given assignments to the other teachers in terms of their responsibility for the unit. The "planning teacher" will assume major responsibility for the organization and implementation of the unit. Thus he or she will, for example, take care of most of the large group discussions or presentations.

While this unit is operating, one of the other teachers will be planning ahead for the next unit, which might be a science unit on electricity. In these units all types of methodology and groupings can be brought to bear. You can use group projects, individual learning projects, individual learning packets, learning centers, contracts, print and nonprint media, dramatics, art, music, physical education, and anything else available to add depth to the unit.

We have a suggestion, an initial organization that will help to carry out the program. We'll try to diagram it and discuss the diagram (Fig. 1).

FIGURE 1   SOCIAL STUDIES AND SCIENCE SCHEMATA

A	B	C
Content applicable to general knowledge, probably appropriate for the whole group.	Small group interest areas (committee work).	Individual projects. Each child would choose an aspect of the unit that interests him or her particularly and design a means of perusing this interest. This would also be controlled by a time limit.
Can be handled through large group instruction, packets that each child completes, or general assignments.	In this column different topics relating to the unit would be offered. The children would make two choices from these topics. They would be assigned to the topics as committees, getting their first choice where possible, and given definite guidelines concerning the committee's responsibilities, and a deadline for completion.	
This column would be required of everyone.		

There are some points to consider. If you feel you've got to give tests, they should be related to the items in column A. This column will also help develop grades in terms of class standing if you feel you must.

Column B committee work can be profitable or very blah. The mistake we make most often with committees is failing to define their task. When we've got six committees, in effect we've got six plans to write. Of course as children become experienced in committee work, the directions can become more flexible and general, but initially they should be very specific.

First, a chairman should be appointed for each committee. We'd suggest saving the election of chairmen until some other procedures are learned. For that first committee, appoint a chairman you feel will make it work. Then each committee should be given a detailed outline of its responsibilities. A sample below shows what to include:

1. Objective—this committee is to identify six of the major forms of entertainment preferred by the Mexican people.

2. The committee must describe these activities, explain why they are so popular, and the extent of their popularity.

3. The committee must then prepare a means by which this information can be given to the other students in the class.

4. The committee has two weeks.

Basically all you want to say is what must be done, and how much time is allotted to do it. This effort will pay off in management of the program. We'd suggest that initially that is the item of greatest concern.

When you feel comfortable managing the program, then you can branch out and explore all the possibilities of the approach. One excellent byproduct of committees is the development of learning stations for use by the other children. Remember everything you can get developed in a way other than through your own effort is going to add to your program, and enable you to branch out and expand the child's learning opportunities.

Column C doesn't require a great deal of in-put on your part, except, perhaps, in helping the child identify an area or a project he can do. You will have to evaluate the final results. A word of caution: try to be objective in your evaluation. Establish criteria for evaluating these projects, such as accuracy and effort. Try to avoid the notion of evaluating on beauty and artistic talent. These look great, but some lack accuracy of detail and content, and all children are not artists.

We've got heterogeneous groups of children of different ages working on

53

areas of similar interest, and making decisions and developing group and individual responsibility. If you think back to chapter I you'll remember that that's the name of the game in the open concept. It probably is best exemplified in the social studies and science programs, and we should not miss the opportunity to make it work.

As you can see, this approach provides the child with an opportunity to develop some skills in terms of large group operation, some responsibility in terms of a small group task, and some responsibility in terms of personal commitment. Thus we can organize a program that deals with content and at the same time attempts to meet the social skills related to the implications of social studies for living.

One consideration we have to examine with any approach is that a child will be in the same primary or intermediate unit for three years, thus we must cycle the curriculum. We believe this will give us a chance to develop three year cycles of curriculum, providing us with optional content choices. We believe content is relevant and accurate in an inquiry-centered approach; teachers and students should be given more latitude in its selection. We also believe there is enough happening in the world that it would be foolish to repeat a topic for a child three years in a row.

If we get to a cycled option-oriented curriculum, it is imperative that we be prepared to sequence those skills related to social studies and science applicable to the examination of content. In part two of this book we've included a sample social studies skill sequence to give you an idea of the kind of thing we're talking about.

If you just use the sequence as a guide for teaching lessons you'll probably do a better job of skill development than your text has been doing. One way to approach the sequence is to develop Individual Learning Packets for each skill area. This will enable the children who can work independently to progress along the sequence at their own rate, and help you identify those children who will need your help in for example, a small group presentation.

You will need to check-off the sequence as the child completes it. This will provide you with a continuous record of his progress.

There are other ways to organize approaches to topics, through learning centers, packets or even individual topic selection. It is probably a good idea to try different approaches. If you only repeat an approach three or four times a year you will prevent the problem of boredom resulting from doing the same thing over and over.

This chapter has hit the four major areas of the curriculum. Has it left you breathless, or speechless, or confused? We hope it has left you excited! These things will work, either in your classroom or with a team. We'd like to say "Try it, you'll like it," but the philosophy discusses decision making for oneself, so all we can say is, "Try it, and see if you like it."

We know there are other areas of the curriculum to be discussed. We will do that in the specials' chapter. Our first concern, however, is the organization, management, and methodology applicable to the basic academic program of the classroom. We hope we've been clear about what to do. If we haven't, send us your questions and we'll answer them if we can.

Why don't you sleep on it and tomorrow get up and get started! How? By reading the next several chapters, of course. They will define methods that you can use to help implement and enhance the program suggested. You won't be able to sleep? Well, o.k., then go ahead and read them *now!*

Checkout is an uninterrupted one-to-one time.

Team teaching is teachers planning together to provide the best learning environment for children.

5

Team Teaching

WHAT DOES A teacher say when she feels so good about teaching she is almost reluctant to leave the building after school? And how does she explain the fact that it is June 1 and she is still cheerfully going to school in the mornings. Well, you could say the lucky person just might be involved in an adventure called team teaching.

Team teaching, especially in an open situation, is an experience teachers do not forget. We won't! Who's we? We thought you'd never ask! It's Ray, Gwen and Anita coming in at 8:15 A.M. to plan, to communicate, to scream, to share, to respect, to fail, to succeed, to learn, to search—always to search for a better way.

It's also Gwen, Anita and Ray sitting down at lunch to continue planning, communicating, screaming, sharing, respecting, failing, succeeding, learning, searching—always searching for a better way.

And last but not least, it's Anita, Ray and Gwen at 4:45 P.M. leaving—tired, but fulfilled, knowing that today they planned, communicated, screamed, shared, respected, failed, succeeded, learned, searched—for a better way.

You say that's great, but I still don't know what team teaching is! It's really very simple to us, although there have been extensive books written on the subject. Team teaching is simply a group of teachers working and planning together to provide the best learning environment possible for their children.

Teaming offers options for varying group sizes and flexible grouping of children. Team teaching to us is not, "I teach while you loaf. You teach while I get coffee."

However, if one of our team mates had a rotten cold we'd be glad to teach 57 for him any time. Or if one of us has gotten bogged down with check-outs, another will certainly bring her some coffee, or help with the check-outs. That's why *caring* and *sharing* are necessary in any team.

Why should you change what you've been doing? Everyone of us asked the same thing at one time or another. "I've been effective in my own classroom, why should I change!"

1. Why? It works for one thing! Research has been conducted and many studies show team teaching is a very effective way of teaching.

2. It's more efficient, for another. There is less repetition when a team organizes and plans together. Before we began teaming in math, we sat down and discovered that in one day all three teachers had taught or reviewed multiplication. Isn't that ridiculous? With teaming that can be avoided.

3. It's more fun. Don't knock it until you've tried it. Someone is always up when you're down and vice versa.

4. It's a good way to train student teachers or strengthen weak teachers. Caution, though, if the team is too heavily weighted it is impossible for it to function. For instance, two more capable people can pull along a third weaker one, but with two weak people on a team it is very difficult for

the one more capable person to survive and keep the team functioning.

5. It's a perfect way to learn from one another. As a member of a team you are constantly in a give-and-take situation. Perhaps you will give someone a neat suggestion for a punctuation packet and she'll give you an approach to use with a child with whom you've been having difficulty.

6. It allows teachers to use flexible grouping for improved instruction. By the use of skill sequences and optional organizational plans, a child's needs can be closely met. See the chapters on scheduling and organization and on skill sequences for more specifics.

7. It builds on teacher strengths. If one particular teacher is great in one area, science for instance, the team pulls from her strength. If a teacher has a weakness, the team can help make up for it.

8. It provides more correlation and continuity within subject matter. Everyone knows what everyone else is doing, because they're planning it together.

9. It means better teaching because three people can plan the unit instead of one. By the time you as a team pool *all* your resources—families, friends, acquaintances, neighbors and club members, your team simply *must*

produce a better and richer environment for children, whether it's borrowing Aunt Ida's crocheted afghan or using neighbor Bill's slides on Argentina.

10. It builds team spirit and improves morale. We just wish we had nickels for each person who's said to us, "I don't know why I ever wanted to teach in a self-contained classroom," or "I'll never go back." If your team clicks, it's an experience you'll never forget! We promise! If your team doesn't click . . . well, that's another story and it is covered later on in the chapter.

11. It causes each teacher to question what she's been doing professionally. A teacher on a team sees two or three other people teaching, guiding and relating to children. They may have newer approaches, other techniques which work and work well. It really has made us all wonder at one time or another "How could I have been so blind?" or "That approach Ray used worked beautifully," or "I'm going to try to use more patience like Gwen." However you still remain you and you do many things right which they notice and use.

12. And most important of all, it causes every teacher to take a look at himself personally. Each person expecting to work on a team should be willing to ask, "Am I doing this the best way?" "Is there a better way?" "Am I being honest?" "Am I communicating?" "How can I cooperate more?" We think if a teacher on a team has a good experience, one of the most important rewards he reaps is a great deal more knowledge about himself as a person.

Now, that's all great for teachers. But what about the children? What does it do for them?

1. First, children have more teachers; they're more likely to find one to whom they can relate. A quiet child can relate to a quiet mannered teacher, or a boy with only a mother at home will gravitate to a man on the team.

2. A child's motivation can be increased because of various teachers' approaches. As we all know, most children want to please their teachers, especially ones they like. Certain adults can motivate certain children—a fact we as parents and teachers have known for a long time. Too bad we're just now doing something about this little bit of information.

3. Children will be working at their ability level because of flexible grouping and less repetition.

Now teachers and children like team teaching, who's left? Oh, yes, the parents. For parents team teaching provides a three or four person evaluation team to note their child's scholastic achievement as well as his social and emotional growth.

There are then advantages for everyone. But are teams always that fantastic? No! How do they get that way? Hard work and give-and-take, among other things. But, since we've been observing in school districts where we've conducted workshops, it's been relatively easy to spot good teams and to see problems—some of which could have been avoided.

The first *must* in a successful team is for the teachers to get along. Some teams click; others don't, and we've observed a few similarities in the good teams:

First, the one thing good teams seem to have in common is a similar philosophy of education. Sound strange? Maybe, but we've observed teachers getting along well together who feel the same about children. Their backgrounds, teaching techniques and methods for helping students learn may be completely different, but if they believe in the importance and uniqueness of children, they seem to be able to work around all obstacles in order to create the best situation possible for their students.

Second, there must be a strong commitment to job, career, open education, or whatever you want to call it. Now, this doesn't mean complete and total abandonment of family, friends, hobbies, or relaxation. It simply means there must be an eagerness to cooperate, to give-and-take, to communicate, and a willingness to put forth the greater effort necessary for team teaching.

Third, the people who work on a team must be able to look at themselves. People with weak egos or those with poor self-concepts could have problems.

Fourth, the team should be selected ahead of time. They should get to know each other before they try to get to know a new program.

Fifth, *They Must Have Time To Plan.* Cooperative ventures take cooperative time to plan. Schedules, units, children's problems—all these need to be discussed during planning time.

Now what about size of teams? Teams of two, three or four seem to function well. Teams of five and six work out fairly well. Teams of seven and more are poor. Why? No one has a chance to get a word in edgewise, that's why! How can you communicate and contribute if you don't have a chance to utter a peep?

Another thing we've noticed is that the success of teams depends to some extent on the team leader. It is certainly important therefore to select carefully. The principal can select the person, the teachers can elect the individual, or the position of team leader can be rotated. However you decide to do it, the team leader shouldn't be selected because he or she is nice. The qualities to look for are:

1. A doer, an action person

2. Enthusiasm for the idea

3. A natural leader among people

4. Sensitivity to people and their needs

5. Fairness

6. Someone who's not afraid to get mad

7. Someone who has the knowledge or training to know something about where the team is going

8. Common sense so the team can avoid some pitfalls in achieving their goals

On a team, teachers are busy. There should be a structure or organization to avoid repetition and confusion. If teachers think about teaming and the many team responsibilities they will have, it might be helpful to list the responsibilities of the members as well as the team leader. Following are those responsibilities as we've delineated them. You will, of course, want to adapt them to your situation. We have included the teacher's responsibilities, the team leader's responsibilities, and the role of the principal.

PROFESSIONAL TEACHER'S RESPONSIBILITIES

1. Guiding and instructing children

2. Planning individual and group lessons

3. Preparation of contracts, packets and learning stations

4. Helping to plan "curriculum" in team planning

5. Contribute in decision making of team

6. Take responsibility for discipline, clean up, etc.

7. Interacting with other team members in team planning sessions

8. Keep records of individual students up to date

9. Pre-planning units for team

10. Relate to individual children

11. Added responsibility for special projects—outdoor education, parent involvement, newspaper, etc.

12. Share in handling large group—70 or more

13. Assist in preparing notices and other materials to be sent home

14. Be involved in continual program evaluation

15. In-service training for self

16. Previewing and familiarizing selves with available materials for use in program

17. Assist visitors

18. Involve parents in program

19. Preparing for parent conferences and report letters

20. Assist in keeping parents informed by participating in parent meetings

21. Be open and honest

In addition to duties performed by teachers, a team leader assumes other responsibilities:

1. Coordinate whole program for children and teachers

2. Develop alternate schedules for consideration by team members

3. Develop fundamental routines for consideration by team members

4. Schedule special events

5. Plan alternative approaches for integration of art, music, etc.

6. Act as organizer

7. Prepare agenda for and conduct planning sessions—point out options

8. Report on program and progress of team to principal and other interested people

9. Represent team when asked

10. Delegate responsibilities equally among team members

11. Initiate discussions at team planning

12. Make small nitty gritty decisions

13. Make final decisions if team members can't agree

14. Encourage team members to communicate and share

15. Bring problems out in the open for discussion

16. Plan parent conferences

17. Arrange field trips

18. Be open and honest

As you look at some of the above responsibilities, you may be thinking, "that's the principal's job." And it may well be. It all depends on your administration. The necessity for a team leader stems from the fact that someone must be available to make decisions. That person must be available *all* the time and must understand the problems. If a principal has that kind of time, is involved directly, and is actually teaching on the team, perhaps he could do some of those things. If not, however, a team leader must be appointed.

What, then, is the role of the principal? In some ways exactly the same; in others, it will be a little different. The principal's, or director's, responsibility is one of support, guidance and decision making. Some of his tasks would be:

1. Finding out about new materials, kits, etc. which could support and improve the program

2. Planning and carrying out parent education meetings and making sure parents understand the program completely

3. "Selling" the program in the community to parents, lay people, school board members, and fellow administrators

4. Planning and organizing a parent involvement program to bring parents into school for the teachers to use as they choose

5. Coordinating a testing program for the school

6. Supporting and encouraging the teachers

7. Accepting only supportive people, people who buy your program, to work in the building

8. Being a responsive listener to your team leaders

9. Being open and honest

As you work on teams you'll think of other responsibilities for teachers, team leaders and principals, but these will get you started.

One last thing to consider should be team planning time. As we've stated, any team which actually works together needs to plan together. However, if you call yourself a team, but each of you has his area and his children, and never the twain shall meet, then forget it! You aren't teaming and you don't need *team* planning time.

As you remember from the chapter on organizing and scheduling, each team should get at least a two hour period per week to plan. In order to get planning time we put our special subjects back to back one afternoon a week, i.e. a child goes from art to music to physical education on that afternoon and his "regular" teachers are thus "freed up" to plan.

Other teams have considered alternative plans for teaming because this plan makes integration of the special teachers into the program very difficult. When the team is planning, the special teachers have the children and they are unable to sit in on the team meeting. However, the way we solved that problem was to meet over the lunch hour with the art teacher or any of the specials who were interested in being involved in the program. So in spite of the difficulty with integration of those people, we believe this 63 to be the best way of getting time to plan. And since we were given two hours to plan we were more than willing to begin planning on our lunch hour. (We ended up planning over every lunch hour anyway.) We also continued to plan long after the 3 o'clock dismissal, and it was not at all unusual for us to plan til 4:30 or 5:00 P.M. on our planning day (and other days, too).

Some teams prefer to meet every morning before school, every day at lunch or every evening after school. They like to plan for thirty to forty minutes each day. We didn't choose this approach because we felt it allowed insufficient time to accomplish anything.

Other teams have chosen to free all teachers but one. That teacher monitored the children, who watched a movie. We dislike this approach for the obvious reason that one member was always missing and had to be filled in later. Also we felt it was unfair to make decisions with one person absent.

Another approach which probably makes the most sense, but might be objectionable to parents is an early dismissal one day a week. And if the time must be made up, this can be done by cutting down on the child's lunch hour if he has too much time, or by adding fifteen to twenty minutes to each day in order to make up

time lost by a 12:30 or 1:00 dismissal. In some cases no time will have to be added because some children already attend more than the minimum time requirement.

As with every other part of this book, you will have to adapt the ideas to your situation in order to schedule planning time which makes most sense to your school.

Now, we promised to talk more about what to do if your team has problems? If your team doesn't work smoothly we recommend the following:

1. Try communication. Talk to the person who is causing the problem and find out why; get him to talk about it.

2. Try the above again. We cannot over emphasize the importance of communicating and talking out the team's difficulties.

3. Ask your principal to help, to sit in and observe to see if he agrees with your perceptions. Then ask for his suggestions.

4. If the team just cannot seem to pull away from the problem, don't give up. KEEP TRYING! If one person gives up, it's so easy for another to follow suit.

5. Give it time. Time heals many ills. But if your ill isn't cured, grin and

bear it, keep your chin up, and at the end of the year ask for a transfer and try again. It's definitely worth another try. The next time might be the charm.

To sum up the merits of team teaching we have chosen the following heart-warming description by Judi Sheer, a teacher in the Elizabeth Jenkins School.

WHAT IS TEAM TEACHING?

What is team teaching? Wow! What a power-packed question! Very briefly it means caring, understanding, sharing, but most of all it means communicating. Communicating feelings and thoughts on program, policy, and procedure. It means growth and development, and the compromise and frustration that comes from the great phenomena of inter-personal relationships. It's a special feeling we have for one another built on mutual respect and trust.

Being a new staff member in an open-space lab school could be an awesome and frightening experience (could be, heck, it was!). Team teaching after five years in a self-contained classroom had me a bit bewildered. I was anxiously looking forward to it, but I don't mind admitting I was scared to death.

I kept telling myself to be confident, self-assured, and all the other positive

kinds of things your brain loudly tells you. I'm convinced it's loud so that you don't hear your knees knocking together or your heart pounding like thunder.

Looking back now (one-half school year later) those fears have certainly dissipated. They have been replaced by several realistic comments.

To begin:

It's wondering how to present that math lesson differently and walking in to find other people pondering that same question.

It's having a loud, lengthy disagreement-type discussion and then going out for lunch.

It's sitting and listening to someone who is concerned about a particular problem or situation.

It's staying until 7:00 P.M. to discuss and make changes in the program.

It's concern over kids' problems.

It's having to "get outside of yourself" in order to solve some problems.

It's being in a good mood when no one else is (and vice versa).

It's oversleeping on a dark, cold winter morning, rushing to school to find that someone has gotten you a cup of coffee and there it is steaming away on your desk.

It's solving the world's problems over your lunch hour.

It's someone who will take over for you or you for them if the need arises.

It's being flexible.

It's being sometimes frustrated.

It's having a sense of humor (definitely important!!).

It's deciding together.

It's sharing together, but it's much more than working together. It's mutual respect, concern, trust, honesty, and openness.

You get so much out of it—you learn about yourself and the way others see you.

The kids benefit because among the team's resources are vast experiences and ideas. What you are good in and enjoy—just very well may be my weakness. You might groove on molecules and I dig teaching pronouns. Writing about it is one thing but living it is entirely different.

If you get the opportunity to team teach be prepared for an adjustment. You have to think about others now, you're not the only one running the show. Be prepared also for the most exciting, rewarding, and enriching experience of your life. Try it, I hope you like it!

*Children work on their
individual projects too.*

CHAPTER VI

The Cultural Arts and Complementary Personnel

THIS CHAPTER DEALS with a much maligned segment of our program: art, music, physical education, industrial arts (where it exists in our elementary schools), reading specialists or consultants, remedial reading teachers, counselors, foreign language teachers, and librarians or media specialists.

Some of us have all of these, and some of us have none. We don't mind saying that, to our knowledge, the true role of these people in an open program has yet to be developed. There are several reasons for this, we think, and we'd like to discuss the most obvious. The primary reason for the lack of integration of these programs into the system is planning time. When you get involved in the kind of program described in this book, you must have time to plan.

Society has avoided providing school for the children four and a half days a week, leaving one-half day for the teachers to plan. We feel this is a sensible approach and will try to justify it later in the chapter. However, educators have decided that the way to get planning time is to send the children to art, physical education, and music, freeing the teachers from the responsibility of children and giving them planning time. We believe this is a satisfactory solution at present; first, because it works, and second, because the cultural arts programs have not been developed yet to function on a practical basis without scheduled time. We won't presume to offer such a plan completely, but we do have some ideas about beginning it.

Perhaps initially, we should offer some rationale concerning the place of cultural arts in the school program. We believe that for many children, and maybe for all, the cultural arts program is just as important as the 67 academic program. There has been a tendency in our schools to suggest that cultural arts programs are frills. This is not true. Many children in our schools are going to be very successful, are going to be involved in very high level jobs, are going to be involved in crucial decision making, and are going to be involved in the pressures of our society. One of the ways that these people will have to free themselves from the pressures which they, themselves, have chosen to undergo, will be derived from the cultural arts. People who might otherwise become greatly disturbed and overwrought with pressure may paint to relieve the pressure, go bowling to relieve the pressure, or listen to music to relieve the pressure. We submit that in these peoples' lives, cultural arts will be just as important as their ability to read, to think, and to generalize. We can no longer relegate these important aspects of our curriculum to second rate status. They must be built into our programs. We must then take a look at their role in the curriculum, the approaches we have taken with them, and come up with some plan to make them fit, to be better integrated, not only into the curriculum but into the lives of the children.

We will begin our discussion of cultural arts by suggesting ways they can be involved in the program even if they are being used to free the teachers for planning. Of course, when you send your children to cultural arts on a scheduled basis to relieve yourself of the responsibility of the children, so that you can plan, you are basically not in touch with the cultural arts people. They are working with the children while you are planning. With this kind of organization we have a tendency to forget that in our planning sessions we can still provide opportunities for the cultural arts people to extend our programs from the classroom into the arts. We have a tendency to plan social studies programs without realizing the implications of the cultural arts for the social studies. For example, if we are planning to do a unit on Mexico, in our planning we ought to consider what, specifically, we could request of the art teacher, the music teacher, and the physical education teacher, in terms of activities that would relate to a unit on Mexico. We believe the music teacher and the art teacher and the physical education teacher would be glad to deal with topics related to Mexico in their classes if we would alert them to the fact that we are going to be dealing with Mexico.

How can we alert them? We have to talk to them at lunch time, after school, before school, or just send them a note telling them that for the next three weeks the students will be dealing with Mexico. Ask them if they could relate any parts of their curriculum to Mexico. We realize that this is certainly not total integration, but it is at least a start in helping the cultural arts people to recognize that we know they are there, we care that they are there, and we care about the part they play in the children's program. If we start this way, perhaps this can lead to better ways to integrate cultural arts into our program.

Of course, as long as we continue to schedule children into the cultural arts program, we are going to have the problem of integration. The alternative to that is, of course, an unscheduled cultural arts program. In order to get into an unscheduled cultural arts program it will be necessary for the art, music and physical education teachers to examine their programs with the same scrutiny we have applied to our academic programs. They must come up with sequences of learning, with a record-keeping system, with option-oriented programs that will provide opportunities for the childern to function at their level and with their interests. They could superimpose a skill sequence over this type program so the children would not miss the skills necessary to function in their program. We believe this can be done in each of these areas. As a matter of fact, teachers have already begun. In the next section we will discuss each area separately, and try to define for each area those crucial things which need special examination.

MUSIC

Music is perhaps the area of the cultural arts most difficult to change.

The reasons for this are hard to identify. Recognizing our limited knowledge of music, we realize that some music teachers will not agree with some of what we say. But, we feel that music, like any other area of the curriculum, deserves to be examined so that it can best provide experiences for the child to improve his skills and experiences to lead him to the joys of music. Music, like reading, math, science and all other areas of the curriculum, must have the development of attitude as its principal goal. Each child should leave school with positive attitudes about music. Only through positive attitudes will he be willing to explore the potential of music.

Why is music a part of the curriculum? That question needs to be pondered and to be answered. If a philosophy of music is developed, it would seem that a program that meets that philosophy would be simpler to develop than a program that has no philosophy. We are not saying that the music programs to date have no philosophy. We are saying that we ought to look again at our music programs in terms of the philosophy we espouse. If these are inconsistent then we need to re-define our programs.

One of the most vital needs in the music curriculum is a sequence of skill. This need not be a sequence of skills based on a publishing company's needs: written on paper, put between covers of different colors, and labeled as first grade music, second grade music, and third grade music, etc. This will not do! We cannot believe that music skills and chronological age are so closely related as to be totally inflexible and immovable. Reading skills do not develop in terms of chronological age, math skills do not develop in terms of chronological age; in fact, no skills develop chronologically. But when we examine our music programs we find that eight year olds are expected to be at the same level of understanding in terms of music skill, the same level of performance in terms of music skill, the same level of interest in terms of the types of music, and the same level of attitude in terms of their attitudes towards music. If inflexible levels based on chronological ages do not make sense in any other part of the curriculum, then how can it make sense in the music curriculum? The music curriculum must function through a sequence. When this is developed, it will be possible to put eight-, nine-, and ten-year-old children into the same music class to deal with their skills on any specific level, and to have them function in musical activities related to their interest.

The technical details of this approach will not be dealt with in this book. Our point is that in order to develop music as an integral part of a program for children, we must first develop a philosophy of what music is to do, then design an approach that will in fact do that. We think the key to that approach is a skill sequence in music that enables the music teacher to keep track of where the children are in the skills. We believe that music has a skill orientation to it which can be managed through a skill sequence. We also believe music has an interest factor related to it, and that students of varying abilities can be interested in the same activities. They can be interested in listening to the same kinds of music, interested in performing on the same kinds of instruments, interested in learning about the same kinds of instruments. We think the music program must be designed sequentially in terms of skills, and at the same time provide a wide variety of activities and options so that the children can pursue an interest in music. The music teacher can then reinforce this interest knowing something about the skill levels of children. We repeat, we do not believe that these skill levels can be totally related to the child's chronological age. At this point in our educational system, we know too much about individual differences to continue to believe that, and to continue to function in that way.

Once a curriculum is developed with these ideas in mind, the second item of concern is to move from scheduled music classes to unscheduled music. When people hear the word "unscheduled," they become a little excited, because teachers have not tried enough of this approach to be able to specify exactly how it would work. We will discuss nonscheduled specials in some detail later in this chapter.

We would sum up our comments about music with these remarks. Music can play a vital role in each child's life. If in our attempts to teach him music, we teach him to dislike it, or we don't teach him all the facets of it, then we have failed in our purpose, which, simply stated, is to build positive attitudes in each child about music.

ART

Of all the special areas, the art curriculum seems to offer the best potential for immediate integration into an open concept program. Certainly it will be necessary to develop skill sequences in the art area. These, of course, will have to be developed by people familiar with the skills and materials related to the elementary school art curriculum. A skill sequence will have to be developed in each of the various media as they relate to the elementary school child. It is possible in an art program to set up a room with five or six options so that as groups of children come, they can choose the medium that they wish to work with. The art teacher can then plan large- or small-group instructional units in the use of the media in the centers. This instruction can precede the children's involvement in the interest areas, or can go on simultaneously with the operation of various centers. For example, centers can be set up involving water colors, puppetry, clay, paper cutting, pastels, and yarn. The children could choose an area and the teacher could get everyone started except the group working with water colors. She would then take time to give this small group the instruction in the skills of water color that is appropriate for their developmental level. They would then proceed to work in the water color center. This approach would require some type of skill sequence, so that a record could be kept of each child's proficiency in the various media. Perhaps your art teacher would be willing to begin by offering two options to the children for each art lesson. Art has an advantage over music because of the availability of a variety of media from which the child can choose. This enables the child to choose materials that are easy for him in terms of providing him with some success. Art doesn't require the skill level that music does in order to develop a "harmonious" product. Art also has the advantage of being judged by the maker in terms less dictated by society. It is basically more personal and offers success opportunities to more of the students than the music curriculum can. Most art teachers are quick to see this, and willing to at least begin to offer some flexibility in their program.

In school the ultimate purpose of art, as in music, is to develop a positive attitude in the children concerning the various opportunities available to them through art.

PHYSICAL EDUCATION

Physical education, like art, offers a multitude of opportunities to develop skills and deal with the child's interest at the same time. Physical education offers a wide variety of activities for the child to pursue. It can offer individual activities, dual activities, small-group activities, and large-group activities. It can offer individual competition and team competition.

The physical education program also needs to be sequenced. The sequences need to be developed in each area from large muscle control to small muscle control. Skills must be sequenced from the area of controlling the body to controlling the body with an implement, such as a hockey stick. Skill sequencing in the physical education area will provide the necessary record-keeping to prevent a child of eight from receiving the same basic instruction in soccer for three consecutive years. Rather it will permit the child to move on to advanced soccer skills, if he is ready, and keep the child who is not ready functioning with the basic skills.

Like art and music, physical education must develop an attitude that will encourage the child to pursue those areas that are of interest to him. It should prepare him to look forward to the potential for his recreational life as he matures.

INDUSTRIAL ARTS

Industrial arts is a relatively new addition to the elementary curriculum. In fact, in most schools it is not even considered a part of the elementary curriculum. But there is an increasing interest in industrial arts in the elementary schools, and more and more schools are adding it. It does bring a new dimension to the special areas of the curriculum. Certainly the skills connected with the various tools would need to be sequenced. Industrial arts offers some areas that overlap with the art program; these should be worked out between the two teachers in order to prevent duplication. We have no objection to duplication, *per se,* except that each of these areas has such a variety of experiences to offer the children, that to duplicate might deprive the children of exposure to an area that they would profit from and enjoy.

As it develops, the industrial arts curriculum goes beyond the construction of wood and metal products. It enters into the world of mass production and environmental awareness. It is generally a high interest area for the children. It also has the basic purpose of developing positive attitudes toward the various media available to each child. It offers the child another option from which to begin to choose those things that are important to him.

FOREIGN LANGUAGE

Most elementary schools don't have foreign language programs. Many have had them and then dropped them. Perhaps they are economically unfeasible or perhaps we made the mistake of trying to make the program fit everyone. The basic question again in this area is how do we sequence the learning so that we know where the child is and how can we keep track of his successes? Another problem in this area is continuity in terms of instruction. If we set up a foreign language program of fifteen minutes once or twice a week, we can't expect any carry over. The child cannot function in Spanish, for example, for fifteen minutes and then deal with English for the rest of the week until the next fifteen minutes of Spanish, and still remember much of the Spanish. Foreign language must be a daily part of the child's program. This has been economically unfeasible with a graded organization. With a flexible program, and concern about the child's interest, there may be a place in the program now, where there was none in the rigidly scheduled graded program.

It seems like we keep repeating this, but the purpose of the foreign language program is to develop a positive attitude that will interest the child in pursuing foreign language in his later school years. Certainly he should not fear it, as many of us learned to do in our high school or college encounters with foreign language.

READING SPECIALISTS OR REMEDIAL READING TEACHERS

Almost all of you have a remedial reading teacher in your district. We can't help but believe that this must be a frustrating job, at least the way it's organized in most districts. It seems we have permitted this position to evolve into a teaching position. The children who need remedial help are identified. There are always too many for one person to handle, so some of the students can't get service. The reading teacher feels sorry or guilty about this and takes more children than she can handle. This means that each child gets less service. Then a schedule is developed that permits the reading teacher to work with each child fifteen minutes twice a week. We insist on taking this approach, knowing that every book on remedial reading stresses the point that the effectiveness of the teaching is related to the amount of attention extended to the child. They stress that, like foreign language, it is imperative that the child work on his skills daily, in an organized and sequential manner, or the results will be disappointing. Here

73

is another example of doing something that we know is ineffective, just so we can do something. We admit this is better than nothing, but it is certainly not better than doing what makes sense.

Why have we taken this approach? We believe it's been forced upon us, as have so many other things we do, by our graded system, and our attempts to be "fair." The question is, fair to whom? The children? We think not.

The usual approach is that if there is time to work with 24 students in the school, and if there are twelve rooms in the school, each room may send two kids to remedial reading class. Each teacher decides which two will be sent, and many of us decide it's a great time to get rid of Billy Smith who can't read, and it will be so nice to get him out of the room, even if it is only for fifteen minutes twice a week. The point of this is that the programs are not organized correctly; the wrong children are going and they aren't going often enough to make any difference.

Can anything be done about this? Yes, there are some things we can do even if we don't change the program. We can permit the reading teacher to test and identify specific reading problems with children. She can then design a program for the child that the regular teachers can follow daily, or that the child can follow daily. She can also

provide materials for the teacher and the child to use that will help the child. Further, she can encourage the use of materials that will fit the needs of the different learning styles of the children. In other words, she can help teachers and the district by designing programs and selecting materials that will help the children.

In an open concept program she will become a member of the teaching team. She will help identify reading problems. These can be implemented in conjunction with the communication skills program. Rather than being remedial the program can be preventive.

Finally, we get a reaction! It's o.k., we're ready! We will no longer need a remedial reading teacher. If the program has each child functioning at his level, regardless of what that is, how can he ever get "behind." It seems the only thing these kids have gotten behind is the rest of the class, and the social studies books. With a continuous progress, diagnostic based, individualized program they can't get behind. They may not move ahead very fast but they can't get behind, and we will work with them wherever they are.

With three or four teachers dealing with the children, more expertise will be available to identify the problems, and more strategies available to bring to bear on the problem. A resource person in reading will probably be needed to help with the serious problems, or to help identify materials that the teachers can use to help the children, or to help design a program for a child who is having problems. These things will be ever so much more effective in a setting where the reading teacher is functioning with the team, where there is dialogue, and where everyone's efforts are coordinated. You see, the reading teacher's position, too, needs to be examined in terms of why it exists, and how can it best accomplish those things it is supposed to accomplish.

THE COUNSELOR

We know that few of you have counselors in your elementary programs. Counselors have become crisis oriented. Their help in the crisis is very valuable, but we wonder how many of the crises could have been prevented if we had used the counselor to do that job she is intended for. In most cases they function like the remedial reading teacher and the foreign language teacher, that is, trying to do an impossible job in the way we are trying to do it now. Counselors too, must become members of the teaching team. They must be able to bring developmental counseling techniques to bear on the school situation. They just can't do this when we isolate ourselves in our individual classrooms. It seems like we are designing these pro-grams for the convenience of the teacher, rather than the children. We know we are helping some children, and we wonder if we could not help these, and many more, just by taking a different approach.

The counselor must be involved on the teaching team. She needs to be designing approaches the teachers can use with children on an ongoing daily basis. She needs to be a resource. She needs to observe behavior firsthand, and not treat it with second-hand information. So many times counselors get a distorted view just by the fact that they only see the child on a one-to-one basis in their quiet office. How many children have you seen in this type of setting that really challenge your patience? It is usually a peer group, or teacher and child confrontation that leads to the "problem" behavior. The counselors need to get out of their offices and into the mainstream of the school to see the behavior patterns, at least then they will know the problem they are dealing with.

We've heard one suggestion that seems to make sense, although the counselors probably won't like it. The suggestion is that counselors put their desks in the hall and not have an office. This would put them in the mainstream, wouldn't it?

We have seen counselors functioning as members of the teaching team, designing methods and materials to help children with problems, and we will say, from our point of view, this has helped the children. It has also helped the teachers and the counselor to become sensitive to the children, and to become more sensitive to themselves.

THE SCHOOL PSYCHOLOGIST

If we use the counselor in the way suggested above, the school psychologist then begins to play a more integrated role in the program. He can work with the perceptions of a group of people concerning a child's behavior. He can bring more sophisticated testing techniques to bear on the child. He can work with the counselor and the teachers, the child and his parents, to develop strategies for the whole group to use with the child to help him. The psychologist's perceptions would be better because he would be dealing with more data. He could see the child function in the open setting, and be much less conspicuous than in the self-contained classroom.

We have also seen a school psychologist functioning as a part of a team. His expertise along with the counselor, the teachers, the parents and the child can result in the observance of real change in the child's behavior. The real beauty of a team is that you *can* see change in children and you know that you are a part of the process that helped the child. Isn't that the name of the game?

THE MEDIA SPECIALIST OR LIBRARIAN

The media specialist must play a key role in the open concept program. She must function as a member of the team. The media center can only be the hub of the program if the media specialist is willing to cooperate in making it the hub. We are all familiar with the problems of some of these people. Some of them seem to feel personally responsible for every piece of material in the center. This sense of responsibility reaches the point where no one is able to use the material. We have, in fact, seen library doors locked at 10 o'clock in the morning in elementary schools of 500 or 600 students because the librarian wasn't in the building. We already discussed the business of trust, so we won't go into that again. But that means no child in that building can get into the library unless the librarian is there. How much sense does that make? Every librarian we've talked with in the last several years says that they want the children to feel at home in the library. They want to develop good attitudes about using the library and they want the material to be used, etc. We hear all those things that we think we should say, all the right things. Isn't it funny how we all know what we should say? We wonder if perhaps we might not consider practicing some of the things we say we believe in.

One of the biggest impediments to the library serving its function is the schedule. How can we schedule each class one-half hour a week in the library and expect it to be available to serve the school. Some of the things we hear children say would be funny if they weren't so sad. "I wish I could read a book, but I guess I'll have to wait til next Tuesday when I can go to the library." Or we hear the teacher or librarian, "You must pick out a book, that is why you're here." And we've got students picking out books for the sake of picking out books, children dreading the one-half hour in the library because "today we are going to learn to use the card catalog." They don't learn to use the card catalog that way. They learn how to use it when they need it, not when the librarian decides they need it. We wonder how many of them make the decision never to need it.

The more we think about this problem, the more we become convinced that it is largely a problem of area identification. This is the library, and all the materials must belong here. Maybe it's the business of putting shelves all along the walls which can't be moved. Then the materials can't be moved either. Maybe it's our way of putting things on the shelves in numerical order, instead of groups of materials related to the things we are studying about. We can't help but wonder the effect it would have if all the shelving were portable, say book carts. We know one thing for sure, the little children could then reach the books. What if all the equipment, film strips, slides and things like that were in portable storage carts? What effect would that have on the library? What if the library material were stored throughout the building, and the whole building were to become the media center, how would that work?

We know what the first cry is going to be: How will we keep track of anything? How will we know where things are? How are people going to find anything? These are certainly legitimate questions. But we also think some of them are appropriate to ask about our present organizations. It is easy to find teachers who are asking the same questions about their present media centers where everything appears to be lined up and beautifully organized.

Librarians also worry about losing things, and they still lose them, breaking things and they still get broken. It is interesting to note that the few people we've talked with who have freed the materials to be used, and simplified their record keeping system, always report that they end up with more material than they start with. How can this be possible?

In an open concept program, we've got to examine some of these possibilities. The media center must become the central focus of the program.   77

It must be available. It must be used. In order to do this it must be unscheduled. It must be open to students and teachers at all times. The "stuff" must be there for the people to get their hands on. Things must be organized to function as a part of the curriculum or must be available to be organized this way. This suggests that the media specialist must also have a skill sequence to guide the record-keeping necessary to show what skills students have mastered and which ones they need to master.

Acropolis Books Ltd. (publishers of this book) has a new book out called *The NOW Library*. This book, by Mary Margrabe, is an excellent beginning look at the place and organization of the library in an open concept program.

The primary problem confronting the special areas is one of scheduling. As long as we use these people to free the teachers for planning, the schedule is going to get in the way of integrating their programs into the curriculum. The only way to avoid this is to have all the teachers in the school at a time when the children are not there. This idea is catching on in some parts of the country. There are some districts that have early dismissals every day, and some that have a four and a half day week for the children. These approaches provide time for the teachers to plan together.

If we can take this approach, the result is unscheduled specials. The incidence of this approach is so rare that we have never seen it. Such a program would have to function in terms of the special teachers offering options that the children would choose. Some of these might run for several weeks, others for several days. A child in such a system might not be involved in music for two or three weeks, but over the length of the school life, he would receive the same amount, and in many cases more, of the special areas. Essential to this approach is a record-keeping system that is easy to manage, and that will identify those children that are avoiding a specific area. Skill sequences would help greatly with this approach. They would not only help us to keep track of the children, but used in conjunction with diagnostic tests, would enable children who already know about a skill to move to other areas without repetition. We hope in the next couple of years to pursue this problem and see if it is possible to organize it in a way that is possible for the teacher to handle. We think it holds tremendous potential for helping the special areas to achieve the goals they are concerned about, that is developing positive attitudes and some level of proficiency in each of the areas.

Basically, this chapter has tried to make the point that the special areas are important to each of our children.

These areas need to be integrated into the main stream of the educational program. They are not frills. Some attention must be given to their place in the program. Finally, we feel the open concept of education gives the special areas a vehicle through which they can achieve their stated purposes.

Children have different abilities in all areas of the curriculum.

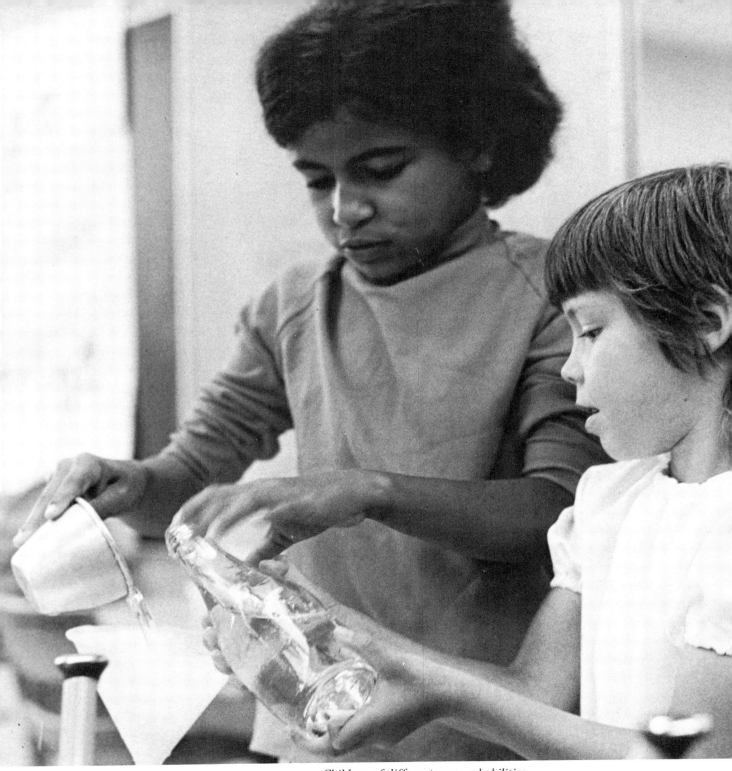

*Children of different ages and abilities
learn to work together.*

CHAPTER VII

Nongradedness and Continuous Progress

PERHAPS THE EASIEST thing to change in our educational system is lockstepping children through grade levels. For several decades, so-called experts have been zeroing in on this system and its basic core, the text-book. However, easy as it would be to change, this seems to be the one part of current organization that hangs on. We've found schools that will go to team teaching, will use skill sequences, who are happy about the open building, who want to use their media, who are trying to individualize their programs, and who still insist on graded pods. It seems no matter what we say or how we say it, they smile politely and organize into graded pods.

Another interesting point in this whole area is that we know age is probably the least important factor to consider in the child's educational evolution. We hear and read repeatedly that chil-

dren develop socially, emotionally, and intellectually at different rates and yet we insist on corraling them by age.

We also talk, with gusto, about the whole child, picking him up where he left off, and individualizing our programs. Yet we expect our schools to cover a known body of content, then we divide the content into separate areas and place these areas in grade levels.

The fact that children differ has been recognized only because children have performed well or poorly, but teachers should have been considering those differences as vital elements to plan around. Children who have not progressed according to the group have been retained in grades. Therefore, the traditional school advocates of the self-contained classroom have recognized individual differences to a small extent and have been more concerned with the "group."

This whole idea of gradedness is, in our eyes, the greatest hypocrisy of our educational system, and we can't understand why the refusal to change it is so vehement.

If the graded system is wrong, the obvious question to ask is what then will replace a graded system? As its name implies, nongradedness means *no* grades, that is, no first grade, second grade, third grade, etc. It does not have anything to do with marks or report cards. Nongradedness is an organizational pattern which places children of varying ages together in an administrative unit.

This term has many meanings to many people. Goodlad and others have written books on the subject (see bibliography). In a purely practical book such as this we have chosen to stay away from the philosophical implications of the concepts in open education. (You get enough philosophy and theory in graduate school.) Therefore we will deal with the part of nongradedness which has application in our schools.

We know each child must start where he is and develop at his own rate. Grade levels make this very difficult.

A viable alternative is to break the grade level syndrome, and develop continuous sequences of skill development and flexible curriculum packages. Thus the term continuous progress emerges. Continuous progress is the type of curricular approach we must take with a nongraded organization. Simply stated, it means we must develop and use systems that will enable us to keep continuous track of each child from the time he enters school until he leaves. Is there a way to do this? Yes! Is it available now? Yes! What is it? (We thought you'd never ask.) Skill sequence! Yes, skill sequences and we've devoted the whole next chapter to them. Imagine that!

But, now, back to nongradedness; we think the following list certainly gets to the point concerning why our schools should be nongraded. (See Fig. 1.)

Convinced? Good. Now, how do you do it? This is the simplest part of open education to achieve. To do it, you just do it. Replace graded groups with nongraded multi-age groups. This can, of course, be done in a traditional building. Instead of having a first grade class and a second grade class and a third grade class, put these 75 children in three rooms with three teachers. Create a primary unit, function as a team—get it all together and you're now nongraded. (Easy, wasn't it?)

If you're in an open situation it's even easier. We began by grouping children into a primary unit including five, six

FIGURE 1

ADVANTAGES OF A NONGRADED PROGRAM

1. Provides opportunity for children of different ages to work and play together and encourages cooperation with the older and more able students helping the younger or less able ones.

2. Younger children become motivated to do things the older ones can do intellectually, physically, etc.

3. Each child works at his own level and at his own rate of speed. There is no ceiling for the bright child and no unattainable goals the slower child must struggle to reach within any period of time.

4. Progress is continuous and on-going as are diagnosis and evaluation of the child.

5. Children meet success, seldom failure. And a student *cannot* "flunk."

6. If the school's program is also ungraded (no marks or report cards), there is less competition and children learn for learning's sake, not for grades.

7. Immature older children can choose younger children as friends. And an 8 year old can play basketball with the 10 year olds if he has advanced physical skills.

and seven year olds (K, 1 and 2), and an intermediate unit including eight, nine and ten year olds (3, 4 and 5).

We initially organized these children into homebase units. In order to get an almost equal number of students from each age group in each of these units, we took the three grade level lists and placed one child from each grade into the new multi-age homebase. The homebase groups were merely administrative groups and helped with keeping track of attendance, lunch money, and things like that. We did, however, find that there were some curricular approaches that fit nicely into the homebase approach.

The next step was to destroy the graded list. The only copy remained in the office. Then when people came and asked for "third graders" we said we had no record like that but that we could give them intermediate children or primary children.

Amazingly enough by the second year the teachers, parents, secretaries, nurse—everyone—were adjusting. The children when asked would say, "Yes, I'm in the intermediate unit"—if they were in school. If, however, they were talking to Mom, Cousin Neil, or Aunt Nancy, they gave their would-be grade level because they learned that most adults didn't understand primary and intermediate.

An important fact is that heterogeneous homebase grouping was used for everything except skill lessons. We feel strongly that for skills, students should be grouped homogeneously. In a math skill lesson, for example, third, fourth and fifth grade children might get the same lesson if they all have the same need. To repeat, math and communication skills were taught to groups of children who needed them. Social studies, science and all other areas were approached with nongraded groups.

Perhaps it seems overly simple, but that's all there is to nongradedness. It means grouping children into multiage units. It means grouping children for reasons other than age. It means making it easier to do the job schools were brought into existence to do.

8

Skill Sequences
and
Diagnostic Testing

WE HAVE MADE a case and an assumption so far in the book that you will be working in a nongraded (multiage) school. Since we've already developed the rationale for this organization in the chapter on nongradedness, we will devote this chapter to a very key item in any nongraded organization—skill sequences and diagnostic tests. If you have the children in three units in the elementary school; i.e., kindergarten, primary and intermediate, each of the latter two of these provides a three year educational setting for each child. This structure means we must develop a system of record keeping that will show us a continuous record of each child. The term continuous progress is derived from this effort. It is very consistent with educational philosophy of today, that is, that we keep a continuous record of each child's progress. The tool that enables us to do this is a skill sequence. A skill sequence is just what the name implies: the skills in a subject area listed in sequential order in terms of difficulty, relationship to each other, or dependence upon each other.

Skill sequences basically are developed in two ways: a leveled sequence, and a topical sequence. A leveled sequence has the skills listed in levels which can be correlated to specific levels of development in terms of the child. A topical sequence has the skills sequenced within topical areas. Thus each subtopic of a major area has an individual sequence. Perhaps the enclosed examples and specific exploration of each will help you to see the difference.

The skill sequences offered as examples have been used in several programs. They should not be presumed perfect. Their use has resulted in revision. Further use should revise and strengthen them even more. They are

*Children should be continually diagnosed
before they are taught.*

a good baseline or starting tool. If used with this in mind they will serve an excellent function in your program. We will discuss the use, advantages and disadvantages of each type in detail. This will enable you to examine your situation and see which type fits you, your children, and your situation best.

LEVELED SKILL SEQUENCES

We will discuss leveled sequences for communication skills and mathematics.

Figure 1 in this chapter is the first page of a leveled communication skills sequence, derived mainly from a sequence developed by the Frederick County, Maryland, School District. This sequence has thirteen levels. Each level has sub-topics within it such as Phonic Analysis, Structual Analysis, etc. The complete sequence is found in part 2 of this book.

Figure 2 in this chapter, also derived from the Frederick County, Maryland, schools, is the front page of a placement test correlated with the skill sequence. This test is important when you begin to use a skill sequence in a program that is already established and will involve children who have spent some time in a graded program that does not use skill sequencing. The placement test will enable you to locate the children on the sequence approximately where they belong.

Each level has a test. The children simply take the tests until they reach a test where they make more than one or two errors. This is their beginning level. The entire test is included in part 2 of this book.

We're sure you can see that if we begin the program with five year olds on the sequence, then the placement tests become somewhat unnecessary as we will use the sequence to keep a continuous and accurate record of the child's progress from age five through twelve.

But, let's continue. Once you have determined the various levels of the children in the unit, the next step is to group them by levels. For example, you and two other teachers are an intermediate team dealing with 75 youngsters, ages 9-10-11. Your testing comes up with the following results:

level 3 = 10 children
level 4 = 15 children
level 5 = 12 children
level 6 = 15 children
level 7 = 12 children
level 8 = 11 children

Your team examines these results and ends up with skill groups as such:

teacher A - levels 3 & 8
teacher B - levels 4 & 7
teacher C - levels 5 & 6

Of course this is only one of several possible choices available to you, but

FIGURE 1

COMMUNICATION SKILLS SEQUENCE

LEVEL O

AUDITORY DISCRIMINATION

1. Identifies sound intensity by discriminating between loud and soft sounds.
2. Identifies pitch by discriminating between high and low sounds.
3. Identifies quality of sounds through their distinguishing characteristics.
4. Compares many sounds to determine variations in duration.
5. Identifies the sequence of sounds.
6. Identifies word pairs that are the same and word pairs that are different.
7. Identifies words which rhyme.
8. Identifies alliteration in oral discourse.
9. Distinguishes likenesses and differences in initial consonant sounds.

VISUAL DISCRIMINATION

1. Discriminates size differentials, e.g., big-little; tall-short; fat-thin.
2. Discriminates shape differentials.
3. Identifies position of an object in a series.
4. Identifies internal details of a picture.
5. Identifies colors.
6. Identifies first name in manuscript form.
7. Identifies likenesses and differences in words.
8. Identifies words and spaces in written language.

VISUAL-MOTOR COORDINATION

1. Demonstrates effective big muscle control.
2. Demonstrates effective hand-muscle control.
3. Demonstrates effective eye-hand coordination.
4. Distinguishes between right and left.
5. Demonstrates left-to-right eye movement with return sweep in identifying objects, letters, words, etc.
6. Demonstrates ability to focus on close work.
7. Demonstrates top-to-bottom eye movement.
8. Demonstrates left-to-right, front-to-back progression.

LISTENING SKILLS

1. Demonstrates ability to listen and form associations with related items from one's own experience.
2. Demonstrates ability to listen closely enough to oral discourse to identify the organization.

FIGURE 2

NAME _____

EVALUATION INSTRUMENT–LEVEL O

MAJOR CATEGORY: AUDITORY DISCRIMINATION

1. Given the following pairs of words stated orally by teacher, student responds orally by stating whether pairs are the same words or not:

car - car	yes - yes
dog - big	went - want
fat - vine	this - this
look - look	then - where
house - horse	thing - think
of - off	zoom - zoom
and - can	our - out

2. Given the following pairs of words stated orally by the teacher, student responds orally by stating whether the word pairs rhyme or not:

cake - lake	cold - kite
mark - feet	hill - will
plate - door	rug - rode
call - fall	sit - hit
back - cow	nest - tree
ran - fan	bad - walk
cat - sat	look - talk
duck - tack	neck - nice
may - way	not - got
night - green	down - brown
sing - hen	bell - book
ten - pen	find - sand
let - met	fun - sun

MAJOR CATEGORY: VISUAL DISCRIMINATION

3. Using the following shapes: circle, square, and rectangle, student responds orally to the following kinds of questions with correct responses:

   a. Show me something big, little, tall, short.
   b. Find something that has the same shape as this . . . and hold up the various shapes.
   c. Line up the children at the fountain. Tell the student to touch the one that is last; the one that is first; the one in the middle.
   d. Put your finger on the door knob, on the window pane, on the waste basket.

4. Given color chips of red, orange, yellow, green, blue, purple, brown, black, student names the color of each one.

5. Given a printed list of 5 first names, student points to his own name.

89

let's examine this one to see how it might work. You all agree on the above arrangement. The next item to examine is the schedule—when can you schedule skill groups. The three of you decide that skill lessons will be offered on Monday, Wednesday, and Friday from 9:00 to 9:30. Isn't that very structured, you're saying. Yes, it is, but remember you are beginning, and you'd better know where you're at or you'll miss the potential that is here for using the flexibility within the structure.

Now what happens? You're teacher A, you've got levels 3 & 8, a total of 21 children to work with on Monday, Wednesday, and Friday from 9:00 to 9:30 on skill development lessons. You, at this point, have several options: you can work with each level for fifteen minutes of each period or you can work with one level for twenty minutes and the other for ten, or you can work with each level for one-half hour on alternating days. What we're suggesting is to first organize your time.

What will the other students do while you're not working with them? Remember they are on a contract and have a lot to do.

After your time is organized, then you need to examine the levels on the skill sequences, and decide with which skill you'll start. The children come together at the specified time. You've

planned a lesson on the skill you've chosen. Part of your plan is a short diagnostic (pre-test) to be given to the students. You check this immediately and the children who already understand the skill go to work on their contracts and you teach the skill to the ones who failed the test. After teaching that skill, you make another diagnosis (post-test) and record on each child's skill sequence his success or failure with the item. If this is done from the time the child enters school, we will have a continuous record of the attempts we've made to teach each child a skill, and the success and failure of our attempts.

Once this is begun you then work continuously through the skills recording progress as you go. You can make use of any materials in your building to teach the skill and eventually should consider organizing them. Some of the easiest materials to organize are the duplicating masters you've already got. Get some parents to title a manila folder for each item on the sequence, pool all your dittoes and let the parents sort and file them in the folders. Put the folders in a filing cabinet accessible to everyone. This will be an immediate source of materials for diagnosis, reinforcement and evaluation. Then, as the children move through the skill areas, they will move to different teachers, but we will have an accurate record of their successes and failures. Also, we will have assurance that our presentation of topics has been systematic, and organized; we will be certain that we have not left gaps in the child's skill development presentations; and we will be able to show all of this with two simple marks—let's say an X and an O. What this suggests is that when the child demonstrates that he has mastered the skill, at least for the present, we will put a dated "X" next to that skill—i.e. 9/16/73. If he fails to demonstrate mastery of the skill, we put a dated "O"—i.e., 9/16/73.

Perhaps you are beginning to see that when children arrive in your intermediate section, they will bring with them skill sequences marked and dated with successes and failures and you will not only be able to pick up where the successes stop, but also be able to attempt to reteach the failures.

When we reach this level of sophistication in our schools, we will no longer be bombarded with questions of accountability. We will be able to show black on white accountability that is far more meaningful than can be shown with grade-equivalent on a standardized test. Thus you have a picture of a leveled skill sequence. However, by now, you've probably uncovered the one major problem with a leveled sequence, that is, that placing a child within a level presumes his skill in all topics within that level to be similar. We all know that's not true. However, if we tried to keep track of each child in three or four levels at the same time, we'd get lost in jumbles of numbers. This weakness noted, the leveled sequence is very easy to begin with, as it enables us to manage and specify what we are teaching. It is such an improvement over our haphazard skill organization that this flaw seems minor. This sequence can even be controlled by the diagnostic approach suggested for each lesson. Of course if you recall in chapter IV when we discussed communication skills, we suggested the creative writings as good lead-ins to skill development. If we combine this creative writing feedback with the skill sequence, we get a manageable and accurate diagnosis and lesson plan guide all wrapped up in one neat little package.

That's great! Isn't it?

Now for the math skill sequence. The enclosed sample is from Fort Frye Elementary School, Beverly, Ohio (Fig. 3). It is a leveled sequence. You can find the entire sequence in part two of this book. There are dozens of these available elsewhere. Again, the important thing is not the sequence but the use of the sequence. The math sequence, if leveled, should be approached the same way as the communication skill sequence. We should place the children on levels and organize the levels for which each teacher will assume responsibility, schedule a math time, and away we go! If each teacher begins with the groups by diagnosing and working with small groups on similar skill problems, using a contractual approach to guide the children who already know the skill, the program will be manageable.

The problem of the leveled sequence in mathematics appears to be more serious than the communication skill sequence. A leveled math sequence includes the following topics in each level: whole numbers—addition, subtraction, multiplication and division; fractions—relationship, addition, subtraction, multiplication, division; decimals—relationships, addition, subtraction, multiplication and division; geometry; measurement (all areas); percentages; and special topics (Roman numerals, metric systems, etc.).

It is obvious to any teacher that children in level 6 are almost certainly not going to be equally adept in each of these areas. So what is seemingly a minor problem in terms of a leveled communication skill sequence seems to be a much bigger problem in a leveled math sequence.

As suggested, the diagnostic approach to each lesson will help with this problem, but not eliminate it entirely. The record keeping approach would be the same as with the communication skill sequence.

TOPICAL SEQUENCES

The shortcoming noted in the leveled sequence led us to develop topical se-

quences. As noted, the topical sequence organizes each topic separately. A topical sequence needs no levels. The first page of a topical sequence is shown in (Fig. 4). It was synthesized from six sequences including the one from Frederick County shown in this chapter. The entire sequence is included in part two of this book.

The communication skills topical sequence is organized into the following areas: Phonic and Structural Analysis, Structure of Language including Use of Language (English), Written Language Skills, Oral Language Skills, and Comprehension. Each of these areas is sequenced K-6. Since there are close relationships inherent in some of these, we chose to list related lists parallel to each other; thus Phonic Analysis and Structural Analysis are listed on the same sheet parallel to each other. This enables us to use them separately or in relationship. Structure of Language, Oral Language and Written Language are listed on the same sheet entitled "Use of Language" because of their relationship. Again, this enables us to deal with them separately and also as they relate to each other. Comprehension is listed separately.

With this approach it is possible to keep records of where the child is in each area and demonstrate a profile of his standing at any one time in the skill areas. An example of this might help: a profile sheet would bear the child's name, a heading for each topic,

FIGURE 3

MATHEMATICS SKILLS

Readiness Level:

Upon successful completion of the *readiness* level the child will be able to do the following:

To count in sequence 1-7

To recognize numerals 1-7

To correctly form numerals 1-7

To make sets equal by adding or taking away

To recognize the four basic shapes in different positions

To recognize a penny, nickel, and a dime

To count items in a set, using one-to-one correspondence

Level One:

To arrange numerals 1-7 in proper sequence

To recognize sets and subsets 1-7

To do cardinal and ordinal counting 1-7

To associate sets, numerals, and number words 1-7

To supply the missing addends for sums 1-7

To solve the addition and subtraction facts through 7, using counters if necessary

To solve simple number problems based on a picture sequence or a continuous story

Level Two:

To read and write numerals 1-9

To arrange numerals 1-9 in proper sequence

To associate sets, numerals, and number words 1-9

To do cardinal and ordinal counting 1-9

To supply the missing addends for sums 1-9

To solve addition and subtraction facts through 9, using counters if necessary

To solve the multiplication and division facts through 9

Level Three:

To use zero as a place-holder for the empty set

To solve vertical addition facts with sums through nine

To tell the value of a penny, a nickel, or a dime

To make equivalent sets using pennies, nickels, and dimes

To add and subtract using money

To add columns of 3 numerals with sums through 9

To count to 100 by 10's

To count to 50 by 5's

To count to 50 by 2's

FIGURE 4

PHONIC ANALYSIS

____ 1. Discriminates between consonant sounds (s [hard] k,d,f,g, [hard] h,j,l,m,n,p, r,s,t,v,w,y,z) and matches sound with the letter.

____ 2. Identifies words which rhyme and states additional rhyming words.

____ 3. Discriminates between final (b [hard] c or k,d,f,g [hard] j,l,m,n,p,r,s,t,v,z) consonant sound and matches sound with the letter.

____ 4. Matches the sound and letter for consonant digraphs in initial position (ch, sh, th, wh).

____ 5. Initial digraph
th-voiced
th-unvoiced

____ 6. Demonstrates ability to substitute consonants in the initial position using rhyming parts.

____ 7. Demonstrates ability to substitute consonant digraphs in the initial position.

____ 8. Identifies letters which are vowels.

____ 9. Discriminates between consonants and vowels and matches the terms *consonant,* and *vowel* to the appropriate symbols.

____ 10. Demonstrates ability to substitute consonants in the final position (d,k,l,m, n,p,r,t,x).

____ 1. Identifies compound words.

____ 2. Forms compound words from two known words.

____ 3. Identifies "s" signaling plurality.

____ 4. Demonstrates sensitivity to syllables in polysyllabic words.

____ 5. Identifies the word endings, *s, d, ed,* and *ing.*

____ 6. Identifies number of syllables heard in a word.

____ 7. Identifies compound words when made from one known and one unknown word.

____ 8. Identifies by naming the structural parts—"root" or "base" word and "word endings" (s,d,ed,ing).

____ 9. Identifies the singular possessive and distinguishes between the plural form and the singular possessive of words.

____ 10. Identifies and applies meaning to new words formed when the suffix "er" has been added to the root word.

and numbers for each topic correlating to the skill within the topic. The profile (Fig. 5) would show that the child seems to need some concentrated help in Phonic Analysis, Use of Language, and real help in Comprehension. If these profiles were completed yearly with different color lines, it would also show a clear picture of several years of skill development at a time. This profile in addition to the skill sequence marked with X's and O's in the child's folder would begin to approach a system of accountability that is not only manageable, but, if we must (ugh), computerable (a new word we invented to mean you can get a machine to do it—after you've done it!).

We know you're asking if the topical sequence solves the problem of varying abilities within levels, how can we manage it? Well, we're going to discuss that next, but remember we're discussing both ways with the notion that you'll pick the one that's best for you. Some feel the leveled sequence is a little easier to manage, others don't— remember, make your own decision.

Probably the easiest way to manage a topical sequence is to do it by topic for a specified period of time. Let's use the example of teachers A, B and C and 75 students ages 9, 10 and 11. You decide to use a topical skill sequence in communication skills. The team plans to spend three weeks working with all the children in Phonic

Analysis. The Phonic Analysis sequence is divided into segments of ten skills each. You develop a test or use pre-printed dittoes to test items on this sequence in groups of ten. A test covering the first ten items is given to all the children. Twenty students do poorly on this test, using any criteria your team wants for the cut off. These 20 children become group 1 and they will work with teacher A somewhere between items 1 and 10 on the sequence for the next three weeks. Teacher A, using the diagnostic teaching approach described earlier in the chapter, can begin on item 1 and bring the children together during scheduled skill lessons, pre-test the group, keep the students who need help, and send the others off to work on contracts.

The 55 children who are left take a test on items 11-20; 25 of them need help in this area. Teacher B will work with them for the next three weeks. Teacher C will take the remaining 30, test them and be generally responsible for their skill development. Near the end of the three weeks the team may decide to spend the next two or three weeks on comprehension skills. Tests are designed, administered, and the children regrouped for this area. These decisions are continually made by the team throughout the three year span of the child's stay in the unit.

We're sure you see that the placement tests must only be administered 95

FIGURE 5

PROFILE CHART

Communication Skills Sequence

Structure of Language

Phonic Analysis	Structural Analysis	Use	Written	Oral	Comprehension
1.	1.	1.	1.	1.	1.
2.	2.	2.	2.	2.	2.
3.	3.	3.	3.	3.	3.
4.	4.	4.	4.	4.	4.
5.	5.	5.	5.	5.	5.
6.	6.	6.	6.	6.	6.
7.	7.	7.	7.	7.	7.
8.	8.	8.	8.	8.	8.
9.	9.	9.	9.	9.	9.
10.	10.	10.	10.	10.	10.
etc.	etc.	etc.	etc.	etc.	etc.

Child's Name

once. For example, while the teachers spend three weeks on Phonic Analysis with the students, they are marking each child's sequence with X's and O's to indicate his successes or failures. At the end of the three weeks, each child's phonic sequence will be marked and when the teachers decide to return to Phonic Analysis they simply need to check the Phonic Analysis records, group the children and go.

One point to consider in this approach, as in the leveled approach, is the creative writing and daily work feedback. This work will continue to reveal areas of weakness in each child's development. When these areas are dealt with in conference or as a part of the class routine, you should try to remember to mark them on the child's skill sequence.

A topical math sequence would be basically used in the same way. The first page of such a sequence is Figure 6. The sequence is included in its entirety in part two of this book. It is organized into whole numbers—addition and subtraction; whole numbers—multiplication and division; fractions—addition and subtraction; fractions—multiplication and division; decimals—addition and subtraction; decimals—multiplication and division; percentages; measurement—linear, liquid, etc; geometry and special topics—Roman numerals, metric system, etc. The teachers on the team will make the decision concerning the time to be spent on each area, then test to get started, regroup the children, mark the X's and O's and go!

We're sure you can see the special advantage a topical sequence offers the child in math. He can be well along in the addition and subtraction of whole numbers and at step 1 in multiplication and division. This gives him a chance to function at his level. When we use a profile it gives us a chance to show where he needs more help and where he is proficient.

A topical skill sequence in social studies has somewhat the same advantages. We've included page one of a sequence developed by Annville-Cleona School District, Annville, Pa. (Fig. 7). The complete sequence is included in part two of this book.

The topical sequence also offers more freedom from the possibility of becoming slavishly attached to moving from one item to the next on a sequence. If we insist on this approach our sequences can become as deadly as textbooks. We should follow in some order, but use sequence as a record-keeping device and a guide to teaching, along with the analysis of the child's regular work. This should enable us to deal with skill needs and record this on the sequence at any time. The topical sequence is easier to manage with this approach as it is not leveled, and being topical it is easier

FIGURE 6
TOPICAL SEQUENCE MATH

1 Differentiate same, different; top, bottom; small, large; over; under; in, out; etc.

2 One to one correspondence

3 Write missing numerals in an incomplete sequence, i.e. 1, 2, 4, 5

4 Facts numbers 1 to 10

5 Reads numbers one—ten

6 Matches numbers of objects 1—10

7 Uses the number line

8 Cardinal numbers to 10

9 Writes numbers 1—10

10 Tells number before and after a given number

11 Tells number in between two numbers

12 Matches number word with number 1—10

13 Deals with 10's

14 1 - 100 counts

15 1 - 100 writes

16 1 - 100 numbers before, after and in between

17 Uses > and < in proper order

18 Identify and write 100 - 200

19 Cardinal 0 - 100

20 Supplies number one more, less or in between 100 - 200

21 Counts by 10 to 200

22 Count by 5 to 100

23 Counts by 2

24 Reads and writes number to 1000

FIGURE 7

SEQUENCE OF SOCIAL STUDIES SKILLS

Map Skills

I. Earth as a Globe

    A. Model of earth is called a globe

    B. Globe is "round" so we call it a sphere

    C. Globe is a map as well as a model of our earth—map or drawing on globe shows where things are on the earth

    D. Globe is more accurate than flat map—e.g. Greenland

    E. Hemispheres
        1. Half a sphere is called a hemisphere so half of the earth is called a hemisphere (hemi-half; sphere-ball)
        2. Two we live in—
            a. Northern
            b. Western
        3. Land and water hemispheres
        4. Eastern and Southern

    F. Rotation—day and night concept

    G. Revolution—of earth around sun
        1. Causes 4 seasons in the year
        2. Seasons in Northern Hemisphere are opposite of those in Southern Hemisphere
        3. Tilt of earth's axis—axis is imaginary rod thru center of earth

    H. The surface of earth is curved, although appears flat

    I. Compares a picture of the earth with a picture of a globe

II. Directions

    A. North toward North Pole—South toward South Pole on ANT map

    B. When facing N., east is always to right—west is to left

    C. Cardinal directions
        1. North
        2. South
        3. East
        4. West

    D. Intermediate directions
        1. N. W.
        2. S. W.
        3. N. E.
        4. S. E.

to locate the specific skill. For example, a child's creative writing suggests he needs help with skill 17 on the written language sequence. You help him with it, and are satisfied he's got it. You pull out his record and put a dated X on skill 17. When you do this you notice he's only completed the sequence to skill 11. You should still mark skill 17. When he gets involved in the sequence again he'll begin at 12 and as he gets to 17 we will have a chance to retest that skill, to find out if the success was permanent.

As we use skill sequence this kind of rechecking needs to be done. Every time we do it we should mark the sequence as this will give us a continuous record of our efforts and the child's successes and failures.

Of course it will be necessary to begin organizing your materials to relate to the skill sequence. This will take time but you can get your parents involved in making folders to correlate with the topical sequence. Put the dittoes you have into folders and store them in a central place for everyone's use.

Eventually we are going to develop a way to coordinate skill sequences with dittoes, kits, tapes, texts, film strips and any other materials we've got at our disposal. This will greatly enhance our skill development programs. Our next book will show you such a design.

In the title of this chapter, we suggested that we would also discuss diagnostic testing. We've suggested that diagnosis ought to be a part of every skill lesson as it relates to the skill sequence. You can use preprinted dittoes for this, puzzles, games, the chalk board or anything. Please try one of the many methods you already know to diagnose a child's competency in a skill before you try to teach it to him.

We've talked about a number of things in this chapter. Perhaps we should capsulize them.

Skill sequences will help us to organize our teaching record-keeping system for the skill areas.

There are two basic kinds of skill sequences: leveled and topical. Each of these has its particular strengths and weaknesses. You should examine them and choose the one that seems right for your setting. We need to incorporate diagnostic testing into our use of skill sequences.

Sequences are available in communication skills, math and social studies in part two of this book.

Examples of both a leveled sequence and a topical sequence are offered for communication skills and math. The social studies sequence example is topical. We've discussed how to begin using these as a part of your program. We'd emphasize the word *begin,* and repeat, as we have many times already, that the first concern in a flexible program is your management of time, materials and children. We feel you should get a handle on the structure of managing these areas, and when you do, the fantastic options available for exploration will become evident to you. When you move in this direction, you benefit, the children benefit, education benefits, our society benefits, and education becomes for our children what society says it ought to be.

If you feel you need a rest after all that, take one, and get ready for what comes next!

Many times diagnostic testing is done individually.

Children work on individual contracts which have been mutually agreed upon by the child and his teacher.

9

Learning Contracts

MOST TEACHERS, interested in individualizing instruction, are willing to try, but they say, "I am just one person. I have 30 children in my class. How do I individualize instruction with 30 children and no aides?" Well, take heart, folks, because contracts can help you do just that.

We think the first step should be to define contracts. Since we found little in the existing literature concerning learning contracts, we had to formulate our own definition. To us a contract is a mutual *agreement* between a child and his teacher or teachers covering a specified amount of work to be completed within a certain time. Contracts should be individual and should meet each child's needs. There should also be a time of accountability—a check-out time.

The next question seems to be: Why contracts? What's the purpose? As we

already said, contracts help individualize instruction. They allow you to give choices to children, and they give you T I M E—that precious commodity which is difficult to get when you are responsible for children. With this time you can teach individuals, small or large groups, sit and chat with a child, discuss a problem—all hopefully while you're sipping a well-earned cup of coffee. (How much improved the mornings in our schools would be if we all could have a cup of coffee in the class room.)

Contracts help the children do some pretty important things too, for in stance:

1. develop responsibility and account-ability

2. learn how to budget their time

3. learn how to handle some of their own learning

4. learn how to use self-control and self-discipline.

Sounds impossible? It isn't! It isn't even far-fetched.

The use of contracts also encourages a free atmosphere, because when 77 children are given choices on those 77 contracts they can be working on 60 different activities—or if you think 60 activities would give you Excedrin Headache 99, you or your team could, of course, limit them to ten or twelve activities.

Contracts encourage creativity and resourcefulness, too. If you give the children a choice about what their follow-up activity is going to be, several may choose to do a puppet show. Well, in order to do a puppet show they must be creative. They have to come up with puppets and costumes, they have to decide the dialogue, and they have to use the resources available to them in order to have a good follow-up activity.

And last but not least, contracts encourage learning. Children very quickly realize that a contract is better than an assignment. They get to have some say in this contract and that is much better than getting an assignment.

O.K., now that you think contracts are marvelous, beautiful things and you want to use them, how do *you,* the teacher, begin?

First, you have to determine how well the children work independently. This is different for each child, so you just have to give them an opportunity to work independently and see how they do. Some will do well and act like they've been on contracts for years; others will need some guidance and reminding; some will need continual guidance and encouragement. The latter might not be good candidates for contracts, at least not to begin with.

The second step in putting contracts to use is to survey the materials that are available to you and to the children. Find out what kits you have, what materials you have, develop your own materials, develop some packets, make some learning stations, and put these things on a contract. But find everything you can use—records, filmstrips, sound filmstrips, filmloops, etc.

After you've surveyed the materials which are available, the next thing you have to do is examine the schedule. Look for the blocks of time available. Do you have a large block of time for each child? Do you have just a small block of time? How many hours would the children have for contract work? (Refer to Chapter III for more information on scheduling and organization.)

The next thing you do is make up the contract form. Put down all the materials and kits you have, organize worksheets into numbered folders, include names of books, workbooks you'll want them to use, and include a place for learning stations and reading activities, etc. (Refer to sample contract (Fig. 1) for more ideas.)

Be very *specific* when you make your contract. Remember, whatever is on that printed contract doesn't have to be written by you. We visited a school where it was taking the teachers 20 minutes just to fill out the contract. That's 20 minutes the teacher could have spent talking to the child. Also, remember there's much the students can do—name, date, etc. (In case we haven't told you yet. Rule #1 among our team is: we never do anything the children can do, including checking their own papers. This means we can spend our time doing more meaningful things with the children.)

After the contract is made up, last but not least, you must explain to all the children what they're going to be doing. They should understand *completely* their responsibility in fulfilling the contracts.

We've given you purposes, advantages, the first steps you must take, and now we think the next question is what do you do with the children in your self-contained classroom? Or if you're lucky enough to be in a non-graded, team teaching situation for the first time, how do you actually start with the students?

First of all, it seems to make sense to start out with a group contract for most of the children. Maybe it shouldn't be called a group contract, because it would be very difficult to get a group to agree to a contract. Therefore, you might call it an assignment, but at any rate you have most of the children doing the same thing. It probably is what most of the kids have been doing—it could include basal readers and workbooks. When this group assignment is proceeding smoothly, you might want to offer some group choices. Possibly at 10:00 A.M. you may want to offer a choice between A or B. For example, A-Illustrating a story, B-Writing cinquain poetry. Then possibly you could offer choices A, B or C, etc. That way everybody has at least something new to talk about.

While the group works on the same thing, (or choices, if they're ready) explain contracts to one or to a few depending on whether you ate a hearty breakfast and are feeling especially strong and well-fortified that day. Go into detail and help the children understand every item on the contract, and what their responsibilities are. When one child or a few begin to work on their own, the other kids see them getting choices, planning their learning and their days, and of course they want to do the same thing. It rubs off and becomes contagious. After those few on contracts can handle it well, start a few more and let them work with the "old pros."

FIGURE 1

COMMUNICATION SKILLS CONTRACT–INTERMEDIATE LEVEL

1. Name_____ 2. Date_____

3a. Weekly _____3b. Daily _____ 4. Checkout Day _____ 5. Time _____

6. a. _____ Reading Titles   Pages
   b. _____ c. _____
      _____   _____
      _____   _____
                Total

7. Group reading with (teacher) _____

   on (day(s), time) _____

8. a. _____Follow-up activities b. Nos. _____
                                        c. Other _____

9. a. _____ SRA Reading
                              b.   Color _____
                              c.   Number _____

10. Imperial Reading Kit
    b. Red _____ c. White _____ d. Lesson Numbers _____

11. Creative writing with (teacher)   a._____
        on (days, time)   b._____
        c. Topics _____
        d. Creative writing list (nos.) _____

12. a. SRA Spelling _____
                              b.   Color _____
                              c.   Number _____

13. Spelling with (teacher)   a. _____
        on (days, time)   b. _____
        Worksheets   c. _____
        Spelling list   d. _____

14. Skills
    a. with (teacher) _____
    b. on (days, time) _____
    c. Worksheets _____

15. Handwriting with (teacher) a.
    b. Where _____
    c. on (days, time) _____
    d. Learning station (activity numbers) _____

16. Learning Stations _____

17. I agree to do the work on this contract
    Signed _____

18. Work completed _____

19. Teacher's signature _____

20. Parent's signature _____

21. Comments:

Well, they're "off and running," now what? If you are especially fond of chaos you could just let them alone for a couple of weeks and you'll have *more* than enough chaos. However, we wouldn't like to see anyone lose a job over chaos that is entirely avoidable. You wouldn't send five or ten year olds out on an African safari by themselves and you don't send them out on their first contracts alone either (unless you really don't like where you work and you like extended vacations). They need guidance, reminders, encouragement, and lots of praise for what they *are* doing right (which might not be too much at first). We found the more of the above we gave them the more they improved. We walked around and encouraged verbally, were always available to help them over those first stumbling blocks, and we were there for check-out, zero-hour, panic time, or pat-on-the-back-time, whichever.

In the beginning of this chapter we said children learn something about self-control, self-discipline and budgeting time. Well, during their contract time all these fantastic learnings take place—at a snail's pace or at supersonic speed, depending on the child. How does this happen? Let's try to explain.

During his first contract (hopefully a short-term one, an hour or two, perhaps a morning) he finds he is on his 108 own. There he is—no one guarding him. Wow, what a feeling! He may even be in another room. Now is the crucial time—he must make these next important decisions himself and they will be crucial. "Shall I work, or shall I play?" Now, of course, you could be a Nervous Nellie, step in, and map it out for him. "Now Horace, you can work an hour, relax fifteen minutes, work an hour, relax fifteen minutes." Or you can let him find this all out for himself by experimenting.

But, let's hope you let Horace alone. He'll probably follow one of several patterns:

1. He'll do nothing but *work* like a demon for the contract time and be completely exhausted OR

2. He'll do *nothing*, period, and push the Panic Button when you say, "Horace, it's 10:15 and I can check you out now," OR

3. He'll do nothing sometimes and something sometimes which is what you hoped for. Remember three things first, though: just because he fell into one of these patterns doesn't mean he'll stay in it. Second, because he's doing it himself it'll take longer; and third, he'll remember the good and bad events longer and more vividly because he was responsible for them himself.

We've watched children last year and this year take off and work a contract with fantastic success and we've watched children struggle all year and just begin to develop the ability to work independently. Also we've seen Nervous Nellie teachers and other teachers. The children guided by the *other* teachers have done better in the long run and have learned lots more about how to discipline and control *themselves* and lots more about budgeting time than the students under Nervous Nellie. We're not sure whether under Nervous Nellie they learned anything about responsibility. What do you think?

After you've guided and encouraged, then comes the inevitable day of reckoning—check-out day. You find out how well the children did. Some will have contracts completed, some will not. But here is where you find out not only if the work was done, but how well it was done and if reading was done, was it comprehended?

Because of time you'll probably have to stagger your check-outs throughout the week, but it's awfully important that the child has a check-out day and time that is constant. We do not believe in open-ended contracts or contracts that can be extended. Those do not teach accountability or responsibility. They teach only excuse-making.

Check-out time then is an individual conference with a child in which you examine and discuss the child's work,

praise his efforts, encourage him to try harder if necessary, determine if a contract was not completed, why not, and agree on an amount of work to be done in the next contract. It is also something else—it is unique in that it is a one-to-one time, a confidential, friendly time to chat and discuss the thoughts and feelings of that child. It should, if at all possible, be uninterrupted.

There are several things to remember about check-out time and the giving of a new contract:

1. All children are *different!*

2. Some can do more work than others within a given time.

3. All children cannot handle contracts of the same length of time. Some need daily contracts, others might work a two or three week contract. They probably will handle longer contracts in time.

4. Primary contracts should be somewhat different than intermediate contracts. (More information will be found later in this chapter.)

5. The first few contracts are little more than guesses on the part of the child and the teacher, because neither has any idea of the child's potential for working independently.

You can usually tell when a child approaches you for check-out whether or not the contract is complete, especially on the first couple of contracts. In September of this year, one tiny eight year old came to me and said, "Can I have another check-out day?" I asked Nancy why and she said, "I don't have anything done on my contract." And since Nancy had just started using a contract I *gently* asked why again. And she said, "Well, you know that play I was in?" "Well, I took all my time practicing it and making costumes and I didn't have time to do my other work." At this point I asked Nancy if she had learned anything and she said, "I learned not to have play practice all week." She now works like a little trooper taking breaks and chatting, but the contract gets finished. Nancy learned quickly. For some, it doesn't happen that fast, but they *are* learning those skills we mentioned, slowly but surely. We think there are many adults who, if they had been given the same opportunity, would be better able to handle responsibility, better able to control themselves, and better at budgeting their time. How many of you put things off till the last minute? We do!

And at this point, we're sorry to say, we have a few children who can't handle contracts and can't work independently. But our fervent hope is that if these children had started out at five years of age, they would be able to handle the responsibility much 110 sooner, and in a few years when our school has been open four or five years, we'll be able to prove it.

One of the groups where contracts require extra planning is primary children. There are several ways to facilitate the use of this technique. One is verbal contracts. But it seems that these young students will have trouble remembering a commitment if, indeed, they even understand it. Our feeling is that if they can't understand what a contract is, they certainly can't understand fulfilling it. If this is the case, let's not kid ourselves and call the work they're assigned a contract. If there's no agreement, then it's an assignment, not a contract.

But, for the students who can understand, contracts will work. Again they should be individualized. And for the children who can't read, there are still some things you can do.

But first—primary children who can read. Their contracts will be similar to those discussed—only simplified.

Now, second—primary students who cannot read. If you want the children to contract their work period or reading period simply use symbols instead of words. In this case the child might get an individual contract that might have colors or symbols on it (Fig. 2). In most cases primary children will have trouble holding on to their contracts so they might be posted on a bulletin board or door where the child

FIGURE 2

SAMPLE PRIMARY CONTRACT

I agree to do this work.   Name _____

ACTIVITIES	LEARNING STATIONS
X	I

GAMES	WORKSHEET OR WORKBOOK PAGES
B	Numbers 3, 6
	READING
	Pages
	READING BOOK
	Fun With Dick and Jane 5-7
	OTHER
	Green Eggs and Ham 10
	Total 12

Work Completed _____   Teacher's Name _____

can refer to them, especially if their contract extends more than one day.

Another way is to contract the kids in groups. To do this simply prepare blank charts and name cards for one day (see Fig. 3), or subdivide the charts into separate parts corresponding to the days of the week (see Fig. 4). In this case the teacher and the child would agree and place his name in the appropriate slot or slots which could chart his course of action for fifteen minutes or five days.

All available materials and kits for the students could be photographed with a Polaroid, symbolized, and each game or kit would have to be numbered or coded in such a way as to be absolutely clear to students and teachers.

Eventually you'd want the games and activities to be classified, too, so while you're numbering and symbolizing, why not classify at the same time?

Most primary children are capable of using contracts. However, remember the age and ability range of the children; some will not be able to use even the simplest contract. If, though, some of the primary children could use the more difficult contract of the intermediate children, for goodness sake, let them.

We have included our communication skills and math contracts (Fig. 1 and 5). Since they will probably need to be revised or adapted to your situation, perhaps a detailed explanation of the contracts might help you do the adapting.

Let's look at the communication skills contract first (see Fig. 1). Intermediate children come to check-out with the first five items completed.

Item number 3 allows a child to use this contract on a daily or weekly basis. Together you decide which is better for each individual and the child then checks one or the other. And if it's a daily contract, you fill it out together every day.

Now to item number 6—Reading. Blank 6a is for the total number of pages to be read on this contract. This should be agreed upon by the teacher and child. Item 6b is the place where the child should fill in the title(s) of the book(s) he's read. Blank 6c is where he puts the number of pages he's read in that particular book or magazine. If he reads from more than one source, he repeats the above procedure, then totals the number of pages to make sure it matches or exceeds 6a.

On to item 7—Group Reading. We included this section for one of our teachers who like to have group reading. A word of caution, though, group reading can be used for appreciation

FIGURE 3

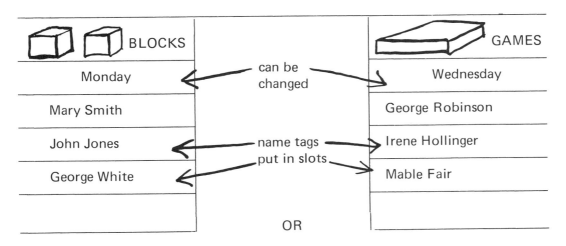

BLOCKS		GAMES
Monday	← can be changed →	Wednesday
Mary Smith		George Robinson
John Jones	← name tags →	Irene Hollinger
George White	← put in slots →	Mable Fair

OR

FIGURE 4

	LEARNING STATIONS				
	Mon.	Tues.	Wed.	Thurs.	Fri.
Number 3	Mary Ann Sue Sal	Ira Bob		Jim Cassie	
Number 4 (numbers can be changed)	Ray Dale	Mary Sue Jack		Harry	Arlene
Number 5	Dick Yvonne		Sally Bev Audrey	Elsie	

FIGURE 5
MATH CONTRACT

1. Name _____ 2. Date _____

3a. Weekly _____ 3b. Daily _____ 4. Checkout day _____ 5. Time ____

6. Merrill Math Skilltapes

    a. Topic_____

    b. Part _____ c. Steps _____

7. Programmed Math Text or regular Math Text (circle one)

    a. Book _____ b. Units _____ c. Pages _____

8. Group Work with (teacher)_____

    a. on (subject) _____

    b. on (days, time) _____

9. Worksheets in folders _____

10. Learning Stations _____

11. Other _____

    S.R.A. Comp. Skills Kit _____

    Cross Numbers Kit _____

    Math Applications Kit _____

    El. M. Kit _____

    Arithmetic Fact Kit _____

12. Work Completed _____ 14. Parent's signature_____

13. Teacher's Signature _____ 15. Comments _____

purposes of a fine, funny, or appropriate story, but beware of the Ghost of Round Robin and his reading-around-the-circle-type reading groups. This can be deadly and can serve no function. Reading for expression is a no-function purpose. How many of our kids are going to be an Orson Welles, or a Richard Burton? Practicing oratory at age six, seven or eight is slightly ridiculous. Don't we really just care about whether or not the child really can read and comprehend? As we said in Chapter IV, if you want to use oral reading for diagnosing reading difficulties, o.k., but that's the only legitimate reason we can find. And if you want to diagnose, why not do it individually?

Number 8 is the fun part of the contract. After a child finishes the reading obligation in his contract, he may choose to do a Follow-Up Activity on any of the books or magazines he's read. He can choose from any of the 66 activities from the list (Fig. 1, Chapter IV), or he may choose to do an activity of his own. Item 8a tells how many follow-ups he should do, 8b tells which numbers, and 8c tells what his idea is if he uses his own. The Follow-Up, though a break for the child, is a learning activity in itself, and it adds to the child's enjoyment of the communication skill block of time.

Item 9a gives the number of S.R.A. Power Builders the child agrees to do in the S.R.A. Reading Kits. 9b and 9c tell which ones he did. This part is also filled out by the child before check-out time.

If you're lucky enough to have other kits, they should be listed specifically and with enough detail to save you writing time. The Imperial Reading Kits are Item 10 on the contract. 10a tells how many lessons the child should do, and 10b identifies the kit the child is in and 10c tells the lessons he did.

Creative writing Item 11 deserves special mention. Creative writing can be done in two ways basically. You can assign a child several creative writings from a list with the option of choosing from the list or choosing his own topic. Or you can motivate for creative writing. The latter takes more time but you can set the mood, and really encourage the use of imagination. We're not saying you won't get creativity without motivation, but at least *one* of the authors of this book thinks you'll get more *creative* creative writings with motivation. Creativity can be increased—this has been proven, and one of us thinks motivation can do just that for creative writing.

For instance, you could simply ask the children to do a writing on the Creatures From Outer Space. OR you could darken the room, play the music from 2001, get some unusual things for effects, turn on some flashlights, 115 pretend you're in a rocket ship, and your creative writing could then be, "Now write a story on the things you're seeing as we're drifting through space. OOps—watch out for that *falling* star. Wow, that space ship came dangerously close to us. Was there anyone in it? What did they look like?" Then give the children some time to think and even more time to discuss and share ideas and then give them a date for the assignment to be due. No one should have to create in half an hour. Let them turn the papers in anytime within the week.

Now to Item 12, S.R.A. Spelling, another good kit which is individualized. 12a tells how many spelling wheels; the child fills in 12b to tell you which wheels he's done.

If you teach group spelling from a text, or in small groups by topic it would be scheduled in Item 13a, b and c. If you have any practice sheets they would be entered in Item 13c. 13d is the most important spelling item to us. When a child brings his creative writing to you, it is full of words that that child comprehends and uses. What better reason for learning to spell those words could the child have? They're usually the words the child uses most, therefore needs most. Also it individualizes your spelling program. You're certainly meeting the children's needs. If in a creative writing the child mispelled "can't," "under," "those," and "train," you

can copy them off the creative writing onto his contract, plus some others you or he might want to add (13d).

Item 14 would be Skills—comprehension, word attack. This is another topic in itself implying a skill sequence which will be covered in another chapter. Item 14 then is where you tell the child his scheduled times for skills. Item 14c is for the papers or worksheets you may want the child to do to reinforce the skills he's just been taught.

Item 15—Handwriting. Handwriting is up to you. We've tried grouping the children according to need. In a self-contained classroom you might have a group of three who need to practice "m" and "n." Then all the children might need to learn how to make a capital "Q." In a nongraded situation you might have 20 who need beginning cursive, 35 who need to review slant, and 14 who need to practice size and spacing. That's when you gather them together and give them what they need, no more, no less. 15a, b and c will tell the child where he is supposed to go for those lessons. Another way of teaching handwriting might be individually through learning stations. This could be a part of the contract, and they too would have to do only the lessons they needed. And of course there is the child who is exempt from handwriting, because if your criteria are neatness and legibility, many of the older kids will meet those criteria and should be excused from handwriting.

On to 16. If you found some specific needs in C. S. (communication skills, remember?) that your children may have, you could make some learning stations to help teach them. For instance, you may find your kids don't know anything about homonyms, or homonyms may be the next skill on the skill sequence, so you could do a learning station on them. If you have more than one station, you may have to number them, and 16 is the place the children keep track of the stations they're to do.

Item 17 is a very important item on the contract. The child agrees to do the contract, but it seems more like a real contract or more important if the child signs his name and indicates his acceptance of it. When he signs he accepts the responsibility for the work on the contract and agrees to do it in the time specified.

Item 18 is for you, the teacher, to show whether the work was completed or not, and if it met with the standards set as acceptable. You can put an adjective here to tell how the work was completed. We think if the work was not done up to standards, you'd want to make note of that in Item 21, Comments.

Item 19 you, the teacher, sign when the work is completed.

Item 20 is the parent's signature. When the work is finished or on a day you all agree upon, the papers and the contracts go home for the parent's signature. Friday has been a good day for this. The parent may keep the papers, but since the contract is a valuable record of the child's progress, it should be returned and kept.

Last but not least is a place for comments by the teacher or the parent. Of course these comments should be discussed with the child.

And that pretty well wraps up the communication skill contract. You thought we'd never finish? Well, we think the communication skill contract is the most important, and because it involves so many skill areas it is complicated. It is also the hardest to do. One good thing, though, after you have a decent communication skill contract put together, the other subject areas are relatively simple. So if you've taken all those other snack breaks, perhaps on this break you ought to go out and run around the block. You could also review your square roots while we get ready for math. What's a square root? Don't ask me, I'm the one who feels talented when I get 7 x 7. As a matter of fact, the other day our team of teachers cheered when I got that exact multiplication fact correct.

O.K. you had a break, let's look at the math contract (Fig. 5). You'll see that Items 1-5 are exactly the same as the C. S. (we're abbreviating communication skills) contract, so we won't mention them.

Item 6 refers to Merrill Math Skilltapes, which is a kit put out by Merrill which can be used for teaching skills or reviewing them. 6a, b and c are necessary for the child to know which cassette tapes he's supposed to do.

Item 7 deals with a programmed math book or a regular math text. A programmed math book, as I'm sure you all know, is one which the child can use to work at his own pace. It is also self-correcting; we have found them very valuable. Any pages in the child's text could also be included in Item 7, any you want the child to do to reinforce a skill he's learned.

Let us insert another note at this point about skills, especially math skills. Very few children can teach *themselves* skills. They can teach another child a skill if they know it, but very few children should be sent out alone to discover the skills on their own, and NEVER should this be done without close teacher guidance. What we're trying to say is a ditto paper will not teach a concept in math to most children. Dittos should be used for practice, review, or reinforcement, but just because a child does a page of addition problems doesn't mean he understands the underlying concepts. These

must be taught individually or in small groups.

Item 8 on the math contract is the place where skill lessons are scheduled. Now, if your children are on contracts and you have several groups working separately, you'll want to have them scheduled at least three times a week for skill lessons. This item tells the child where he's to meet his teacher and when.

Item 9. If you have any worksheets you want the children to do as reinforcement you could number some file folders, put them on a window sill, and record the number of the sheets you want the child to do at this place on his contract.

Item 10—Learning Stations. If you have some activities or math games, you could set these up in a learning station where the children could be involved while you're working with another group.

Item 11—Other. This is just what it says. If you think of some things that don't fit anywhere else they could be included under Other.

Items 12, 13, 14 and 15 are the same as on the C. S. contract.

We're in the process of revising the math and C. S. contracts, which is something we feel should be done. In any skill area contracts should be continually evaluated and revised as you evaluate and revise the whole program.

One last item we didn't mention—a reward. What do the children get if they do their contract well and on time? The only thing we've given the children is free time. If the child's contract is completed and done well at check-out, he is given ten minutes of free time. The child can do with the ten minutes what he wants. He can even save it up. We use a form to keep track of it (See Fig. 6).

With C. S. and math contracts we have agreed upon work to be completed, and it is done and done well. Let's assume that you agree with us at this point about the value of contracts. In what subject area do you begin? We think it makes sense to begin with C. S., perhaps not in all C. S. areas, perhaps just in reading. Then after you've gotten the children working on reading contracts, add spelling, then handwriting, and keep on adding the areas mentioned in Chapter IV. Then you're an expert. A math contract will

be a breeze for you. In our first year at the Elizabeth Jenkins School, we successfully managed contracts in C. S. and Math only. We didn't even think about contracts in Social Studies and Science. That was our goal for our second year.

As we said before, contracts are marvelous things, but I guess the most amazing thing of all is the amount of learning that began to take place at the beginning of the year. It continued to take place, and the learning was extended by the children themselves. It was an incredible thing to watch. The children extended and increased the amount of work on their contracts. It came from them; it didn't have to come from the teachers. If this isn't self-motivation, self-discipline, and self-direction, then those terms aren't familiar to us. And if contracts can help us get this much from children, don't you think they're worth a try? We do! We feel that they are NOT a Mission Impossible. They are a very possible mission. As a matter of fact, we just hope this chapter has made you feel excited enough about them to try them.

FIGURE 6

Name _____

FREE TIME

How Much?	Subject?	Teacher's Sig. (when given)	Teacher's Sig. (when taken)

CHAPTER X

Packets

WE'VE TRIED TO identify several specific techniques for individualization in the book. This chapter presents another of those—Packets.

Perhaps you'll recognize them as being called I.L.P.'s (Individual Learning Packets), or L.P.'s (Learning Packages), or just plain (as we've chosen to call them) packets. In this chapter we will discuss the different types of packets, their construction and use in the program. We feel that the basics of packet construction can be examined briefly, and you should be able to develop a packet when you finish this chapter. If you have further interest, then most college bookstores will have more detailed texts.

There are three basic kinds of packets: (1) an activity packet, (2) a practice packet, and (3) a learning packet. Each of these has a purpose and a particular design. We will discuss each one.

Before we discuss each type perhaps we ought to point out basically what a packet should do, regardless of the type. A packet is meant to be used by an individual child. It should be designed so that a minimum of help is needed. It is a little silly for us to design individual learning activities for children and then spend as much time answering questions about the activity as it would have taken us to teach it.

This is as good a place as any to bring up a point we need to make. We discuss several techniques in the book designed to help individualize learning. There are, of course, many others. It is necessary for all of us to know about as many approaches to learning as possible. However, since we are all human and must function in terms of our energy, and personal demand, it behooves us to make the best possible use of our time. We need to take a look at all the approaches available

121

to us in light of the concept we wish to teach. This will enable us to choose the most efficient and best way to present the concept. We agree that any concept can be presented in any of these ways, and for many children we'll need more than one approach.

On our first attempt though, we should try to use the most effective, efficient and productive method possible. We, therefore, need to examine what we want to do and then arrive at the best way for us to do it. Some of the methods suggested in the book require time to develop. We suggest that this effort is best applied to topics that are likely to be repeatedly presented so that your effort goes further. Of course if you work on a team and involve other personnel such as parents or aides in the program, this becomes a much less critical concern.

The point is if you're going to do a lesson or a set of lessons on Columbus, and you probably won't get the urge for Columbus again for a long time, it is somewhat unprofitable to invest ten hours in a fifteen or twenty minute lesson. Simply stated: know what you're going to do, then choose the way to do it that best fits the time, effort and energy you've got to expend.

One final point—individual learning packets began as just that. However, activity packets, and practice packets somehow came into use under the

guise of individual learning packets. We have included those two packets in this chapter to distinguish them from individual learning packets and to discourage their use as such. They should be used for the purpose they serve. Our enthusiasm for these two types of packets is not overwhelming. We realize however that there may be times and settings when such a design may meet the needs of a child. Therefore, we've included them.

With this in mind we will discuss the various types of packets.

ACTIVITY PACKETS

An activity packet is a set of varied activities packaged for each child to work on. A workbook is a form of an activity packet. Teachers should try to keep the activities in such a packet varied and related to the same topic. A primary teacher might, for example, develop an activity packet on some of the beginning consonants. Such a packet usually includes picture identification, crossword puzzles, discrimination activities, etc. Each child, when ready, receives a copy of the packet to work on at his own speed. This could be a part of his contract. An activity packet basically provides a variety of activities for a child to perform as reinforcement and diagnosis of skills already taught. Activity packets usually have between five and ten activities. This seems to be a reasonable amount for most children to complete in a specified period of time. Students might need to do only a part of an activity packet and these could be identified in the child's contract. Variety stores sell activity books that can give you some ideas about the types of activities which could be included in an activity packet.

PRACTICE PACKETS

A practice packet is based on reinforcement of concepts already learned. It is basically a collection of practice exercises on a specific topic. A practice packet could be developed by an intermediate teacher to provide practice with division with two place divisors. Practice packets include about three to eight pages of practice material, and key in on one or two concepts at the most.

Both practice packets and activity packets need a direction page and both are much more appealing with some kind of a cover.

Several words of caution are appropriate here: These packets should be used very carefully. Practice is sometimes necessary, but how much is an important question. Beware that these packets, which we've seen heavily used, are not merely *busy work!* They should be based on the child's needs and used only *when* and *if* a child needs them.

INDIVIDUAL LEARNING PACKETS

Individual learning packets are designed to help an individual learn a particular set of concepts. The individual learning packet has nine parts, each of which is important as a part of the whole packet. (The sample packet was done by Diane Kyle, a graduate student in an Open Education Workshop at Millersville State College.) We will discuss each of these parts in some detail:

I. The Cover—Each individual learning packet should have a cover. (Fig. 1) The cover should depict the topic in some way. Try to use your imagination, or anybody else's you can get hold of. The cover should say to the child: I am something you should be interested in doing. Use color, cartoons, pictures, diagrams, anything, just try to make the cover inviting. (Fig. 1)

II. Directions—Every individual learning packet must have clearly stated, concise directions. (Fig. 2) This is very important since we expect the child to get the packet and use it by himself. If there are materials to be used with the packet, the directions should specify where they are, and how to use them.

Perhaps an incident we're all familiar with will help to support the need for clear, concise directions. Have you ever sent your own child, if you

FIGURE 1

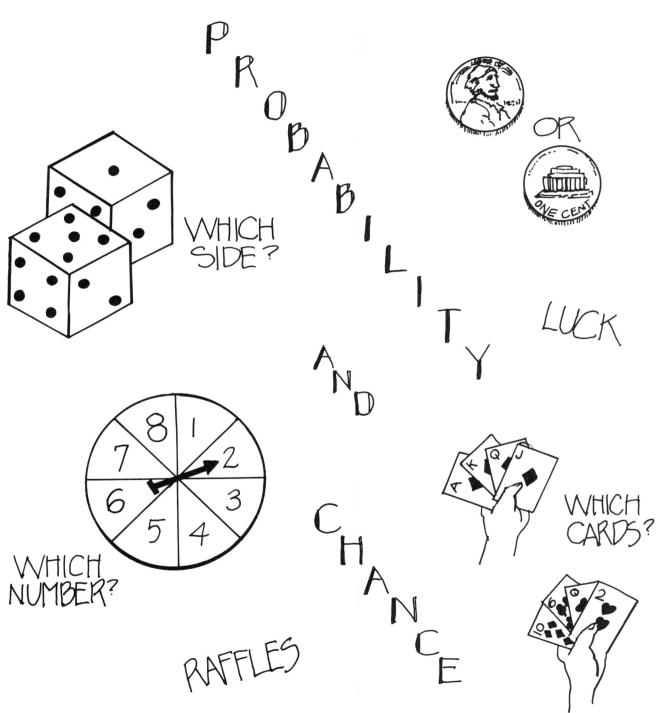

PROBABILITY AND CHANCE

WHICH SIDE?

OR

ONE CENT

LUCK

WHICH NUMBER?

WHICH CARDS?

RAFFLES

FIGURE 2

DIRECTIONS

1. Read this page completely before doing the packet.

2. Read the page entitled "Why Do the Packet?"

3. Take the pre-test and put the answers on the answer sheet.

4. After your pre-test is finished, check your answers on the answer sheet with the pre-test answer key.

5. Each question on the pre-test has a learning activity number in (parentheses) after it. Find the pre-test questions you had incorrect and do the learning activities for those questions. Do those activities to improve your skills.

6. If you had all the pre-test correct, come see me.

7. After you have done the activities, take the post-test. Put the answers on the answer sheet.

8. After your post-test is finished, check your answers with the post-test answer key.

9. Answer the last sheet in the packet honestly. Tell what you thought about the packet.

10. Bring the completed packet to me.

have one, or somebody else's to get something? (Mom) "Bill, bring me the yardstick from my bedroom." (Bill) "Where is it?" (Mom) "On the dresser." (Bill) "Which is the dresser?" (Mom, getting upset) "The one with the mirror." (Bill) "I can't find it." Mom goes upstairs and there, big as life right in the center of the dresser, is the yardstick! This is the child you are writing directions for in the packet.

III. Objectives (Fig. 3)—We hesitate to use this word because right away we get hung up on the "behavioral terms" bit. We've read several of the books dealing with this and are convinced that those authors are the only ones who can state anything in purely behavioral terms. As for most teachers, we ought to feel pretty good if we know specifically what we are trying to accomplish and can state that in terms of what we'd like the child to be able to accomplish.

This part of the packet, though, should not be called "Objectives" in the packet. Try to come up with a way to say what the packet is for, or what it will help you to learn, or somehow personalize it. Your imagination (or someone else's again) can help make even the purpose of the packet an interesting experience. A packet should deal with three to five objectives. If the material you're packaging has more objectives than that, develop a series of packets to deal with the area.

IV. Pre-Test—The pre-test (Fig. 4) should be included in the packet so the child can test his knowledge of the material before he does the packet. Obviously, if he knows the material, he shouldn't do the packet, or if he knows part of the material he should do only the parts he doesn't know. It's a good rule of thumb to have at least two questions in the pre-test for each objective. Yes, that's right, the pre-test questions are derived from the packet objectives (part 3). Thus, if you have five objectives, you will have ten pre-test questions.

V. Pre-test answers (Fig. 5)—What! You say put the test answers in the packets? Of course! Now, if you're not ready for that, then your directions must include where and how to get the pre-test checked. The test must be checked before the child can go on to the next section of the packet, activities.

VI. Activities (Fig. 6)—This is probably the most important part of the packet as this is the part that teaches the child the things he doesn't know, as indicated in the pre-test.

It is important to develop a variety of approaches in the activity sections. There should be at least two activities for each objective, preferably more.

One of the most important considerations in developing packets is correlation of the packet components. All of

FIGURE 3

WHY DO THIS PACKET?

This packet offers you the opportunity to learn:

1. the names of men who first worked with probability

2. the ways our government and business use probability to see how much success they will have

3. to define probability and give an example of a probability situation

4. to express the probability of an event happening as a fraction

5. to give the probability of an event occurring or not occurring

FIGURE 4

PRE–TEST

1. What is probability? (Activity 1)

2. Name an activity you could do that can be tested by probability. (Activity 1)

3. If there are six basketballs in a gym bag and three are brown, two are gold and one is red, white and blue, what is the chance of your *not* picking out a gold one? (Activity 4)

4. Look at this picture.

Which fraction best describes the probability of someone *not* drinking milk? (Activity a)

a) $\frac{1}{1}$ b) $\frac{1}{3}$ c) $\frac{2}{3}$ d) $\frac{1}{4}$

5. Name two men who began working with probability. (Activity 3)

6. In what century did probability start in math? (Activity 3)

7. Jonathan has four pair of pants: two are blue, one is brown and one is grey. What are the chances he will choose a blue pair? a grey pair? a brown pair? (Activity 4)

8. There are four dozen cookies in a jar: two dozen are chocolate chip, one and a half dozen are peanut butter and one-half dozen are oatmeal. What is the probability of your picking out an oatmeal cookie? a chocolate chip cookie? a peanut butter cookie? Express your answers as fractions. (Activity 2)

9. Name three uses of probability in our world today. (Activity 5)

FIGURE 5

ANSWERS FOR THE PRE–TEST

1. Probability is the chance that something will happen in a certain way.

2. The weather: whether it will rain or not.
   Whether you will go to school or not.
   Whether your teacher will come to school or not.
   Whether you will have pizza for lunch or not.
   Plus many more answers.

3. 4 out of 6

4. c

5. Pascal and Fermi

6. seventeenth century

7. 2 out of 4; 1 out of 4; 1 out of 4.

8. $\frac{6}{48}$; $\frac{24}{48}$; $\frac{18}{48}$.

9.
taxes	life insurance
elections	life expectancy
selling products	card games
weather	statistics Any three are OK.

FIGURE 6

ACTIVITIES

1. Go look up the definition of probability in a dictionary. Write down what you find. Then look up probability in the World Book Encyclopedia. Compare the information. With this to help you, write down five things you could do today that have some chance in them. Keep your paper.

2. View a filmloop called "What Are the Chances." This you will find in the library. When you are finished viewing the film, take a coin and toss it up in the air 100 times. Keep track of the number of times it lands on heads and the number of times it lands on tails. List the results in fraction form.

3. Go to the World Book Encyclopedia and look up probability. At the end of the section of probability you will find some names. Go look these up and see what they have to do about probability. Write a paragraph about what you read about each man. Share this information with your friends. You can also check in other encyclopedias for additional information.

4. Do two of the following activities. Compare your results with those of your friends.

   a. Take a coin and toss it up in the air 25 times. Record the number of times you get tails and the number of times you get heads. There are only two possibilities: heads or tails.

   b. Pick a card from a deck of 52 cards and then put it back. Shuffle the cards and then pick out and return cards 100 times. Keep a record of the cards you pick.

   c. Put your crayons in a bag and pick a crayon. Do this 15 times. What were your chances of pulling out a pink crayon? A silver crayon? Record these results.

   d. Take a thumb tack. Toss it up in the air. Record how many times it turns out "point up," "point down," or on the side.

5. Find the article "Probability" from the New Book of Knowledge, pp. 470-474. You only need to read the first page and the last four paragraphs on the last page. List ways probability is used today. Do you know any others? Look up probability in a book in the library and see if you find more uses of probability. Try to make one huge list of uses of probability in the world.

the activities should be designed to teach the objectives of the packet. Therefore, these must be coded into each other. The logical place to do this is on the pre-test. The activities related to each pre-test question should be listed at the end of the question in parentheses. The packet should note in the directions that these numbers appear after each question. When the pre-test is checked, the errors will guide the child to the activities he should perform in order to learn the skill tested by that question. For example, if the child takes the pre-test and misses question one, and the numerals 1, 2 and 3 appear in the parentheses at the end of question 1, then the child should do activities 1, 2 and 3 in order to satisfy that part of the packet. Sometimes you may want the child to do only one activity of three if he misses a question. In such a case at the end of the question in the parentheses you can put (do activity 1 or 2 or 3).

With this type of organization, the child is not doing activities designed to teach things he already knows. He is only doing activities to learn things he doesn't know. The caution we offer is to avoid designing reading and writing activities alone. Certainly include some of these, but try to develop activities of different kinds to add interest and provide more than one option for learning. Perhaps a suggestion about constructing packets would be helpful here. We've discovered that

the first item to deal with in packet construction (once you've decided on a topic) is the objectives. Once these are developed, it seems efficient to then take each objective and develop the test questions and activities for each. When these are completed put them together with the cover, the directions, and the other parts, and your packet is ready to go.

VII. Post-test (Fig. 7)—The post-test is inserted so that the child can get feedback concerning his success with the packet. The post-test is also your way of knowing how well the child performed on the packet.

VIII. Post-test answers (Fig. 8)—Of course the child needs some way to know how he performed on the test. If you still feel you can't include the answers in the packet, then remember in the directions to tell the child where to find the answers.

There are a couple of things to consider in this part of the packet. If you want the child to have further experience with concepts he doesn't understand as revealed through the post-test, then you must include additional activities in your post-test design. That is, your post-test must be keyed into a set of extension or reinforcement included in the packet. These should, however, be fun-type activities and not seem like punishment for finishing.

131

FIGURE 7

POST TEST

1. Mr. Young bought 15 chances on a car raffle. There were 5,721 chances sold. What is the probability of his winning the raffle?

2. In a box, there were four brown marbles, three blue marbles and five red marbles. How many marbles are in the box? Does each marble have the same chance of being picked? What are the chances of picking a red marble? What are the chances of picking a blue marble? What are the chances of not picking a brown marble?

3. What is the probability that the arrow will stop on black? What is the probability that the arrow will stop on red?

4. Name two men who worked with probability when it first started.

5. What was the century when the theory of probability was started?

6. Define probability.

7. Put an X after each sentence that tells of a situation of chance; it has to deal with probability.
   a. the weather today
   b. the results of a basketball game: winning or loosing
   c. when you were born
   d. what you will have for dinner today

8. There are 6 buttons in a box. The chances of picking out a blue button are 4 out of 6. How many blue buttons are in the box?

9. There are 52 cards in a deck. What are the chances of picking out an ace? a 2? of *not* getting a 9?

10. Name two events in your life that deal with probability

11. There are 35 boys on a bus trip. Which number best tells the probability of picking a girl to be the leader on the trip?
    a) $\frac{1}{35}$ b) $\frac{1}{20}$ c) $\frac{1}{15}$ d) 0

12. List three modern applications of probability in the world today.

FIGURE 8

POST TEST ANSWER KEY

1. $\dfrac{15}{5721}$

2. 12 ; yes ; $\dfrac{5}{12}$ or 5 out of 12 ; $\dfrac{3}{12}$ or 3 out of 12 ; $\dfrac{8}{12}$ or 8 out of 12.

3. 2 out of 4 or $\dfrac{2}{4}$; 1 out of 4 or $\dfrac{1}{4}$

4. Pascal and Fermi

5. seventeenth century

6. chance that something will happen in a certain way.

7. a) __X__   b) __X__   c) _____   d) __X__

8. 4 buttons that are blue

9. $\dfrac{4}{52}$ or 4 out of 52 ; $\dfrac{4}{52}$ or 4 out of 52 ; $\dfrac{48}{52}$ or 48 out of 52

10. your own judgment: ask a friend who has already done this packet

11. d

12. elections   life insurance
    weather   business problems
    card games   auto accidents
    taxes   statistics
    life expectancy   Any three are fine.

IX. Feedback Page (Fig. 9)—This page should be available for the child to comment about the packet. It can be a blank page or have creatively illustrated questions or be a check list. The design is up to you. This page is important in revising the packet, as the children will indicate dull activities, activities that don't teach what they portend to teach, poor objectives and any other weakness apparent in the packet.

USING THE PACKET

Now that you've made the packet, you're wondering, "how do I use it?" There are several ways you can use it. If you have made a packet in a skill area, then you probably want all the children to do it. This may seem like a text book approach, but you only make about ten copies of a packet. Therefore, you must organize and schedule your program so that only ten children at a time are working on the packet. You must have other activities, other packets, or write the packet into a contract. In this way ten packets will be plenty. The beauty of the packet is that the child who knows the material takes the pre-test and does not have to do the packet, or only has to do a part of the packet.

If you make packets for enrichment or to supplement your program, these can be used basically in the same way. You probably will not want all the

children to do this type of packet. Therefore, you can reduce the number of copies you need.

As you build up a file of packets, they become much more useful in the program. If you are working on a team or in cooperation with other teachers, as all of you contribute to the file your collection will grow, and the number of options available to the children will grow.

You will, of course, want feedback about the packets the children complete. It is a good idea to establish a system that enables you to see the results as they are finished. This is most easily handled by having the children put the finished packet, or a report of the finished packet, into their folders. This will enable you to see the results simply by picking up the folder.

If you have a laminating machine available, it is a good idea to laminate the packets. This will greatly extend the useable life of the packet.

Packets can be a valuable tool in your classroom. They do require some time to make if you make them correctly. They will, however, be worth it. As you add to your collection they will become an even more valuable tool. When you combine them with learning centers, and contracts, and texts, and kits, and filmstrips and all the wide variety of materials available to us today, they provide us with the

FIGURE 9

FEEDBACK

1. Which activity did you like best?

2. Which activity did you like the least?

3. Which activity did you find the most difficult?

4. Which things didn't you understand?

5. Which face best described "how you feel" about the packet?

---

potential to have the kind of program we want to have for our students.

In summary, we have organized the components of the packet into the following schemata.

PACKET SCHEMATA

I. TITLE PAGE—(Use your imagination, make it interesting, neat, mad, "sexy")

II. DIRECTIONS—(Clear, concise, simple, complete)

III. OBJECTIVES—(Specific, limited number, stated in a provocative way)

IV. PRE-TEST—(Each item coded in parentheses to correlate with activities, each item also related to the objectives)

V. PRE-TEST ANSWERS—(In the packet, or where to locate them if they are not in the packet)

VI. ACTIVITIES—(Try to develop different approaches, not all reading; develop at least two for each objective. Lead into activities by placing the number or letter of each activity in parentheses at the end of each pretest question that is related)

VII. POST-TEST—(Could be the pretest with items in another order)

VIII. POST-TEST ANSWERS—(In the packet, or where to locate them if they are not in the packet)

IX. FEEDBACK PAGE—(Try to make it an interesting way to tell about the packet)

135

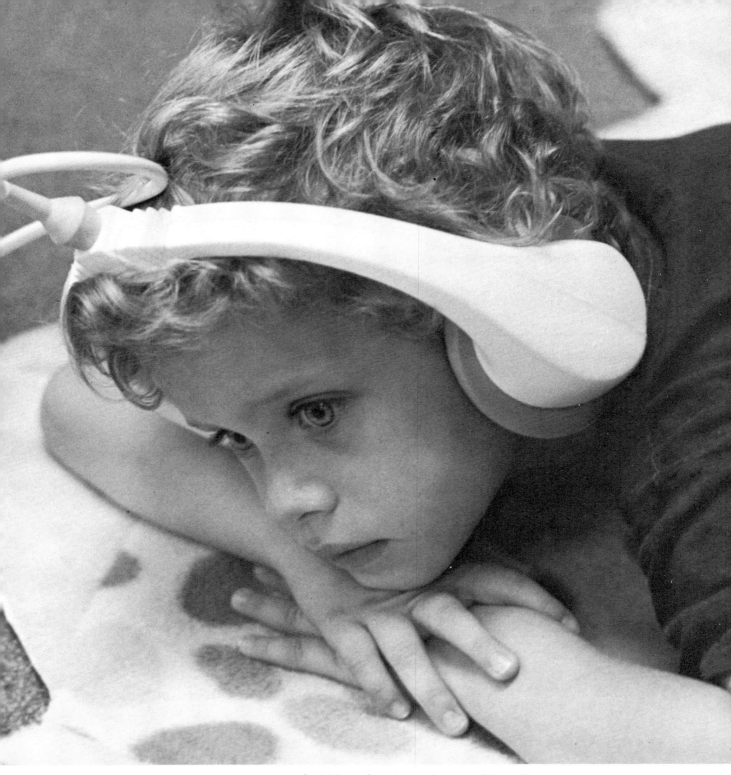

Activities at learning stations should provide for individual differences.

11

Learning Stations
and
Centers

WELL, WE KNEW you'd like Open Education! What? You're still not convinced? O.K.! Then here's another chapter guaranteed to convince you.

If you've been up and about in the educational circles for the last three years, you've heard the terms "learning station" and "learning center." As a matter of fact in the 1960's another term, the "interest center," was the big thing, and could very well be considered the father of learning stations as we know them today.

Those interest centers, however, were very different. Their primary purpose was to provide an area where a child could go to keep himself busy if he finished the work he had been assigned. It might have been a math center where math games had been set up, or a science area where displays of leaves had been placed. It kept the child busy and he could stay there as long

as he obeyed the rules and kept QUIET. It was irrelevant whether the child learned anything.

Its offspring, the learning station or learning center, is quite different. It is, as its name implies, a learning place. A definition will help, and again, this is our definition. A learning station is a gathering of visual, auditory, and/or manipulative materials to reinforce or teach a single concept, or to add enrichment to your program. And though many authors use the terms synonymously, learning stations and learning centers differ. The latter may be defined as a group of learning stations designed to present related or sequential concepts.

Learning stations and centers offer the child a chance to function as an individual. And you thought this chapter was different! We seem to be

137

repeating, but in open education, people care about the child—the INDIVIDUAL child.

WHY LEARNING STATIONS? They are a lot of work; why bother? Learning stations, as we said, help you individualize.

1. A learning station can help you review, practice, or extend a skill.

2. A learning station can help to enrich your program, and help to challenge your high-ability students. With learning stations, a teacher can offer optional topics to challenge the faster children because when you have set up two learning stations, you've altered the pupil-teacher ratio somewhat. In effect you've added two teachers.

3. Learning stations can help you offer more choices. If a unit is divided into sub-topics, three teachers (you and two learning stations) can be handling these three areas at the same time. How's that for amazing? If they can choose from the three, and if there is a list of activities to choose from, children are able to make more of those decisions we keep talking about.

4. Learning stations can provide more fun-type learning situations by adding humor, gimmicks, or a variety of approaches—all of which make learning more interesting to the child.

5. Learning stations can help a child learn individually, at his own pace and according to his ability.

6. Learning stations can help teachers begin to team-teach. They are a beautiful way to begin to cooperate with the teacher across the hall. You can make two stations, he can make two, you can share them with two other teachers and you will soon have eight stations. We've often wondered why we in education have refused to share and cooperate. Most of us stay in our own rooms limited by our own human capabilities and never take advantage of our neighbor's abilities. If you have a good station or bulletin board, why not share it? If you have a good technique or a new twist, share it and that sharing soon becomes contagious. See the chapter on team-teaching if you want more reasons to team-teach. We expect sharing from the children; shouldn't we set a good example. To those of you who already do share, congratulations! Education needs more of you, but you can help even more— why not coax the reluctant lady down the hall to join in "OPERATION CO-OPERATION."

THE BASIC INGREDIENTS OF LEARNING STATIONS AND CENTERS

Every station should have several components:

a. DIRECTIONS

b. OBJECTIVES

c. CONTENT

d. ACTIVITIES

e. EVALUATION

Further explanation of each of these components might help to clarify stations and centers for you.

a. *Directions*—These should be absolutely clear to the children; they can be presented on a sheet of paper or on a cassette; they should be appropriate for the age level of the child you're dealing with. They should be as simple as possible. Prior directions on how to operate the equipment and for general use of learning stations would eliminate the need for that repetition at every station. You should include in those directions such things as: it's a privilege, the child's responsibility, the quality of work expected, directions on the operation of any equipment they will be using, where the children ate to work, standards of behavior, respect for "kids" in other classes, and any special information. A necessary reminder sometimes helps, for instance, WATCH THE HANDWRITING! or a motivational note—WELL, YOU'RE OFF AND RUNNING NOW! or GO GET 'EM TIGER!

b. *Objectives*—As soon as possible after the child gets to the station, he should understand why he's there and what's expected of him. This can be done by the title of the station, or it can be written, pictured, or recorded. Two examples follow:

HOMOMONSTERS
LEARN TO FIGHT THEM AND WIN

or

DUNE BUGGIES
FIND OUT ABOUT THEM
AND
MAKE A MODEL

c. *Content*—We began by saying the children learned through stations and centers. This is where the content comes in. They can read the content, read to find it, watch a film to get it, listen to a record, do an experiment, or listen to someone give it on a cassette. The content is included so the child can get information that will help him reach the goals or objectives of the station.

d. *Activities*—After he has learned, he can extend that learning through the activities. They also must be appropriate for the level of the child, must be individualized, and should enrich the learning experience. Research questions, group discussions, murals, any art activity, making reports, making games, notebooks, interviewing speakers or resource people, and taking field trips are all activities you or the children can choose from. Activities can make or break a station—they

139

are terribly important, and should be interesting and challenging. Here's where you can coordinate the art, music and physical education people. Of course they have to be flexible enough to be interested in the approach, but most of them probably will be; special teachers have been talking about being integrated into the program for years. Now here's their opportunity.

e. *Evaluation*—Here's a bit of a sticky one. We don't believe all learning can be evaluated OR that all of it *should* be evaluated. Learning stations can be, but do not have to be evaluated. Your school district will probably govern how much you evaluate and what. If you must, worksheets can be an activity and an evaluation instrument at the same time which kills two birds with one stone. You can, of course, always give a test, and the product or result of an activity can be evaluated. You can also have discussions individually or in groups to evaluate the learning which has taken place. The best approach, though, is to have the child evaluate himself. Self-evaluation, by the way, is a major goal of open education. When our children can evaluate themselves honestly, fairly, and accurately, think about what open education will have done for the human race. If our children can learn to do this, they'll have one up on most adults, and perhaps fewer of them will end up on black leather couches in psychiatrist's offices. Not

only that but we'll be producing happier, mentally healthier, and more honest human beings.

CRITERIA FOR LEARNING STATIONS

There are certain criteria which if followed will make the stations better and their implementation smoother. They follow:

1. Learning stations should be completely self-directed. If you're using a station as an extension of yourself, the children using it should not have questions about how to do it. If your station is unclear, the children will be interrupting the child or group you're working with. Every detail should be worked out, the materials available, and directions and goals explicitly clear.

2. Learning stations and centers should be self-correcting when possible. In an open situation a teacher's time is extremely valuable, and she cannot afford to waste one minute of it checking work the children are perfectly capable of checking themselves. If worksheets accompany the station, an answer key should be provided at the station.

3. Learning stations and centers must be individualized. There are two ways of doing this. First, you could allow only certain children to do certain

stations according to their ability. However, if you're using a station as an integral part of the program and feel it's valuable enough for everyone to do, then your activities are the key. Activities help to individualize. If directions and content can be provided on a cassette, you can provide appropriate activities for even the problem reader, such as films, filmloops, records, recording his answers or opinions on tape, drawing, painting, or modeling. If a child has difficulty reading, he can work with a buddy. This approach would pair him up with a more capable reader. Be careful of this system though; an impatient or unwilling child might criticize a less able child and do more harm than good. This, of course, is not what you are seeking.

4. Learning stations and centers should be attractive. They should be motivational. If children have a choice, they'll choose an attractive station first. Spend a little time on unusual lettering, attractive colors, interesting pictures, or realia. Sure, it's going to take time, but you can use it over and over again, and the children, if motivated, will get off to a better start.

5. Another motivator—humor and gimmicks. Don't be afraid to let the "kids" have fun. One of our teachers said when we first discussed learning stations, "I can't do them. I'm not creative!" She repeated it over and over. During a unit on Africa, this "non-creative" teacher was to show in a station the distance from the United States to Africa. The "non-creative" teacher went home with a cassette recorder and taped a hilarious flight from Kennedy Airport to Africa. Her husband's voice was the pilot's, her daughters were stewardesses, and they took the kids on a fantastically funny flight, giving them content at the same time. They managed to cover distance traveled and geographical landmarks, etc. That "non-creative" teacher has never lived down those doubting comments.

A student teacher during the same unit did a station on animals in Africa. She, her boy friend, and some jungle sounds albums helped the children go on a "Swingin' Safari."

During another unit a teacher did a station on the Amish of Pennsylvania. Out of plywood he built himself a porch, brought in a rocking chair, pipe, and jeans outfit and chatted with the children about the Amish. Now that station was not self-directed; he had to be there, but the children sure enjoyed it—especially the part where they made homemade ice cream. Gimmicks? Yes! But they sure liven up Geography, History or English.

6. Variety is the spice of life. We've all heard the saying, but it's true. While using stations, children can be

bored by the same approach used constantly. It's so easy to use different materials, media and techniques. Reading and researching are fine activities, but they are tiresome after the fifteenth time. Besides, the poor kid who can't read is really stuck. Use your noggins and think of new ways. Why not let them make a movie? You don't have a camera? Borrow a friend's! Let them sew some colonial costumes, put on a puppet show, etc. Vary the activities. Have a Halloween station in a closet. Have surprises at the end of cassette recordings to encourage listening. We used the Mission Impossible theme quite a lot last year. We taped the music and at one station the kids were told to listen carefully for a surprise. Of course they expected the tape to "self-destruct" at the end, but the tape said, "This tape will . . . NOT self-destruct; it's the last one we have!" Think *fun* while you're preparing stations. The fun station can still "cure," but what's the matter with a SUGAR-COATED pill?

As you read this book a few of you will be thinking up excuses for why you can't do this or that. Most of you, however, will think, "No, I can't do exactly that, but I could adapt it in this way." The examples, suggestions, and ideas provided in this book are not intended to be used as lesson plans. They are to spur your own creative thoughts and ideas. At workshops we've conducted, we've found those two types of people, but we have a solution for you excuse-makers, if you're interested. Read this book once and make your excuses; then, *please* read it the second time and try to adapt, alter and adjust. If that fails, use the book to start a fire in the fireplace. It'll certainly work there.

7. At every station each child should be successful. As discussed before, activities should be provided for each child's differing abilities, or certain children should do only certain stations. See, you also can have a choice, how about that?

8. Learning stations should be relevant to the children. The children should have an opportunity to choose some topics. When was the last time you asked the children what they would like to study? Our curriculum guides should be flexible, should be just *guides* (if we have to have them at all), and should consider the children's interests. Why not include dune buggies or drug units if that's what the children are really interested in?

ORGANIZING FOR LEARNING STATIONS

If you're in a self-contained classroom you will, of course, begin differently than if you're in a non-graded team-teaching situation.

In a self-contained room you might begin by answering the following questions:

1. Learning stations—Who? Probably your most independent workers, children you can trust to work alone, even in an area outside the classroom. Then be ready for the surprise. When we started we found we misjudged many of the children. The brightest weren't necessarily the most independent workers, and the trustworthy ones inside the room were not necessarily trustworthy outside the room.

2. Learning stations—When? Begin when the other children are most occupied. During the first few times you use stations, however, you should be available to help those children using the stations. Of course the subject area in which you've chosen to use stations will have something to do with the time of day you use them.

3. Learning stations—How many children at a time? That will depend on the age and level of your children. It might be one; it might be seven or eight at one time. You can save time at the first stations by explaining generally to all the children as we suggested earlier.

4. Learning stations—What topics? Your first stations should be high interest ones—ones the children would really like to do. Here's where you might pick Dune Buggies or Snowmobiles, or whatever is likely to appeal to your age group. Each and every child should want to do that station. Chances are they'll abuse the privilege a lot less if it's something they want to learn about.

5. Learning stations—How to begin? Once you have two stations then what? The next step would be to branch out into other subject areas. The first could be on anything, the next could be on a communication skill, possibly punctuation; then an estimation station in math. By that time you'll be so good you'll be ready to try them in social studies or science. Try doing a unit teaching one of the concepts by station. Then on the next unit try several stations, and on the third unit use stations almost exclusively. That'll really make you an expert. BUT another word of caution: when we say "almost exclusively by stations" we are not saying never use groups. We must remember these children will live in society, and this involves living and getting along in groups. That plus the learning that comes out of group discussions, group interaction, and social living situations is enough of a rationale for learning some things in groups. In our school we had too little of it our first year, realized our mistake, and included more group work in the second year.

So much for the self-contained teacher, what about you folks in team   143 situations? You'll be able to do a lot more with stations. You probably have two or three teachers, possibly an aide, maybe a student teacher, and if not, let's hope you've got a whopper of a parent volunteer program organized. See the chapter on parent involvement for more help.

As a team, you then decide where your needs lie and which areas or skills can best be taught by stations. In our first year we put most of our stations in the social studies and science program (S.S.S.). We had a coordinator for the unit which we, or the youngsters, had decided on. That person broke the unit down into subtopics, wrote an outline, and assigned each of the other team members a topic. We researched our individual subtopic and set up a station on that subtopic. For instance, a unit on Africa might include six topics or stations on:

Education
Animals of Africa
Culture of Africa
Business and Way of Life
Location of Africa
People of Africa

The coordinator's job was also to gather reference materials for all the teachers, line up resource people, and present the outline of the unit to the team. At this point the team discussed, added, changed and improved the unit. Then we set up the stations.

Well, then, after your S.S.S. program is together in the afternoon, you might want to add stations in communication skills and math.

HOW TO PUT A LEARNING STATION OR CENTER TOGETHER

Learning stations come in many shapes and sizes. They can be free standing on table or floor, hanging from ceiling or against a wall, and they can be three dimensional.

We made many mistakes our first year, and we thought if we told you about ours you could avoid making those same ones. (You can make your own.)

1. Do *not* use tag board—it will eventually cave in, bend, or go limp.

2. *Do* use heavier cardboard from boxes 1/4" or 1/2" thick, TV or refrigerator cartons, plywood, formica, masonite, or any firm material that has strength. Tri-Wall Corporation, 1 Dupont Street, Peachview, Long Island, New York 11803 will ship you 6' x 8' sheets of 1/2" cardboard that can be cut with a jig saw into any shape or size. We put our stations together using that heavy cardboard with 3" or 4" wide bookbinding tape and they are so durable they will last for the next 20 years.

3. The table-top station may be your best bet if you're cramped for floor space. Fig. 1 shows how to put four stations at one table. This is a dandy

way to organize a small learning center with four stations.

4. In Fig. 2, the book-type station is illustrated. It is simplest to make and can be placed against a wall or door, or in the middle of the room, and the back "covers" could be used for other stations.

5. A three dimensional station can be set on a table with all the necessary items on the table beside it. See Fig. 3.

A single desk makes a great base for a small station for use by just one child. A table can service one station or can hold several stations and become a center. That's up to you.

6. The size of the station should be governed by the number of people who will use it at one time. There's no reason for using a large table for a station which can only be used by one child.

7. Cassettes are extremely valuable— to give directions, to give content, or for a child to record his contribution on. Quality cassettes should be made. A poor quality cassette can ruin a station. We use good recorders to record and cheaper recorders to play cassettes back at stations. Cassettes save you the time of writing up extensive directions, they save space at the station to display those directions, and save the problem reader the frustration of not being able to do the station sim-

ply because he can't read the directions. Adjust the pace on the cassette to the purpose. Directions should be given more slowly than content material. Remember an advantage of a cassette is that your children do not have to listen to your voice *only*. Have your husband, friend, parent, or another child record some of your cassettes to provide variety and spice.

8. As you're setting up the station remember that the children can contribute to the list of activities, and thus provide more activities. For instance, at a station on Robert Goddard, one of the activities might be to do a report on Robert Goddard. Then another optional activity might ask the children to read the report on Goddard. Use their pictures to brighten up your stations, too. At a station on rockets they were to design their own rockets and hang them at the station. One of the dangers inherent to learning stations as we see it, is that we're using all teacher-made stuff again. We had gotten away from that and we'd sure hate to go back to rooms void of the children's work.

9. Now, speaking of teacher-made stuff, how talented are you? Well, fear not, oh brave ones, because there's a magic machine which turns even the poorest artist into a Picasso. You know that opaque projector which has been standing way in the back of the supply closet? Drag it out because with that machine you can make a picture as

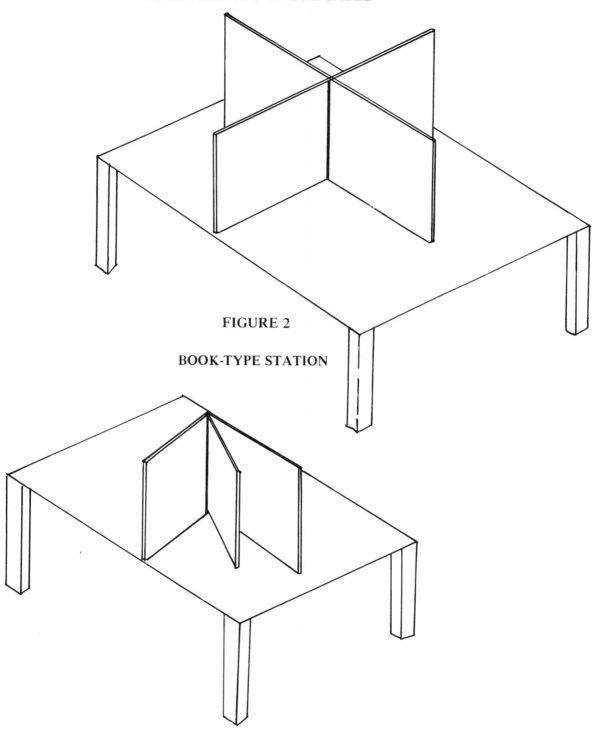

FIGURE 1

FOUR STATIONS ON ONE TABLE

FIGURE 2

BOOK-TYPE STATION

146

FIGURE 3

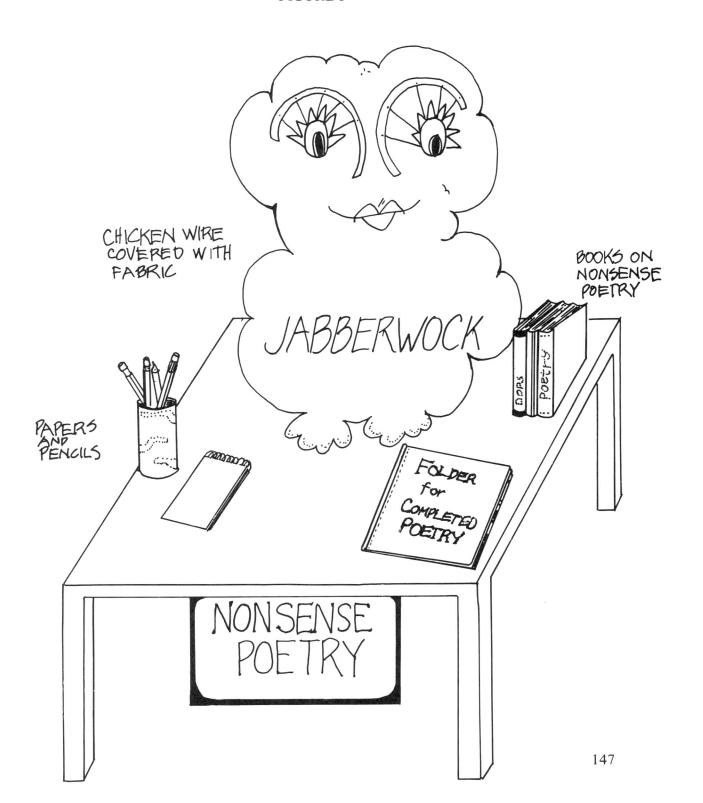

small or as large as you wish simply by projecting the image onto a wall onto which you've taped some white paper, or any color. Simply trace around the image after you've chosen the ideal size by moving the projector closer or further away from the paper. Voila! You've made a perfect copy of Snoopy six feet high. You don't have an opaque? O.K. Use an overhead. Make a line drawing of your object on a transparency and follow the above procedure.

10. When you're setting up the station or center be sure to provide a place for completed worksheets and pictures, etc. Everything that isn't nailed down at a station should be packaged in manila folder, envelopes, small boxes or containers to avoid losing them.

11. It might be a good idea to remove the cassette from the station. If your children have not had an opportunity to use a cassette recorder, they might try to record their voices, which of course will ruin your tape. The best way to avoid this is to make several well-used cassettes available to the children to experiment with at other times.

12. Too many worksheets will turn the children completely off. Our first year they complained constantly about too many worksheets so we used our noggins and began to come up with some other more interesting activities.

However, when the children got the opportunity to do their own stations, would you like to guess how many worksheets two boys dreamed up for their snake stations? SIX!

13. All stations and centers should be numbered and possibly color-coded. For instance, a red card with a No. 2 on it could be placed in a corner of the station. This will aid the child in finding the correct station and in checking off the station when it's completed. The colors could designate subject areas, for instance: red-communication skills; blue-math, etc.

14. An idea we thought helpful was a way we developed for the teachers to keep track of the stations that were done and how they were done. We developed a format. When we did a station on a topic, we filled out a format for it. (See Fig. 4). We all made formats for a learning center as we each did one on our own subtopics. When they were finished, each of us had the complete station, not just one part of it. On the format enough information was included so that anyone could follow the directions and set up that station. We kept these formats on file for future reference.

Hopefully these suggestions will help you avoid our mistakes and keep you from learning those lessons the way we did, the hard way, with thousands

FIGURE 4

FORMAT FOR LEARNING STATIONS

Page one—

1. Diagram the station or stations.
2. Give size, construction, arrangement of materials.
3. Tell how displayed (on table, hung on wall, on floor).
4. Number posters, direction and activity sheets for identification purposes.
5. Include colors used.

Page two—

1. Identify numbered items shown on page one.
2. Give contents of direction sheet, list of activities, pictures, etc.
3. Content—manner presented—read, film, cassettes, etc.

Page three—

1. Give sources of all pictures, posters.
2. Bibliography—list books to use to get background information, books for teacher use, books for students' use.
3. Source of additional materials—number and source for films, filmstrips, filmloops.
4. Include any information which would help persons set up this station.

Page four—

1. Attach any worksheets which would accompany station.

of missing worksheets, dozens of collapsed stations, etc., etc.

In order to make stations a bit clearer, we've included a sample learning station format for you. It was done by a graduate student, Karen Herceg at Millerville State College in an Open Education Workshop. (Figure 5)

RECORD-KEEPING

Record keeping can be done in several simple ways.

1. The teacher can keep track of the children by placing a check-off list at the station itself. (See Fig. 6)

OR

2. The children can keep a record in their notebooks of all the stations they do. (See Fig. 7)

3. There can be, and probably should be, a master list of stations broken up according to subject area with the childrens names, too. (See Fig. 8)

FIGURE 6

Title				
Christmas Around the World				
Mary	x	Tim	x	
Sue		Harold		
Sally	x			
Jim				
Harry	x			
George				

150

FIGURE 5

THE NEW STONE AGE: WHAT'S IT ALL ABOUT?

FORMAT FOR A LEARNING STATION:
SEVENTH GRADE
SOCIAL STUDIES

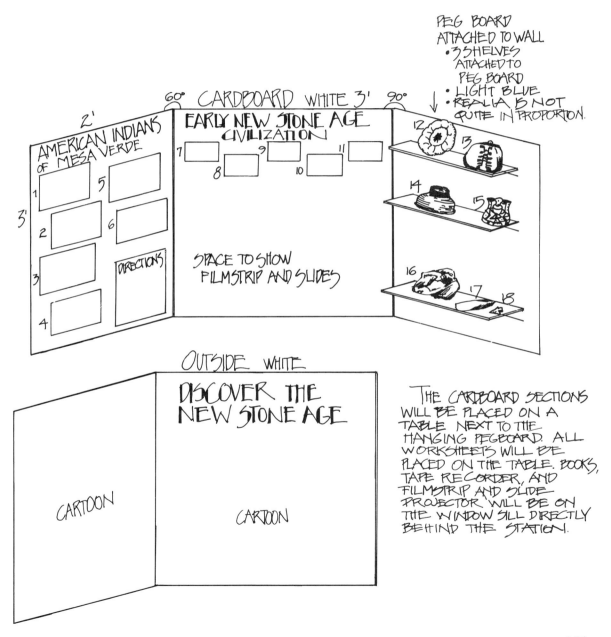

IDENTIFICATION

Large picture cards (6"x9") are pictures of the diorama at Mesa Verde Museum, Mesa Verde National Park.

1. The Basketmakers

2. The Developmental Pueblo Period

3. The Modified Basketmaker Period

4. Early Man in North America

5. The Great Pueblo Period

6. The Cliff Palace at Mesa Verde (post card)

Small picture cards (3"x5") are post cards of the Indian ruins at Aztec, New Mexico; they have nothing to do with Aztec Indians.

7. Large Kiva

8. Great Kiva

9. Artist's idea of what took place in the Great Kiva

10. Burial ruins

11. Overall view of the pueblo at Aztec

Realia: these items were mostly obtained in the southwest.

12. Round, woven grass dish

13. Reed basket with lid

14. Black pot

15. Wedding vase

16. Adobe mortar

17. Charred wood

18. Arrow head

DIRECTIONS

1. Read the New Stone Age information in at least one of these books:

   World Background for American History, pp. 28-33.
   Discovering Our World's History, pp. 10-15.
   The Social Studies and Our World, pp. 59-74.
   Building the Modern World, pp. 30-35.
   Long Ago in the Old World, pp. 8-19.
   Out of the Past, pp. 29-40.

2. View filmstrip "Early Man," part I of the Time-Life Series.

3. View videotape "Stone Age Tribes of Mindanao," a National Geographic TV special.

4. Do worksheet #1.

5. Check your answers (in folder tacked on bulletin board).

6. Do worksheet #2.

7. View slides of Mesa Verde and listen to accompanying tape.

8. You may now change answers on worksheet #2 if you want to.

9. Check your answers.

10. Do worksheet #3.

11. Check your answers.

12. Examine the EXTRA ACTIVITY sheet and do one of the suggested activities.

BIBLIOGRAPHY

Eibling, Harold, *et al. World Background for American History.* River Forest, Illinois: Laidlaw Brothers, Publishers, 1968.

Fraser, Dorothy. *Discovering Our World's History.* New York: American Book Company, 1964.

King, Frederick, *et al. The Social Studies and Our World.* River Forest, Illinois: Laidlaw Brothers, Publishers, 1970.

Reich, Jerome, *et al. Building the Modern World.* New York: Harcourt, Brace, and World, Inc., 1969.

Southworth, Gertrude and John Southworth. *Long Ago in the Old World.* Columbus, Ohio: Iroquois Publishing Company, Inc., 1959.

Wilson, Howard, *et al. Out of the Past.* New York: American Book Company, 1959.

ADDITIONAL BIBLIOGRAPHY

Howell, Clark. *Early Man.* New York: Time-Life Books, 1965.

Osborne, Douglas. "Wetherill Mesa Yields Secrets of the Cliff Dwellers," *National Geographic,* CXXV (February, 1964), 155-211.

Shafer, Burr. *Through History with J. Wesley Smith.* New York: Scholastic Book Services, 1953.

MISCELLANEOUS

"Early Man," part I, Time-Life Series Filmstrip.

"Stone Age Tribes of Mindanao" is a videotape of the *National Geographic* TV special, made at Garden Spot High School.

Slides and tape of Mesa Verde prepared by Frank and Karen Herceg (my husband and me) from slides we took in July, 1969.

Pamphlets about Mesa Verde and Aztec National Monument were prepared by the National Park Service and are available from them.

Pictures were obtained at Mesa Verde and were prepared by the National Park Service (cost: $1.25).

Baskets, pottery and adobe were also obtained in the Four Corners area. These are present-day craft items that are made in the same patterns as those of hundreds of years ago.

The charred wood and arrow head are local products. The wood is from my parents' fireplace; the arrow head was found in a field near Bowmansville, Pennsylvania.

Post cards were purchased at the above-mentioned monuments.

WORK SHEET I

1. What are three major differences between the Old and New Stone Ages?

2. What were the geographical features of the areas typically settled by NSA people?

3. What were NSA economic systems based on?

4. Why did NSA people build permanent houses?

5. List as many ways as you can to show how climate affected the way NSA people lived.

6. What did NSA people worship? Why?

7. Who was the religious leader in NSA societies? What were his duties?

8. Why was government needed in NSA societies? How did it develop?

9. Is there any proof that NSA people ever had fun? Explain.

10. List as many jobs as you can that existed in the New Stone Age.

11. Why do you think the NSA was generally very short in comparison with the Old Stone Age?

WORK SHEET II

Study the large pictures in the station.

1. Of all of them, which is the only one that could indicate an Old Stone Age society? Why?

2. Briefly tell something about each of the other pictures that shows they are of New Stone Age societies.

3. Put the pictures into chronological order (use the numbers) starting with the oldest and ending with the most recent.

Study the small pictures in the station.

1. Briefly explain what each one is showing.

WORK SHEET III

Study the realia on the shelves in the station.

1. Briefly explain

   A. what each thing is.

   B. what each thing is made of.

   C. what each thing was used for.

EXTRA ACTIVITIES

1. Make models of NSA tools.

2. Make models of NSA baskets.

3. Make models of NSA pottery.

4. Make models of a NSA house.

5. Develop a play about the NSA, find people to work with you, and prepare it for in-class presentation.

6. Make a NSA diorama.

7. Develop a series of cartoons or a comic strip dealing with the NSA.

8. Make a display showing how to make adobe, or thatch, a fish net, canoe, cloth, etc.

9. Pretend you are living in the early days of the NSA. Write a story of your life or keep a diary for a set period of time.

10. Do more research into the Mesa Verde Indians and report on them, or develop some other activities such as these about them.

11. Develop your own Stone Age game that would be a good activity for others to use in reviewing this information.

12. Find an example of a NSA society that still exists. Give a report on it and explain why (you may use your own opinion) those people have not progressed out of the NSA.

FIGURE 7

Name — Susan	
Station Titles	Check-Off
Christmas in China	x
Radio	
Volcanoes	x
Hawaii	
Snowmobiles	

FIGURE 8

	Learning Stations									
	C. S.			Math				S.S.S.		
Students	Punctuation	Creative Writing		Estimation	Stock Market	Monopoly		Weather	Apollo	Creative Expression
Sue										
James										

Record-keeping is a simple thing. Often we're tempted to make it more complex, but we must remember, all the time we spend filling out papers and forms is time we could have spent with the children.

CHILDREN'S STATIONS

As we said, we want to put the students' work on display. What better way than to let them do their own learning stations? In our communication skill program, we offer a research project to those children ready to handle it. They pick the topic, learn research skills, and when their research is complete, choose a method of sharing what they've learned. Many times they'll choose to do a station. Now their stations aren't perfect or always terribly neat, but with a little guidance they can do some very nice stations which offer you and the other children more stations.

If you have younger children whose research and findings will of course be more shallow, you can let them "hunt" for information for several days during Communication Skills (C.S.) or S.S.S., and set up a station to share their knowledge. Some of them will be able to set up a fairly nice station which even older children might enjoy going to, just for fun. Let the children do stations! It's beneficial to them and you.

We sure hope you're convinced that learning stations are worthwhile. If you're not, try some and perhaps you'll be sold. For more detailed information on the use of centers, see Voight's book (bibliography). For samples, Forte's books are a good source (bibliography).

Parents need to know teachers care about their child.

12

Parent Education

THE SEGMENT OF the population most overlooked by educators is the parents. The problem with overlooking them is that the parents really make a difference in the success or failure of new programs. This is particularly true as you attempt to move toward open concept education. The problem is that the parents have read books and heard people talk about open education. They have, in many cases, inferred from these sources that open education is irresponsible education. The notion is that children in such a program do anything they feel like doing, and teachers in these schools really don't care if the children learn to read and write, as long as the children are happy. With parents having these ideas about open education it is almost dangerous to mention it. We are, therefore, faced with not only the problem of helping parents understand the new program, but with changing their minds about it. This

is unfortunate: however, it can be done. It can be done by carefully planning a program that will inform and involve the parents in the evolution of the program. The catch word is "involve." Teachers have been very hesitant to involve parents in the schools. We have been afraid that they will try to take over. You know the story; teachers are the professionals, and they will make the decisions about education. We are not suggesting that we depart from this stance, but we can benefit from parent perceptions of what the educational program should accomplish. Why not welcome all the feedback we can get?

This chapter will attempt to offer some suggestions for designing a program that will help the parents understand and get involved in the program. The parents who are involved in the program are going to end up as your best public relations agents. Believe   161 us, schools can use all the good press they can get.

We have a book coming out shortly called *The Parents Guide to Open Education* (to be published by Acropolis Books, Ltd.). When this book is published, it will be a big help in developing a program for educating parents about open education.

However, until you can refer parents to this book (you will, won't you?), you are going to need some guidelines for developing a program of parent education. This chapter should help with developing such a program. We will discuss some general ideas concerning parent education and will then outline a program of large- and small-group presentations to be used with parents.

In education, one of the mistakes we have made is trying to start new programs without knowing exactly how we intend to do it. The problem with this is that when parents ask us questions we don't know the answers. We then get defensive, and as a result have ended up developing negative attitudes about the program before it has had a chance. Therefore before you schedule parent meetings you must know what you are going to do.

The first idea you must clarify for the parents is the rationale for the program. Tell them why you want to develop a program of open education,

why it is important to have such a program, and how it will benefit their children in terms of preparing them to function in our society. What you are trying to do in this session is to help the parents understand why it makes sense to develop a program of open education. This is a very important step in the process and should be done well, because this is where you sell the program. We call this session philosophy or rationale.

It will help if you have anticipated some of the questions parents will ask in this session and have answers ready for them. If these questions don't come up in this session, they will in others. Some questions to anticipate are:

1. Will there be standards, control and discipline in the program?

2. How will my child adjust to the more structured program of the middle school or junior high school?

3. How will I know where my child is in comparison with the rest of the children?

4. How will my child be graded?

5. What kind of a schedule will my child have?

6. What are you going to do about homework?

7. Will you expect the quality of work that the child is capable of?

You may hear other questions, but we're sure you'll hear these.

Some of the points you ought to stress in your answers are:

1. There will be standards of behavior. The standard will be developed in terms of each child's individual rights. A positive approach will be taken.

2. The child going to the more structured school will adjust very well. In fact he will have the following advantages:

   a. The open concept program emphasizes the development of responsibility, and this should benefit him in any setting.

   b. In the open program flexibility will be emphasized. This means that the child will have opportunities to develop the ability to adjust to different people and situations. Rigidity is easier to adjust to than flexibility. In fact the child's flexibility will help him to adjust to rigidity.

   c. The open program emphasizes self-concept. A positive self-concept is the most potent weapon a child can have in the structured school.

   d. The open concept program emphasizes work habits and study skills as opposed to memorization. Kids with good work habits and study skills perform very well in a structured setting.

   e. (Don't forget this one!) If a child in his lifetime can only see the beauty of the sunlight for 10 minutes, it would be wrong to deprive him of this just because the rest of his life will be spent in darkness.

3. The child will be on a skill sequence and you will know where he is at any time in any skill area. You will be able to point out the progress he's made over a month, a semester, a year, or several years. It is more important to be aware of the kind of progress the child is making than to compare his progress with that of other children.

4. The child will preferably not be graded. He will be constantly diagnosed and teaching will be keyed into the areas of weakness revealed by these tests. If grades must be given he will be graded in terms of his progress and ability rather than in comparison with the other kids.

5. The schedule is discussed in chapter III. The point to make with parents is that there is a schedule.

6. Homework in an open program assumes a different posture. It could be

better described as work at home. It will be assigned to reinforce skills diagnosed as weak, to provide practice in skills recently taught, or just to complete work not completed during the daily program. The point to emphasize in work at home is that it will be (only) work each child needs or wants to do and not a mass assignment.

7. In addition to behavioral standards, the program demands performance standards. Each child's work will be evaluated in terms of his capacity to perform. Substandard work will not be accepted from any child. This evaluation will be based on the teacher's best judgment in terms of each child.

Next, the parents need help in understanding the terms connected with the program. Explain the terms team teaching, nongradedness, continuous progress, skill sequences, diagnostic testing, contracts, packets, learning centers and individualization. To do this you can prepare a parent's dictionary, develop an overhead presentation, or any other approach you can think of.

The third thing you will need to discuss is school organization. The school will have nongraded units, there will be a specific number of children and teachers in each unit, and the units will be located in various parts of the building.

Explain that each team will have a team leader with specific responsibilities.

Discuss the various options for scheduling. This can be done with sample schedules on ditto. Perhaps for this part of the program it would be best for each team to meet with the parents since primary and intermediate units schedules may be different.

Next you should consider discussing each area of the curriculum. Begin with communication skills. Explain how you will integrate the reading and language arts into a unified program. Chapter IV will help you with this. Use a similar approach with math, science and social studies. These areas are best handled in unit meetings since there will probably be some variation in the approaches used by each team. Include in these sessions procedures for record-keeping. Also explain what you would like parents to do with the work the child brings home. Tell them how you are going to handle the work the child does in school. Explain how they will see the work. Will you send it home weekly or are you going to keep it until conference time? If you are going to have conferences, how will they fit into the programs? You will also need to inform the parents of the system you are going to use to report the child's progress. You will need to show them how the skill sequences fit into the reporting system. Explain how you intend to convert the child's performance into grades if you must give grades.

You will next need to explain how contracts will be a part of the program. How contracts work, and how they will differ according to the ability of the child to accept responsibility. The parents should also understand learning centers and packets, and how they will be used in the program. You should also include an examination of the special materials and kits you will use in the program. A good way to do this is to bring the parents in and set up stations for each of these areas, divide into small groups and rotate through the stations. Teachers or children or both can man the stations.

You need to explain the special areas of the curriculum such as art, music, physical education, the media center, reading specialists, and other areas your school might offer.

Finally, you need to help the parents understand how they can help with the program. The chapter on aides and parent involvement will be a help with this topic.

There are some films that should help in your program with parents. Some of these are:

Charlie and the Golden Hamster, I.D.E.A. Films, 32 Gramercy Park, South—New York, N.Y. 10003

Why Man Creates, Pyramid Film Productions, Box 4018—Santa Monica, Cal. 90406

Team Teaching, I.D.E.A. Films, 32 Gramercy Park, South—New York, N.Y. 10003

Square Education, T.Y.O. Productions, Dr. John Tyo—715 Crawford Avenue, Syracuse, N.Y.

It is also a good idea to begin a collection of books that parents can read in connection with open education. These can be included in the media center and the parents can sign them out.

You might want to organize this whole program in conjunction with your parents organization. However you decide to do it, it is going to take some time and should end up as a planned program of activities spanning one or two years. It is not a bad idea when you are involved in planning to meet in "coffee klatch" groups in the parents' homes to set the tone for the new program and to begin to discuss the type of parent education program necessary to help parents understand and want to participate.

The main point in the development of a program of parent education is to know what you are going to do and how you are going to do it. Thus, when questions are asked you will know the answers. If you don't know an answer, 165 however, just say you don't know, and you will certainly find out or get help in finding out.

If you are getting help in the development of the program, make sure the parents know where the help is coming from and why the people offering the help are qualified to give it. It is very important to include these people in your program of parent education.

Be sure to plan the program so that there is some sequence to it. The basic idea is to keep the parents informed so that they feel as though you are trying to help them understand what you are doing, and that you are trying to involve them in it.

There are four approaches you can use in getting the message to your parents. You can use these approaches singly or intermix them. We will outline sample agendas using these four approaches. The approaches are:

1. Reading—providing books and articles for parents to read

2. Stations—setting up stations for visitation and having the parents rotate through them.

3. Large group—large-group meetings where you explain the program

4. Small group—small-group meetings with parents to explain the program

In addition, films, filmstrips, resource people, articles, and slide shows are some materials you can use.

Here is an agenda that will give you an idea of how to organize a program. This basic pattern will fit into a program for the parents in your self-contained classroom, a program for the parents in your school, or in your school district.

I.   PARENT EDUCATION AGENDA

Large group sessions

Session 1.   Two hours
              Philosophy or rationale—Definition of terms
              Questions and answers

Section 2.   Two hours
              Organization of the school
              Scheduling in the various teams
              Movie—Charlie and the Golden Hamster
              Questions and answers

Session 3.   Two hours—Curriculum Areas
               Communication Skills   This could take two sessions. Discuss how
               Math   these programs will be organized and what
               Science   they intend to accomplish.
               Social Studies
               Questions and answers

Session 4.   Two hours
               Learning Centers and Stations
               Contracts—Packets, Kits and other special materials

               Start in large group and explain that you have set up stations through
               which the parents will rotate. Man the stations with teachers or students
               or both.

Session 5.   Two hours
               Reporting to parents, record-keeping, skill sequences
               Questions and answers

Session 6.   Two hours—Cultural Arts Programs
               Get these teachers to explain their role in the program. This can be done
               with small groups rotating.
               Questions and answers

Session 7.   Two hours—Parent Involvement Program
               Question and answers

II.   PARENT EDUCATION SESSIONS

Mixed Approach

Session 1.   Two hours—large group
               Philosophy, rationale, definition of terms
               Questions and answers

Session 2.   Two hours—large and small groups
               Large group—Origin of school and film, Charlie and the Golden Hamster.
               Small group—Scheduling within each team—Each team meets with the
               parents of the children assigned.
               Questions and answers

Session 3. Two hours—small group—team oriented meetings
Curriculum Areas: Communication Skills
Math
Science
Question and answers
(This could take more than one session.)

Session 4. Two hours—team oriented meetings
Learning Centers and Stations, Packets, Contracts, Kits and other special material
Questions and answers
(This session is effective if the parents are actually involved in using these approaches perhaps on a rotating basis. This could take more than one session.)

Session 5. Two hours—large group
Reporting to parents, record-keeping, skill sequences
Questions and answers

Session 6. Two hours—small group—team oriented meetings
Parent involvement
Questions and answers

These two examples will help you organize a program of parent education. Please don't underestimate the importance of such a program. Include it in your overall plan of program development. Believe us it is effort well expended—it really is!

13

Parent Involvement

IF YOU DECIDE, no . . . WHEN you decide (we'll think positively!) to open up your self-contained classroom, or if you are to become part of an open school, you must already have a firm belief in individualization of instruction. Very shortly after you begin to individualize your program, you'll come to a shocking realization: the more you individualize, the *more* you *need* to individualize. As the only teacher in a classroom we're sure you've sat down at one time or another and wrung your hands and said, "What can I do? I am only one person. I have only two hands." Sound familiar?

You need this chapter. One person CAN only do so much. HELP! We hear your cry and help is on the way. It seemed to us at our school that help could best come from the people who were most dedicated. (Besides we didn't have any budget for aides.) The parents were interested; they had a stake in their child's education, and they cared; they didn't all show it in the same way, but they all did care. Now, how can you take advantage of their willingness to help, and how can you organize a parent helpers program which will be beneficial?

We soon learned that parents were more capable of helping if they understood the program fully. For this reason it was absolutely necessary that the parents be educated as we suggested in the previous chapter. We will then begin by assuming that your parents have some knowledge of the program.

The second step is to have the parents observe. In order for them to have a complete understanding, it will be necessary for them to see the theories being applied in everyday situations. 169

With an open philosophy you need all the
help you can get – high school students,
student teachers, and parents.

Our most efficient, loyal help came from a group who had spent a great deal of time observing, and clarifying our aims and objectives. They believed in open education, and they were willing to put forth some effort to see it work. Friends, you can have an educational program and you call it open education, but you will need help to make your program a good one.

Because of parental support and involvement during the last two years, our school's program is probably two years ahead of where it would have been without them. Convinced? Good! Then, let's go on.

Third, after the parents have observed they can begin by doing little things. One parent reminiscing the other day said, "I just hung around. Someone always found something for me to do." That was the way she got involved our first year. And, we think during your first year it might make sense to have your parents assist you that way. You will be so busy getting your feet on the ground and finding your own way in and around contracts, learning stations, etc., that any kind of explicit parent program may require time you don't have.

If you are in a self-contained classroom this is the way you would develop your parent program. Parents could help you with some of the things listed in Figure 1, and depend-ing on how much time you are willing to devote, perhaps they could help you with some of the instructional things in Figure 2. Probably, however, you'll have your hands full organizing them to help with the non-instructional program.

But for those of you who are on teams and in nongraded, continuous progress schools, you will want to handle your parent program in another way and work toward a larger-scale program. As we said, your first year will be a difficult one for everybody. Notice we didn't say unrewarding or impossible? The kids will be learning and all will be adjusting. Therefore, your first year will be occupied with getting the program going.

During that first year, assure the parents that they are welcome. YES! EVEN IN YOUR FIRST YEAR! If you try to keep them out they will become suspicious and rightfully so. We think that schools today are asking for trouble by not having their doors open at all times; one's first question is why? So, during your first year invite them to plays, or teas, or science exhibits and rather specific things which are well organized and rather systematic. By doing this the parents can gradually be introduced to the greater movement and noise level aspects of open education. Please don't forget the fathers; try to arrange a re-play at night for the fathers and working mothers if necessary.   171

FIGURE 1

Name _____ Date _____

1. Collecting lunch and milk money.

2. Collecting supplementary books and materials for instruction.

3. Collecting and displaying pictures, objects, realia and models.

4. Collecting money for charity drives, pupil pictures, trips, etc.

5. Proofreading class newspaper.

6. Ordering and returning films, filmstrips and other AV materials.

7. Distributing and collecting materials from supply room, such as writing paper, art paper, and supplies and keeping them available for children's use.

8. Procuring, setting up, operating and returning instructional equipment.

9. Building up resource collections and bibliographies for specific units, learning stations, or packets.

10. Obtaining special materials for science or other projects.

11. Keeping records of books children have read.

12. Arranging and supervising indoor games on rainy days.

13. Checking out books from local libraries.

14. Typing and duplicating mass communications.

15. Typing, duplicating and collating instructional materials.

16. Typing and duplicating the class newspaper.

17. Typing and duplicating children's writings and other work.

18. Typing and duplicating scripts for plays and skits.

19. Making arrangements for field trips, collecting parental permission forms, and accompanying teachers on trips.

20. Telephoning and making arrangements for special classroom resource speakers from college or elsewhere and possibly maintaining a file of these available people.

21. Displaying pupil work.

22. Attending to housekeeping chores and supervising clean-up time.

23. Preparing instructional materials, cutouts, master copies, flannel board materials, science materials, social studies displays, concrete teaching aids for arithmetic, etc.

24. Arranging bulletin board displays for teaching purposes, such as flow charts.

25. Arranging interesting and inviting corners for learning: science or recreational reading areas, investigating areas.

26. Keeping bulletin boards current.

27. Developing techniques and materials to meet individual differences such as re-writing reading materials for less able readers, taping reading assignments for less able readers.

28. Supervising committees engaged in painting murals, constructing, researching, or experimenting.

29. Presenting information concerning you and your background, special interests, talents, or skills.

30. Tutoring individual children.

31. Listening to oral reading by children.

32. Reading and storytelling.

33. Helping with the preparations of special programs.

34. Previewing films and other AV materials.

35. Preparing charts of worthwhile, upcoming television shows, specials, or educational TV programs.

36. Setting up learning stations from previously made formats, or helping teacher set them up.

37. Helping children set up learning stations on independent research projects.

38. Helping with follow-up activities.

39. Helping children find materials in media-center when no one is available.

40. Keeping instructional kits, materials, cassettes in order.

41. Preparing new materials for classroom use.

42. Recording content material on to cassette tapes.

43. Helping young children through lunch line.

FIGURE 2

Information sheet   Name _____   Date _____

Occupation _____   Previous Occupations _____

SKILLS OR TALENTS Name (yours or friends or relatives)	Address or Phone No.	Skills	Suggestions on how best to use person's skills
Can speak foreign language Name	Address or Phone No.	Language	Conversational or Instructional
Hobbies or Interests Name	Address or Phone No.	Hobby or Interest or Collection	How could it best be shared

Information sheet page two

NAME	PHONE NO. OR ADDRESS	COUNTRY (IES)	ANY HELPFUL INFORMATION FOR US
TRAVEL (or lived in or native of other parts of this country or foreign country)			
1.			
2.			
3.			
4.			
5.			
6.			

TRAVEL (CONTINUED)

Please put yes or no in numbered boxes corresponding to numbers of above travelers.

	Numbers as above					
	1	2	3	4	5	6
COULD BRING IN REALIA OR SOUVENIRS FROM COUNTRY						
COULD SERVE AS RESOURCE PERSON AND TALK TO CHILDREN						
COULD SHOW MOVIES OR SLIDES TAKEN IN COUNTRY						
COULD SET UP LEARNING STATION ON COUNTRY IF ASSISTED						

NAME	PHONE NO. OR ADDRESS	ACTIVITIES
ETC. (not real good at but could assist with)		

While you are organizing and changing and adjusting, begin to observe your parents while they're observing and working in the school. Why? The second year when you get your parent program going full speed, you will need a parent coordinator. There are two reasons for having a parent coordinator. First, it will be too much for a teacher to handle in addition to her regular duties, and second, some parents will feel more like exhibiting leadership qualities if a parent handles it. Look for a supportive individual, one with ability to lead and organize, and one who is a pleasant person with whom people will want to work. This person should also have the spunk to take the bull by the horns and make decisions. He or she will work directly with one of the teachers on the team to coordinate the efforts and supply help to the teacher who needs it. The parent coordinator will need a committee to get all of this together. Perhaps the teachers will have specific individuals to suggest who they have observed. The coordinator will probably also have several people in mind with whom to share the duties.

Now for organization. The team leader and the principal should sit down and outline the program. Objectives, extent of help, limitations and regulations governing parents in the classroom are all topics which should be input from the teachers and from representative parents. After the meet-

ings have produced a plan, you're ready for action.

The plan must then be presented to the parents. This could be done at the end of the first year during your last parent's meeting. The outline could be presented and the meeting thrown open for additions and changes. The parents could then have time to think about it over the summer, and decide how they want to help.

We did it differently. In the fall of our second year, we called the parents to a meeting to discuss the plan. Figure 3 is the letter we sent asking for their help. (We know you'll have to revise it, but we thought that revising it was easier than writing it.) As a follow-up to that meeting we sent the questionnaires containing information about how each parent wanted to be involved (Figs. 1 & 2) along with a letter of introduction and a motivational sheet (Figs. 4 & 5.)

When the questionnaires were returned, the parents committee sat down and tried to assemble them into a workable system. They devised a master sheet of the noninstructional helpers, and a card file of the instructional helpers. Then the parent coordinator and the team leader reviewed the daily and weekly schedules with the intent of developing a manageable plan. They were successful and after the kinks were ironed out, it worked beautifully.

FIGURE 3

September 5, 1972

Dear Parents,

Well, the new school year is here; the vacation seemed to fly by. The Intermediate team of teachers has been busy mapping out the coming year—planning to keep some ideas, change others, and working out some exciting long-range plans.

This year we want to emphasize parent-school communication. We also hope to strive for more parent involvement. This year we hope to have time to involve you more. The simple fact is we've learned a great deal about individualizing and meeting children's needs, and one of the things we've learned is that we need more people—parents, teachers, aides, Martians—anybody who is willing to help.

When we consider the fact that we have 75 children, that means that we must have at least 120 parents subtracting parents who have 2 children in the Intermediate Unit. That is a lot of people, folks. And all of you have different talents, abilities, skills and backgrounds which seems a wealth of resources to pull from.

In many schools parents are not only unable to become involved, but there are many places parents are unwelcome even as visitors or observers. (Some of you have told us about these schools.) We believe that the school should be a joint concern—a joint effort of both teachers and parents. We are sure that you know by now that you are welcome to visit any day, any hour, but now that our program is underway we want to go one step further. We want you involved, actively. We need you to help in both instructional and non-instructional areas. We feel that by helping us help your child, your benefits are many—your time is used profitably, you gain a more thorough knowledge of your child's program, and hopefully you'll enjoy working with the children and us.

Now we know that some of you are working and have schedule difficulties, but perhaps, there are still some little ways in which you can help us. Then, of course, there are those of you who work part-time, or are taking courses and could give us some time each week on a regularly scheduled basis. Others of you have young children, but could work at home, phoning or typing. And hopefully we can all find some time in the evening once or twice a month (even though we're all tired) to get together and work out some major projects.

This is our year of "getting it all together." We want very much to get you in this year, not just to visit, but to roll up your sleeves and help us provide a better program for your children.

Last year we were really appreciative of the help of many of you, but Mrs. C. deserves special mention. Even though we didn't have time to sit down and map out a specific program for her, she saw a need in the media center, asked if she could help, and faithfully helped all year, assisting the director and helping grateful children locate materials and supplies when the librarian was unavailable.

We would like to meet with you. Therefore, we'd like to invite any of you who are interested in helping to develop a Parent Involvement Program (otherwise known as P. I. P.) to meet with us Wednesday evening, the 13th of September at 7:00 P. M. Please bring your ideas and suggestions. At that time we will work out a sheet to be sent home as a survey of parent's interests, skills, etc. Also a schedule, and just talk about ways to get PROJECT P. I. P. off the ground. (Sounds like a James Bond movie.)

Please fill out the attached and send in to Mrs._____

Thank you very much.

The Intermediate Teachers

FIGURE 4

JENKINS SCHOOL FOR CHILDREN

Dear Parents,

I'm a week late but it's never too late to launch a P. I. P. (Parent Involvement Program). WE NEED YOUR HELP.

In the next four pages you'll find a fairly comprehensive list of ways you can help. The first two sheets lead primarily to instructional tasks; the last two are primarily non-instructional in nature. We need both!

Mrs. C. _____ has agreed to be our P. I. P. coordinator, and will work with the teachers and her committee to organize and set up the program. Please give her your support if she asks. She certainly can't do this alone.

If you can help in any way please fill out the enclosed forms and return to me. Sheets 1 and 2 are fairly self-explanatory and will have to be dealt with almost individually. Sheets 3 and 4 need some instruction. Will you please check the items you would be willing to help with? Then, after we have a chance to tabulate the results, we'll be sending a follow-up sheet requesting the times you can help.

PLEASE RESPOND.

Thank you very much.

Anita Waterman

FIGURE 5

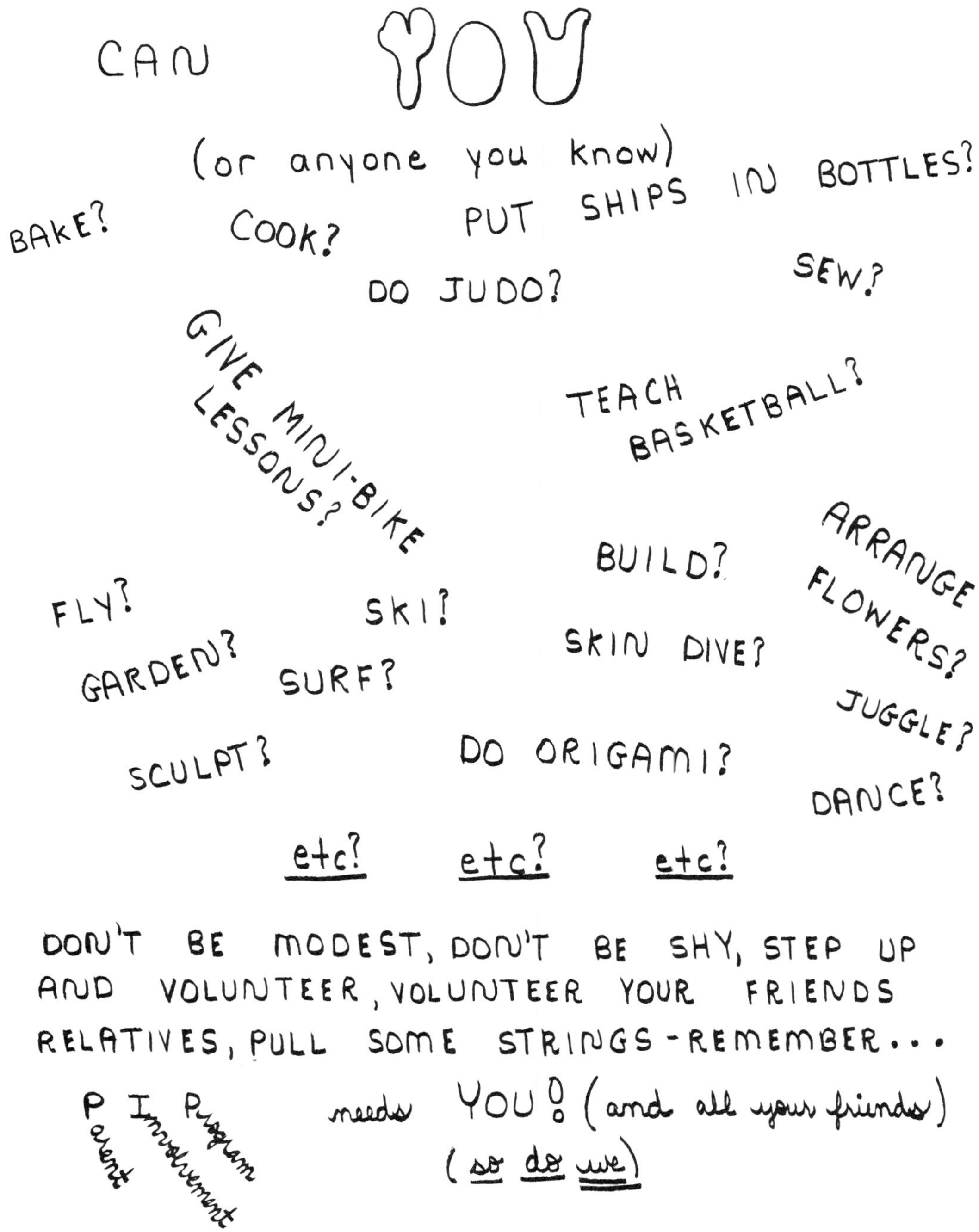

CAN YOU

(or anyone you know)

BAKE? COOK? PUT SHIPS IN BOTTLES?

DO JUDO? SEW?

TEACH BASKETBALL?

GIVE MINI-BIKE LESSONS?

BUILD? ARRANGE FLOWERS?

FLY? SKI? SKIN DIVE?

GARDEN? SURF? JUGGLE?

SCULPT? DO ORIGAMI? DANCE?

etc? etc? etc?

DON'T BE MODEST, DON'T BE SHY, STEP UP AND VOLUNTEER, VOLUNTEER YOUR FRIENDS RELATIVES, PULL SOME STRINGS - REMEMBER...

Parent Involvement Program needs YOU! (and all your friends)
(so do we)

Because of our schedule and our parents it worked out that Tuesday and Thursday mornings were the best times for part-time helpers. There were jobs which were needed on a regular basis and some which were not. For instance, if a parent wanted to do typing or dittoing, we asked her to come in on Tuesday or Thursday, and the teachers prepared the work to be done.

However, another job, the refilling of pencil, paper, and other supplies was done by a lady whenever it was convenient for her, possibly every one or two weeks.

A third task, the filing of the children's take-home folders, was handled in still a different way. This had to be done on Friday, and took most of the day. It also required that the person have a pretty thorough knowledge of the program. The helper came in on Friday morning, filed all the papers and contracts of the kids into "take-home folders" in the kids' mailboxes. What we're trying to say is that the program and the parents have to be flexible. The needs of the program and the limitations of the parents, in terms of time, have to be considered.

Those people who came in on Tuesday and Thursday lent themselves to an important part of the involvement. The team of teachers asked for help and got it. We had two kinds of work placed in two separate bins. One of the bins was labeled NOW and the other bin was labeled SOMEDAY. The mothers who came in finished the NOW work first. Usually that was finished on Tuesday, and Thursday could then be spent tackling the SOMEDAY bin. The mothers were flexible also in that they took turns and took advantage of each other's talents.

One more noteworthy thing. Several of our parents said, "I'd love to come in, but my three pre-schoolers make that impossible." So the parent coordinator arranged for a couple of our moms to babysit for each other and allow each some time away from her little ones. We had another mother who did not want to come in to school to help, but she was willing to babysit for any other mother who did want to come in.

At workshops when we've discussed our P.I.P. program (Parent Involvement Program) teachers always ask about problem parents. We found in our school parents were only tempted to be problems if we let them. Here, then, are some ways to avoid problems:

1. Ask for short term help til you see how they work out. The time can always be extended.

2. Momma Worry who comes to observe and observe and observe (you suspect, spy) is unsure about her child.

Have a conference with her. Try to alleviate her fears. If that doesn't work kindly ask her one morning if while she is observing she'd mind checking a few papers.

3. Don't put moms with their child. However, moms with problem kids would be great for other people's problem kids. They already understand. We had one mom who helped for two years and she always said, "I'm glad to come in and help someone else's child because someone else will help mine."

4. Don't ever put Momma Worry in the same area with her child. She'd be a good person to type in the office.

5. Avoid taking school time for direction-giving, etc. Ask the parents to come in early, or at lunch so you can explain what you want them to do. Another solution if they can't or don't come in when you're not busy, write them on paper or put them on a cassette. As we've said many times, your time is too valuable to waste.

6. What about Talkative Tilly? When she comes have her directions always on tape. Tactfully, always tactfully, suggest you have lunch together and can chat then. If when she comes to teachers to chatter they seem terribly preoccupied she'll take the hint.

7. What about Norbert and Nora Knowitall? Good old Nora was a teacher, or her husband was and they know all about Open Education and Piaget and Silberman, etc. And when they say time after time, "In so and so's book, he suggests. . . ." Rats! After the 50th time, the team gets rid of him or her and bang their heads against the nearest wall (if they can find an empty spot) or they march single file to the nearest tree and climb it. They just might be ready to use drastic number 8. First, however, just try shaking your head and saying, "Yes, that's a good idea" and count to 3,000.

8. Reserve this treatment for the worst, the hopeless and for when your patience is exhausted. If a parent has come to help and turns out to be Impossible Ida, change her job. If she likes to do exciting things, ask her if she can help you do a thorough count of all your supplies, count pencils, tables, etc. *OR* ask her if she'd please clean out the supply room. *AND* always ask Ida to help Mary who just upchucked all over herself and three other kids.

You won't have many Idas. We never have. We've gotten beautiful cooperation from our parents, but we followed the steps outlined in the first part of this chapter. Our parents have helped make our school successful, they've helped us make it better for their kids, and I think they feel as much pride in it as the kids and teachers do.

What about aides? If you're fortunate enough to have aides, (we don't! Mumble, Mumble) we suggest you handle them basically the same way. They're paid, yes, and it's their *job,* yes; but they're people with feelings. If you match them to the tasks they like or are capable of you'll have much better aides.

Aides are around a lot more than parents and therefore become members of the team. If problems arise handle them the same way we suggested in the chapter on team-teaching.

Your first year will probably be very busy and if you have aides, you'll probably be far better off by giving them non-instructional duties from (Fig. 1). The next year the aide can move into instructional-type things.

To summarize then, in an open program, whether that's in a self-contained classroom or in an open school, you'll need help. Use it wisely, have a parent coordinate it for you, and be grateful and kind to people who help you because you sure can't do it without them.

Teacher observation and the child's self-evaluation
are effective means of evaluation.

14

A Record-keeping System, Reporting to Parents, Discipline and Management, and Evaluation

A RECORD-KEEPING SYSTEM

IN A NONGRADED continuous progress program or in your "open" self-contained classroom, the first questions you get are: Does my child learn anything? How do you keep track of all the children?

Thus, a most important part of a good program must be its record-keeping system. If you don't think you want to bother with nitty gritty details like that, it's o.k. with us, but when your administrators and/or parents have you ready to hang up by the thumbnails, don't call us, because we wouldn't want to have to say, "We told you so." Everyone is entitled to know where the children are. If our open program, or anyone's for that matter, cannot show interested parties how and what each child is doing in black and white, then our system is no better than the one we propose to

change. We won't waste time telling you what's wrong with the present system; we'll give you the new one and you can decide for yourself which is best.

We have found several records necessary for each child. A list and an explanation follows:

1. Math Folder—Each child should have a Math folder which houses his math contract, review worksheets, tests, kit booklets, and diagnostic materials. The math workbook could be kept also.

2. Communication Skills Folder—In this folder, put the contract, workbooks, S. R. A. or other kit booklets and practice worksheets, etc., needed in communication skills.

3. Social Studies or Science Folders— The children should use these for

keeping any papers, worksheets from stations, science experiment records, etc., from their S.S.S. (remember?) projects, units and learning stations.

Note: These folders should be kept for the child's use. Of course, the teacher would also put in worksheets or tests the children needed, but primarily these are record folders the children keep track of. Remember, again, don't do things the students can do. What? You remember? Great! You'll end up with a few minutes to breathe in your open situation.

4. Take-Home Folders—Guess what these are? You're right. Back in the chapter on parent involvement we talked about mother(s) who came in to stuff each child's work into his "take-home folder" and put the folder in each child's mail box.

The mail boxes might be worth another note right here. Ours were old kindergarten cubby hole units which were no longer used. One of our student teachers, the Industrial Arts teacher, and the children transformed them into beautiful mail boxes which the students then labeled with their names.

Another important note before we leave the child-handled records. If these folders are to be left in the unit (classroom area), finding a place to keep them becomes a problem. The children can, of course, keep them in their tubs, but that becomes a problem because it makes the tub heavier

as well as creating one unnecessary trip to the tub area. If you are following a schedule and everyone has math at the same time, it becomes rather difficult to get seventy-two math folders from tubs at 11 A.M.

But take heart, help has arrived. A company called Smith Systems has designed a shelf unit for media centers (libraries, as we're sure you know). It is a leveled affair, provides access from both sides and is movable. It's absolutely perfect for kits and is described in more detail in the chapter on the physical plant. But, the best part about these units is an item which can be ordered separately and was originally designed to house 16MM films. It's just a long metal tray with wire petitions and is fantastic for keeping all the children's folders in alphabetical order. Each one holds about 25-30 folders. If you hunt around you'll come upon your own "finds" which are perfect for an open situation.

We feel our program received relatively little criticism its first years because we did have records and we could tell parents (or anyone) where children were. However we tried to keep only necessary items and tried not to keep records just to keep records. The teachers kept the following ones:

1. Contracts—The students' contracts were an invaluable source of information, for instance, how many and

which books the children had read, even which pages. Also included would be a listing of the follow-up activities, parts of kits, and learning stations and so on. We kept the child's contract in his finished folder for referral later and we then had the beginning of a seven year record of each of our children.

2. The Cumulative Folder—This folder simply had medical records, birthdates, transfer information, parents' names and that's about it. One big fear we had with the traditional cumulative folder is in the way some teachers handle it. It is misused, and in some cases the material is distorted and eventually the child, his parents or teacher is hurt. If used wisely it can be a good tool, but beware of abandoning your own judgment of a child, because of what another teacher has already said about him in the almighty "cume" folder.

3. Finished Folders—The teachers kept a finished folder on all the kids they taught. This was simply a representative sample of work which could be used for conferences or for comparisons from one month to another, or from one year to another. This is also where the contracts were kept.

4. Skill Sequences and Diagnostic Tests—Each teacher kept the skill sequences of the children he taught up to date. These were kept in a file in the team office or office area of the room. Along with this were placed the diagnostic tests which have already been explained in great detail in that chapter. The sequences and tests were placed in proper folder—either math, social studies, science, or communication skills.

5. Planning Boards—Along with the skill sequence folder, probably the most important record of all is the planning board. Since it is also described in the above-mentioned chapter, a brief review should serve here. As you recall, the planning board is simply a concrete record-keeping device which parents, student teacher, student teachers, etc. can use to see or chart the progress of each child with each skill in each of the content areas. Different colored pins are placed each time a skill is diagnosed as needed, or taught. This board is the difference between skeptical school boards and accepting school boards; between skeptical parents and accepting parents, and between skeptical visitors and accepting visitors. It seems to be a device which everyone can see and touch; and believe us, we wish we had a quarter for every "Oh, I see now." or "That's really great!" uttered by a doubting Thomas rapidly turned believer.

6. Each teachers' individual records—In an open situation you know now the key word is flexibility and for the purposes of this chapter, that means you "gotta" keep track of who needs

what and who got what. Some people keep notebooks, some people use index cards and some people use their heads. The writer uses all of these. A word of caution—when you're teaming, each of you depends on the other, but each must keep his own records, too, or mass confusion will result. So to those of you who, like the writer, keep mental notes, be careful not to forget your mental notes. This might result in a group of children getting to the wrong place, or a child missing a skill, or a child getting lost during math time for thee days. Our plea is to please keep track!

File cards are easy and seem to work well. When a teacher teaches a group of students in math, for instance, she uses an index card for each of them and in her own system keeps track of each skill she taught them, which chapter tests they had taken, etc. We kept cards on all the children we had for anything. Since you will probably have different students for different things, it seems simple to have a card for each child and clip them or hold them together with rubber bands and label them math group, Christmas group, Civil War group, etc. They could be kept in a metal recipe box for safe keeping.

With learning stations we kept records too. We felt a simple way was to have the children sign a sheet when they had satisfactorily completed the requirements of that station. If there

were a lot of stations we sometimes had a master list of all the students and all the stations, which children or teachers checked off.

Now, if you keep records similar to these, we guarantee you won't be strung up by your thumbnails, but you'll still have people who need convincing. You believe though (don't you?) and enthusiasm is contagious, so your enthusiasm and that of their child will be enough to convince most every skeptic.

REPORTING TO PARENTS

For this part of the chapter, as with the first part, we have decided not to spend a lot of time on the rationale for a new reporting system, but we can't resist a true story about a lovely six year old we'll call Mary. Mary was partially sighted. She had inherited the disability and was able to read only special books with large print. Also Mary didn't have 160 I.Q.; we don't know exactly what it was, but it was nowhere near 160. At any rate, Mary was a beautiful little girl who was unkept, not always super clean, but a darling child who wanted to learn to read. She got as much individual help in reading as her teacher could give her and Mary gave her teacher her all. She tried and tried and tried. What Mary lacked in ability she tried to overcome with effort.

Now, Mary came from a home where grades were important. The grades meant a child was good or bad depending on what kind of marks he got. If a child got an F he was bad and goofing off, regardless of his ability or lack of it.

When the marking period came it was time for the teacher to give Mary a grade for reading. The teacher was brand new, had a lot to learn, but had a fierce love for children, an even "fiercer" sense of fair and unfair. The teacher struggled with all the grades trying to get some C's, so that there were not all A's and B's, because "No class has all A and B students in it," spoke the mighty principal. The teacher managed to give all the children grades except Mary. When the teacher finally mustered up enough courage to ask if it was alright to give Mary a B just to encourage her for her spectacular effort (because Mary was more than six weeks behind in her reading level), the principal said, "NO!" Whereupon this teacher, who sat down with each individual kid to try to explain why they got each grade, called Mary to come sit down, which Mary did willingly. Then a well-meaning teacher tried to explain to an innocent child why she had gotten a D in reading for which she'd receive a spanking from her Dad and teasing from her brothers and sisters.

Mary probably forgot it, because Mary was going to have more tragedy to try to overcome in her lifetime, but the teacher never forgot. And the teacher vowed one day she would be in a school where that kind of torture and cruelty could never take place. I (Mary's teacher) never forgot either Mary's or my tears, and *I* will never give grades to another child.

Grades aren't necessary! Children will work for the fun of learning! They don't need to have competition to work and study. We've seen them. Grades aren't fair and they are a waste of a teacher's time, because they can never communicate effectively a child's progress. Parents want them? Hogwash! We know a district where the *teachers,* not the parents, asked to return to report cards. Parents may question at first, but they'll readily give them up if you offer a good alternative.

And so again, we'll offer some alternatives and you decide which is best.

1. Check Lists—This is a simple skill sequence or a condensed form of a skill sequence listing the most important skills which the teacher checks off when the child demonstrates mastery of those skills, and it is then sent home at report time. Or a checklist can be in the affective areas such as the one we used in social development.

2. Report Letters or Progress Reports—A much more effective way to

communicate progress to parents is this device which can be as simple or as complex as you wish. It can be coupled with a follow up conference and this, of course, increases its effectiveness. We sent out report letters in November and March and had conferences in December and May until each was completed. We used some team-planning time and finished them quickly at home. It was not a big job, at least it doesn't have to be. If in one subject area all the children covered the same units, we wrote a brief description which went on all the children's letters. Usually when this happened it was in the social studies and science area.

Figure 1 is a sample progress report and you'll see the summary in S.S.S. which was the same for each child.

Roman numeral IV on Figure 1 was important, we felt, because it gave the parent some constructive ways to help the child, which concerned parents will appreciate.

As you can see, space was left under each area for comments by the teacher. We felt we did not need much detail, because a conference was already scheduled and at that time we could discuss any questions or problems. However in the beginning we felt the handwritten comments in our reports should be more detailed; so we used Figure 2. Next, though, we began using a skill sequence which led to a change in the report format.

As we said, a teacher can use a report letter in almost any way she wishes. Figure 3 is a detailed sample which was written for each individual child. If you are not following up the report letter with a conference, perhaps you'd find Figure 3 more suitable to your needs, because then more detail would be necessary. This one was written by Mary Ann Heltshe, Elizabeth Jenkins School, Millersville State College.

3. Conferences—Conferences are, we feel, the most sensible, the most effective, the most accurate device we have for reporting to parents. Our first conferences were a big mistake. We knew the team members should all be involved in the conference, but we didn't know how to schedule them so all the teachers were free for all conferences.

We decided the child's home base teacher should hold the conference, and any other teachers who had that child filled in the home base teacher on how the child was doing, his strengths and weaknesses, and would give the home base teacher samples of the child's work to share with the parents at the conference. This was fine and dandy, but in the middle of Billy's conference, Mrs. Jones asked, "How is Billy doing with his 3 times tables." Since Billy's math teacher couldn't possibly give the home base teacher all the math information, Mrs. Smith, the home base teacher, had to tell Mrs. Jones politely that she didn't know, but she'd find out and send her a note. So, the second year

FIGURE 1

JENKINS SCHOOL FOR CHILDREN

PROGRESS REPORT

Name _____ Date _____

I. Social Studies—Science

In Social Studies—Science we have completed a unit on Expression. During the first phase of the unit we investigated the creative process, creative people, and the creative products of architects, scientists, inventors, musicians, playwrights, authors, artists, and businessmen. In the second part of the unit the children were given an opportunity to create and finally they were able to share some of their own creative products with their peers. At present we are studying the Election and have included an outline with this letter.

II. Communication Skills

Your child's needs have been diagnosed and he has been placed on his proper level. He is progressing at his own pace working with appropriate materials and learning activities in our individualized Communication Skills Program. At present he is working on Level _____ on our Communication Skills Sequence.

III. Math

In Math your child's placement was also determined by diagnostic tests. He is presently working on Level _____ on our Math Skill Sequence.

IV. Suggestions for helping your child at home:

V. Conference

Please bring any questions to your conference scheduled for November _____ December _____ from _____ to _____ . If you cannot come at this time, please call Mrs. Baker. Thank you.

The Intermediate Team

FIGURE 2

JENKINS SCHOOL FOR CHILDREN

Progress Report of _____
This report letter is written concerning your child's individual ability rather than group achievement.

   I. *Communication Skills*

  II. *Arithmetic*

 III. *Social Studies*

FIGURE 3

PROGRESS REPORT

Name _____ Report prepared by _____

Date _____

1. Concepts covered during this period:

    Since starting school in September, we have given each child an individual diagnostic test in reading and math skills. Group instruction in the basic skills is given each day as well as individual help with skills. The six and seven year olds work with contracts each week. These contracts for independent work are based on the needs of the individual child. All of the children have become more adept at finding materials and functioning independently. Several units of study have been covered. The children have studied concepts in citizenship and responsibility, ecology, insects and their ways, the discovery of America, and the growth and development of baby chicks. At the present time, we are involved in a study of linear, liquid and weight measurements.

2. Skills developed:

    In reading we've reviewed these concepts with Judy: compound words, consonant blends, digraphs, contractions and antonyms. Judy has mastered the basic sight words she needs to this point. She uses the phonetic skills she has learned quite well. She is doing a beautiful job in her reading and enjoys reading various materials on her own.

    In math we have reviewed these concepts: the basic addition and subtraction facts to ten, place value of tens and ones, money values and telling time. Judy has mastered most of these concepts at this point.

3. Skills needing practice:

    Judy has been introduced to these concepts in reading: vowel sounds (long and short) and their rules, vowel dipthongs and digraphs (ae, oi, oy, etc.), homonyms and synonyms. We have also begun formalized spelling instruction with Judy. She is also learning dictionary skills such as alphabetizing and is using the simple dictionary. These skills will be the basic core of her reading instruction and still need practice with use. In math, Judy has been introduced to two digit addition and subtraction, place value to the hundreds and the number facts to 20. We have also touched upon simple fractional parts. She still needs practice in these areas and money concepts.

4. What you can do to help your child:

    Play spelling games with Judy and read with her. (I'm sure you do this already!) Share poetry with her and play simple number games with money such as making change with coins. This will reinforce her money concepts. Keep doing what you've been doing with Judy since it seems to be working like a charm! She is a delightful child to work with!

Your conference for Judy and Janet is scheduled for:

Thursday, November 30 at 10:30 — 11:30 A.M.
in the Teacher's Lounge

See you then!

THE PRIMARY TEAM

we improved. We scheduled the conferences of seventy-two students before school, during the lunch hour, (with 10 minutes to gobble), during the afternoon, after school, and a few as late as 5:00 or 5:30 P.M. We settled for a phone conference for one or two, because of special circumstances.

What were the children doing? Well, we did it both ways. We sent them home three days after lunch once, and the other time we scheduled conferences during team planning time, and the other afternoons the children worked on contracts with student teachers or parents to help them. What's best? We'd recommend a combination, perhaps sending them home two days and having one afternoon to work on contracts.

Our director asked one day why we didn't let the students sit in on the conferences. So the children had the chance to do just that from then on. Some chose to; some did not. (We had surveyed the parents at the first conferences of the year and most didn't care one way or the other). So, it became the child's decision. We recommend it highly. You'll learn all kinds of things about the child's relationships with his parents and with his teachers.

Who attends the conference? Anybody who can provide some feedback about the child's development. Certainly all the teachers who deal with the child, perhaps an art or music teacher could add something or even the secretary or custodian might have seen the child in an unusual light. If you are lucky enough to have a child psychologist, and all schools should, by all means invite him or her to the conference if he or she has worked with the child. And, last but not least, the child, if he wants to.

We think you'll like conferencing as a reporting technique. Ours have become thirty minutes of friendly, informative sessions with relaxed people giving and getting information which will be of great help to the kids they all care about.

And even though the saying is "last but not least" we're going to modify it and use the expression thusly, *"last and least"* we have . . .

Altered Report Cards—If you *absolutely* have no other means available to report to parents, then try to adapt your report card so that it is at least more humane. Figure 4 is an example of a report card in the process of change from Lancaster, Pa. Lancaster hopes to continue to move away from report cards, so this was a beginning step but we think it a good one. At least, though they can't do it all they aren't sitting back and saying, "We can't!" They're beginning. As with the rest of this book, have the strength of your convictions and begin.   195

FIGURE 4

SCHOOL DISTRICT OF LANCASTER

1973-1974

NAME _____   Grade 1

SCHOOL _____

TEACHER _____   PRINCIPAL _____

MESSAGE TO PARENTS: Your child's development is of concern to you and the school. You are urged to visit the school and talk over the progress of your child with his teacher and principal.

Failure is not indicated on this report. Each child is placed where his ability and achievement show he will work best. This check list is marked on your child's own ability. It does not indicate his standing in the group. His progress is indicated by a check (x) in the appropriate column. Areas not covered during this working period have been left blank. Your understanding and encouragement are necessary for your child to do his best.

READING LEVEL

	1	2	3	Term			1	2	3	Term
Reading Readiness					Third Grade				
Pre Primer					Fourth Grade				
Primer					Fifth Grade				
First Grade					Sixth Grade				
Second Grade					Above Sixth				

S = Progress Satisfactory
I = Needs Strengthening

LANGUAGE ARTS

Evaluation Periods

	1		2		3		4	
READING	S	I	S	I	S	I	S	I
Knows letter names								
Knows letter sounds								
Knows growth in skills: Phonics								
Comprehension								
Vocabulary								
Reads well orally								

Evaluation Periods

	1		2		3		4	
	S	I	S	I	S	I	S	I

LANGUAGE
Expresses ideas well orally . . . .

Shows creativity in written work . . . .

HANDWRITING
Applies handwriting skill . . . .

Prepares neat work . . . .

MATHEMATICS
Identifies and writes number: 1-10 . . . .

1-100 . . . .

1-150 . . . .

Understands current addition facts . . . .

Understands current subtraction facts . . . .

Understands relationships between addition
          and subtraction . . . .

Comprehends value of penny, nickel, dime . . . .

Tells time to the hour and half hour . . . .

Understands place value—ones, tens . . . .

SOCIAL STUDIES
Contributes to unit study . . . .

SCIENCE AND HEALTH
Knows and applies good health habits . . . .

MUSIC
Participates in music activities . . . .

ART
Expresses his own ideas . . . .

Follows directed activities . . . .

PHYSICAL EDUCATION
Shows progress in locomotive skills . . . .

Shows progress in ball skills . . . .

Shows progress in stunts and tumbling . . . .

Shows progress in rhythms . . . .

Shows progress in apparatus skills . . . .

Shows good sportsmanship . . . .

Participates to the best of his ability . . . .

197

Evaluation Periods

	1		2		3		4	
	S	I	S	I	S	I	S	I

WORK HABITS
- Listens . . . .
- Follows directions . . . .
- Practices neatness . . . .
- Begins work promptly . . . .
- Finishes work on time . . . .
- Works independently . . . .
- Works well with others . . . .
- Makes good use of self-directed time . . . .
- Uses materials carefully . . . .

SOCIAL ATTITUDES
- Obeys rules and regulations . . . .
- Shows respect for authority . . . .
- Shows considerations for others . . . .
- Shows self-discipline . . . .

TEACHER'S COMMENTS

1st Period _____

2nd Period _____

3rd Period _____

4th Period _____

PARENT'S COMMENTS AND SIGNATURE

1st Period _____

2nd Period _____

3rd Period _____

This pupil is assigned to_____ beginning September_____

198

One final note on reporting to parents—the take home folders are an excellent way to keep the parents informed weekly. Our first year we weren't able to organize and manage that part of our program, but the second year the "take home folder" idea had top priority. The parents enjoy seeing their children's work and they were able to watch progress all during the year instead of hearing all about it only twice a year at conference time.

DISCIPLINE AND MANAGEMENT

Many teachers would like to open their classrooms and move into open teaching situations, but they fear chaos and "bad" children. But believe us, children in open situations are no better or no worse than children in traditional schools. What is different, however, for some teachers, are the methods of discipline and techniques of management. We hope to give you enough ideas in this chapter to alleviate some of those fears and calm the ulcer your principal is working on because he feels openness means madness.

Step one is to plan ahead. Commit yourselves to the positive approach from the beginning. Look for the good in children and you'll find lots of it. Praise the child who does some good independent work, and some other child listening will try harder himself. Children want to do right. They want to please you, their teachers. Oh, some by age fifteen may make you think they don't want to please, but we all know they started out that way.

Step two is to set standards beforehand as a team for your unit (classroom area). We decided on things like: feet off furniture, no running, listening when someone else is talking, and the golden rule. No, they aren't what you think about when you discuss standards, but those few things were the ones we felt were important and the only ones necessary to preset. We believe the important thing is to set as few rules as possible and to make them sensible. The fewer there are, the better they are remembered. If a situation comes up and becomes a problem, deal with it then, but you can't set standards for situations which might happen.

It will be necessary for the teams and the principal to sit down and set standards for the halls, playground, cafeteria, bathrooms and any other common areas shared by children from several teams. If you don't do this and adhere to it, team A's children run in the hall, Team B's children "butt" in line in the cafeteria, and Team C's children wrestle on the playground which, of course, is unfair. We think teams might have different unit standards but there should be unanimous school standards which everyone adheres to. *Consistency* is a must even within a team.

199

Step three, and still to do before the children come, outline the rights, privileges, special advantages of this unit, room, school, etc. The teachers should agree on these.

Next, as a team, outline the responsibilities of the children. Now when the students have all these advantages what do we have a right to expect from them? We felt our children should take care of their personal belongings and tubs, take care of school equipment, have a reasonable attitude toward school, handle themselves responsibly, and be considerate of others.

Fifth, as a team, discuss what to do with students who break standards. We chose confinement, and restriction of privileges.

Sixth (the team handles this, but usually after the children are in school and everybody's functioning) an open situation allows, indeed encourages, movement and communication, both of which are noisy and disruptive for some people. If this happens, provide areas for them to work. Allow a teacher to wall herself in somewhat, at least temporarily, if she feels the movement or noise bother her. If, however, at the end of a year, she's still bothered, she'd probably be better off in another setting altogether. If a child is bothered, a desk or table in a quiet area should help. On the other hand, if everyone seems upset by movement and noise, look at the schedule. It just may be there's too much movement at one time. Noise, according to us, should be enough to allow communication, but not enough to prevent learning.

Seventh, the team agreed not to punish all for one's behavior.

Eighth, we agreed to trust the students and ask for their help.

Ninth, we agreed that yelling was unnecessary and that it would be quite a disturbance if one teacher yelled at a child in a quiet area.

Tenth, we vowed to find the source of the problems of the "problem students."

Eleventh, we vowed to handle all but the severest problems ourselves as a team and not to send the children to the principal, who wouldn't be aware of the circumstances.

Now, with the children, what happens when they get there? The team has already discussed this aspect and someone, probably the team leader and/or the principal, are ready to handle these topics with the students.

1. The first time you talk to the children, it should be about all the great things about your new system or school. They should know something about the philosophy and terms they'll be hearing, too. So tell them about the

great teachers they'll have, their privileges, rights, the fact that there will be no grades, that they'll be able to move about and talk. They'll be able to make their own choices and decisions as long as they demonstrate the ability and as long as their "thing" doesn't impinge upon the rights of others.

2. That afternoon or the next morning, the related talk on responsibility should be given. Lay out in black and white exactly what you expect and why. You expect them, for instance, to take care of their own belongings, help each other, take notices home, have a positive attitude about school, and in general live and work in school by the golden rule. In both talks the students should be encouraged to enter in and contribute.

3. The next session is an important one. You ask the children to set standards. What? You say the teachers already set them? Yes, that's true, but the teachers set them for their own peace of mind.

We set standards; our children set standards, and guess what! They were exactly alike. Let the students set them and give their own reasons why the standards are necessary and they'll remember them a lot longer than if you dictate preset standards. They use reason and good common sense, and it really works.

4. The children should sit down in another session and should discuss the terms self-control and self-discipline. If you use some good group techniques such as role-playing, you should be able to get this across to very young children. The students should know these are two long-range goals they must work toward just because they are in an open education program. At this session you could also discuss what to do with children who don't follow standards; let the students decide, but be prepared to soften their punishment.

5. Discuss with the students problem areas as they come up. One of the problems in our school is that our children have many, many college students who tutor them, teach them, delight them, and sometimes unfortunately upset them. So we talked about this problem which was building up, and they decided since the school was a laboratory school for college students to learn in, and since when someone is learning, they often make mistakes, and since this is the only reason to have a school like theirs, and since they like it, they'll just learn to cope with the situation. So we talked about some solutions and we solved the problems, and in one rare case I can think of, a nine year old was more mature than a nineteen year old.

One solution the children came up with was really neat. They decided   201 that since a few children were leaving the areas agreed upon and goofing off, they ought to have to stay in "corrals" (those three-sided desks used in libraries and called carrels) which brought up a beautiful discussion about horses and why they must be confined to *corrals.* One child suggested we keep any child like that in a "corral" night and day and make him eat hay. Needless to say, we modified the idea and just used carrels to restrict students who couldn't handle the freedom of movement. (Some children sat next to teachers almost a whole year before they learned how to handle it.)

With children, it seems you must remember the key which was stated in chapter I—you give the students only the freedom they're able to handle and only then when they accept the responsibility that goes along with it.

Some teachers in a graduate workshop on open education came up with the following list of the responsibilities of children which we think is good and will serve as a summary. We also think any child in an open situation would be willing to comply with these.

RESPONSIBILITIES OF CHILDREN

1. Follow standards set by group

2. Budget time

3. Respect each person's rights and uniqueness

4. Take care of materials

5. Share what he learns and knows

6. Set reasonable, attainable personal goals

7. Evaluate his own efforts

8. Help each other

9. Be honest

10. Ask for help when needed

11. Work toward self-control and self-discipline

12. Accept responsibility for freedom

13. Follow the schedule

EVALUATION

Since we have stressed the need for evaluation of the child and your program throughout the book we want to summarize in a few lines our feelings on evaluation.

Evaluation is a constant part of your program. It is ongoing, and we feel when you cease to evaluate and question what you're doing, you're in big trouble. Team teaching helps you evaluate your own and each other's ideas at team planning. Parents will offer ideas and thoughts worth considering; so will administrators. Keep an open mind, listen, and then make your decisions.

And the children? Well if you've read only one-third of our book you know we feel a continuous diagnostic testing program is essential. The skill sequence with its diagnostic tests is a fantastic evaluation program in itself.

We have preached pre-test and post-test and we're sure you know by now you should give pre-tests to find out if kids already know or don't know the skills you propose to teach them. (Don't you wish graduate school profs would do that?) Also a post-test is necessary for *you*. Did you get the skill across to one, to ten, to all?

We know there are some of you who evaluate programs solely by test scores of human children which sometimes then becomes numbers and statistics to you. And to you folks we say nothing. . . .

For us, all the figures in the world don't make a bit of difference or prove open education is good or bad. We'll settle for the smiles on the children's faces, and the happiness in their hearts. And when they demonstrate care and concern for other human beings, that's the only proof we need that open education is good, that it is a Ray of Sunlight in the Future.

204 *Open education is sharing.*

15

The
Physical Plant

WE HAVE DISCUSSED in some detail the many facets of open concept education. We have emphasized that this concept is much more a matter of attitude than it is related to the physical plant known as the school building. We realize, however, that each of you is in a building. Some of these buildings are new, some are old, and some are in between. Some buildings have been designed as "open space" buildings. In most cases this was done for one or both of two reasons: (1) open space schools are about 18 percent less expensive to build than buildings with walls and doors and (2) open space schools are "in." These decisions were made by top level administration. The buildings were built, the children and teachers were placed in the buildings and the realization dawned that to teach in this type of building required some different thinking about organization, about scheduling and curriculum, about the teacher's role, the children's role, the principal's role, and about the parent's role. Administrators then scurried off madly looking for help, and in many cases taking any that came along. Isn't this interesting, how we can always find help.

Help came, in many cases, from those who knew much less than the teachers frustrated by the situation. The result—a lot of bad feeling and bad press for "open education." . . . In fact some open schools will never be open as a result of these uncoordinated attempts at program development. A beautiful thing got all wrapped up in physical plant and people, and educators who should have known better got all "out of joint" and refused to listen, to look, and to examine. Educators ran for the cover of, "but we've always done it this way and that makes it right." Thus open education got all wrapped up in the business of new buildings, and old thinking: "It wouldn't work in our old buildings," and "we didn't want it to work in the new ones." As a result all our non-change agents sat back and breathed a sigh of relief—another challenge beaten off. Once more we won't have to look at ourselves and be frightened by the prospect of what we see.

This is why we wrote this book. Fortunately, there are still people like you, people who wanted to look at what they've been doing, people who believe in the right of each child in our society to derive the most possible from school. There are people who will not only stand up and be counted, but will stand up and shout, "You're wrong, open education belongs in our society, it has nothing to do with buildings old or new, it has to do with children, their lives, their destinies. It has to do with teachers, their goals, and their beliefs. It has to do with parents, their aspirations and their dreams. It has to do with all of us who believe in the dream of what our democracy can mean."

Most of us work in buildings designed for individual self-contained units. Schools have been built this way since time immemorial, not because we ever gave any serious thought to curriculum, but because we gave all thought to one type of organization—the graded one. If open education doesn't work in this type of building, then we would have to build all new buildings. In today's economic world this cannot even be discussed, and should not. Most of our buildings are perfectly serviceable, and should continue to be used. They cannot, however, continue to be used as an excuse for doing nothing. In this chapter we are going to discuss some ways you can adapt an old building to serve the program; some considerations about a new building; some thoughts on planning future buildings; some ideas about furniture and space, floors, walls and ceilings, outdoors, and just doors. We will make a few comments concerning the ideal physical plant, and wrap the chapter up by trying to anticipate some of the excuses we hear.

OLD BUILDINGS

Let's begin by taking a look at that old building. In most cases there are rows of rooms with walls separating them and a long hall. There are several things you can do with this type of building. Of course, the best thing to do is take a tandem of three rooms and remove the walls from the middle room. Some districts are not quite willing to take this step because of uncertainty about the program. In some cases, of course, the room walls are supporting walls and cannot be moved. An alternative in such a case would be to put a large arch (Fig. 1) or large rectangle in the center of each of the middle room walls. Another alternative is to put two arches or two

FIGURE 1   1 arch or door

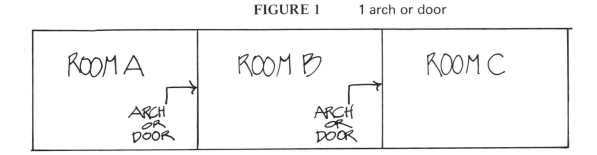

FIGURE 2   2 arches or doors

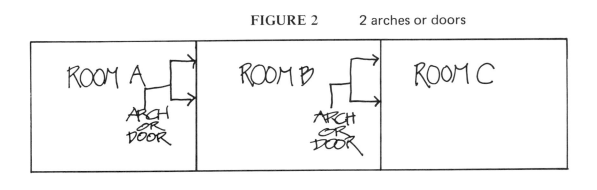

FIGURE 3   Half walls

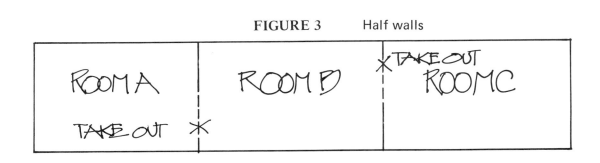

doorways in each wall. (Fig. 2) If the walls are not supporting walls and the district does not want to remove the whole wall, a good alternative is to remove half of each wall. (Fig. 3)

We'd like to emphasize that for each tandem of three rooms, only two walls need to be renovated. In each of these cases the result is a set of three rooms open to each other, providing a space where three teachers can work together, and take full advantage of the potential offered by team teaching. In most cases removing half or a part of a wall is a simple enough task that district maintenance personnel can do, and in most cases it is a reasonably inexpensive procedure. One of the best examples of an old building opened up in this way is in the Manheim Central School District, Manheim, Pennsylvania.

If the district is unwilling to alter the school, the easiest way to get some openness is to remove the doors. This is easily accomplished by removing the pins from the hinges. The doors can be stored and replaced if there should be a need. This will enable at least some free movement among the rooms.

The next thing to consider is how you are going to use the rooms: that is, one area would be the communication skills area, where all the com-

munication skill materials would be available, one area a math area, and one a social studies science area.

Take a look at your halls. Can you use them for learning centers, or small group work? What other areas of the building can you use? Are there alcoves or empty classrooms, or any space that can be set up for individual or small-group work. We have seen hallways in older buildings made into media centers, used for learning center areas, and in some very old two- and three-story buildings, the center halls have been used for large group instruction. There are many things you can do with old egg-crate buildings. With imagination and ingenuity the ideas are limitless.

The one item that can add even more flexibility to your old building is furniture. Since furniture used to enhance flexibility does not differ from new buildings to old, we will discuss all furniture in one section of this chapter.

NEW BUILDINGS

If you're moving into a new building there are some advantages, and believe it or not, some disadvantages. We hope you're one of the rare people moving to a new building designed with a program in mind. In fact, we hope you helped design the program and the building. This type of planning is rare, however, and you're probably getting ready to move into the new building and working on a program at the same time.

A new building offers an opportunity to make real changes. Teachers who really want to change can get involved in the program. Teachers can get involved who are willing to live with the initial shock of change. Teachers can get involved who are willing to plan and work together and bear the frustration that accompanies change.

This sounds like we're saying that a new building gives us a chance to make a big change all at once. That is exactly what we are saying. Of course this means that the teachers involved will have time to plan, learn about, and develop the new program. They need an intensive, well coordinated, well designed program of in-service, such as the "Summer Happening" at Millersville State College in Pennsylvania. They need a commitment from the school district that change is acceptable and encouraged; and they need time. Actually, time is needed to develop a program like the one described in this book.

Usually the new building will be of an open space or semi-open space variety. There are many open buildings being designed today. The reason is, in many cases, that these buildings are less expensive to construct. We've heard estimates as high as 20 percent less. This kind of saving certainly influences school boards in their at-tempts to balance the ever increasing budget.

Another advantage of a new building is the absence of tradition. In a new building you establish precedent, you re-establish tradition, you set the tone of the future. This is a unique opportunity. We would caution you against "going slow." We're not saying don't go slow. What we are saying is that if you're going to go slowly, then know where you are slowly going to get. We have seen too many "go slows" as excuses to continue to do what's been done in the past.

One problem with an open space building results from attempts to use the open space as self-contained units. We've seen ingenious attempts made to close off space into single units. If the same effort had been extended to develop a program for the open space available, these people would have been assured of success.

Thus one of the first considerations in the new school is to look for ways to use the open space to advantage rather than to close it off. The team needs to look at its pod or space and make some decisions about space utilization. These should be made in terms of spaces to accommodate children in the different aspects of the program rather than to accommodate teachers in their individual biases. Avoid any area being identified as any one person's exclusive domain. Rather, 209 identify areas for large-group instruction, small-group instruction and individual instruction. Set up these areas physically to accommodate these concepts. Then in these areas arrange furniture to suit the purpose.

Next, set up areas in terms of materials centers, that is, keep all the math materials in one area, all the social studies, science materials in another area, and all the communication skills materials in another area. The large-group instruction area may also be the math materials area, and the small-group instruction area may house the communication skills materials, or you may choose to house the communication skills material in the media center.

After these areas have been designated and arranged, then each teacher may choose to use one of these areas for his home base. This would be the area where they do their check-outs or meet with groups specifically assigned to them for various purposes. This approach will prevent you from each taking a corner of the space, lining up the desks and doing your own thing to the exclusion of the other teachers. You will also find that it is very difficult to do your own thing exclusively in an open space as there is no place to hide as there was in your self-contained classroom. Try to integrate the media center into your program by considering it as an extension of your classroom. Find the spaces in

the building that will be useful for small-group and individual work areas. We have two sets of stairs in our media center. They make a great area for small filing cabinets; what we didn't realize is that they also make a great area for kids to crawl into, behind the file cabinets to read, to listen to cassettes, or just to be alone. Don't overlook any area in the building; the most inconspicuous area may be a very useful one for the program.

FUTURE BUILDINGS

Now, if you're one of those fortunate people who are involved in planning your own building, Voila! We have some suggestions for you to keep in mind. The first consideration is to leave out the walls. Yes, leave them all out, moveable or immoveable. If this upsets people, then at least leave out all the walls in the pods. Somehow get the media center in the center of the building with easy access from all the pods or areas of instruction. Try to get the building carpeted, all of it if you can, if not all, at least the instructional areas. The only areas that should not be carpeted are the art room, the gymnasium, the cafeteria, and a small area around the sinks in the open instructional areas. Try to influence the construction of the service areas on a lower floor or in a separate wing. This area should house the cafeteria, gym, art room, music room, industrial arts room and any other special service room. This does not mean you can't have art in your classroom, but it helps if there is a place specifically for art and the storage of art materials. Try to influence the construction of storage areas; there are never enough. Ask someone to give attention to the height of the sinks and the drinking fountains. Plan as much uninterrupted space as possible; you'll be glad you have it, especially after you're in the building and have the program organized. Get as many ideas about the building as possible, and then have a committee work them over for ideal recommendations. Prepare a list of options and priorities. Cost and other factors may prevent you from getting everything you'd like to have, know ahead of time what you're willing to give up. Remember, no matter how hard you plan, when you get in the building you will find things you don't like and didn't anticipate. This is true in any building, just remember you have to make many more adjustments in an old building than in one you help design.

FURNITURE

Furniture style and arrangement can be a big factor in developing a flexible program. For example, if you're in that old building, you probably have old furniture. There are many things that can be done with old furniture in an old building. First of all get the desks out of rows and into some other kind of organization. If you take four or six desks of the same height and tape the legs together, you can make tables of them. Use any tables you've got to arrange areas for small group work. Don't assign each child a desk; let them sit anywhere. Meet them first thing in the morning in large groups, this way they can sit on the floor and in chairs and still be all together. Use some of your scavenger ability, ask people for old couches and old rugs that are serviceable. Find out about cardboard carpentry, and let the kids make some of their own furniture. Experiment with different arrangements. Try to get bookcases put on casters. Two of these can be placed back to back, attached with screws and placed on casters. You will need a place for the kids to keep their books and things. Use cardboard cartons that hold twenty-four cans of pop (soda) or (I didn't say this) beer. The children can decorate these any way they want, and they can be stored on the floor or on a bookshelf. We used plastic dishpans in our primary unit. We bought these at a local discount department store at a discount. We only paid 49 cents for each. They're presently in their third year of use. The ideal items to use are fiberglass tote trays that cost from $3 to $5 apiece. Don't forget about a place for the students to hang coats and put boots and stuff like that. One item you can get out of the way is your desk; it does not have to be the 211 dominant piece of furniture in the area. One last point, if you can scrounge up enough carpet, this will reduce the amount of furniture you will need. Try to keep some open space in your arrangement. This will be easier with carpet because in many cases the children can sit on the carpet and prefer this instead of a chair. One item we often overlook is a stool. There are many types from little wooden ones to bench types. Stools will not only add variety to your seating arrangement but will increase your seating flexibility.

If you're moving into a new building you probably will be involved in choosing furniture or at least some of it for the building. The furniture you should consider should be portable, light and sturdy. The most common error seems to be buying too much furniture before the building opens. If possible you should try to influence the administration to buy only the essentials to begin the program. If it is possible to keep some money back this will pay off by letting you buy furniture that you discover you need as you operate the program with children. Avoid buying more than a few student desks; tables and chairs are very practical and flexible. Try to get some round, square, rectangular and trapazoidal tables. For storage try bookcarts for books, and metal carts (such as Smith System carts) for kits and other materials. Don't forget to provide a place for coats and boots.

You will need a place, a portable cabinet, to store tote trays. Concentrate on getting chalkboard space. This can be a problem without walls. Look for portable boards that move easily, are not top heavy, and don't have great big legs sticking out for everyone to trip over. Try to hang peg boards or bulletin boards on every possible place you can. Try the back of carts and cabinets, on doors, or any place you can find room. Avoid elaborate systems of furniture. They cost a fortune and besides looking nice and being something you can show visitors, they don't greatly enhance the program. If we insist on sturdy, light, portable furniture, the furniture companies will soon get the message and develop pieces that will help us with the program.

These same ideas should be kept in mind for the media center. We're convinced that book carts and Smith System type furniture would not only provide greater flexibility to the center, but will play a role in making the center more useful as the core of the program.

Couches and comfortable chairs are a great addition to the area. People have been slow to accept this idea, but see what you can do. How about a couple of bean bag chairs, or big pillows to bring both color and comfort to the setting.

Use the wall space for bulletin boards, learning centers, and displays. Try to get a finish on the walls that won't come off. We must be able to use the walls. You'd be amazed at the number of schools where the teacher can't put anything on the walls, or schools with carpet where no one is allowed to move, let alone paint. We must be free to use the buildings. When we are recognized as professionals, the realization will come to light that we are not irresponsible, and that accidents will happen.

Remember that many things can be hung from the ceiling. Mobiles, learning centers and projects are just a few of the things you can hang. Ceilings have been another place that we have been forbidden to use.

We said we would conclude this chapter by mentioning some of the excuses we hear about buildings. We have just discussed two, the walls and the ceilings. Other excuses have to do with noisy floors, small rooms, uncooperative parents, narrow minded principals, wrong furniture, etc., etc., etc., etc.

We feel this chapter nullifies most of these excuses and offers some ways that you can begin to make your building work for you, the program and the children. After all, this is what education is all about, isn't it?

Sometimes the best learning experience
takes the least space.

16

Where to Start in Your Self-contained Classroom?

WE REALIZE THAT most of you are in self-contained classrooms, and will probably continue to be there for a while. We hope this book has interested you in working for change in your school. In the meantime, there are some things you can do in your one classroom to begin to open up. We'd like to suggest some things for you to consider.

The first thing you should do is take a look at the way you have your room organized. You need to try to get some open space in the room, and develop some space for centers. Are your desks in rows? There are lots of ways you can group them and reorganize them so that you can get more floor space. Make a list of the things you'd like to have in your classroom; carpet, couches, easy chairs, bookcases, etc. Then start to scrounge, ask your friends, the children, storekeepers, the principal, anyone you can think of,

and try to get what you can. When you know what you will have, you can then proceed to organize your room.

The next thing you need to do is examine your materials—what have you got that you haven't used for awhile? What kits do you have? What can you share with your neighbors? Here again, these don't have to be commercial or new. Use the same sources as above and see what kind of neat games and activities the children can bring in. Remember learning stations can be on any subject and if you are doing communication skills the students don't have to be doing communication skills stations, they could be doing a station that grew out of one of the child's magic hobbies.

The next thing you should do is pick out an area of the curriculum and begin to individualize the program in that   215 area. Many people start with communication skills. Some people like to start with learning stations in social studies and science. A necessary last thing you should do is review the standards you've set for your room. Are there any that aren't necessary? Refer to that chapter for more help. We will discuss briefly each area of the curriculum and make some suggestions about where you can start in each of these areas. Remember you probably should only start with one area at a time. When you get that area worked out, then try adding another area.

Communication skills—There are two possible ways we can suggest you begin working with your "top" reading group. Take the approch suggested in chapter IV with these children. Try giving them some longer-range assignments. Try giving them some choices. Move them out of the basal text and get them to make some choice concerning their own reading. Give these students a chance to keep their own records. Work out a system for your records. Try diagnosing some skill areas and let the students do work to reinforce their skills. Use the workbook pages for diagnosis rather than grading.

The second way is to pick out several students as per chapter IX who are very responsible and put these children on a contract. Simplify this contract in the beginning, and make it

for a short period of time. As the children get adjusted to it and start to perform well, then increase the amount of work and time encompassed in the contract. When you get a system worked out for these few students, then add others. Soon you will have a majority of your children functioning in some kind of contract in communication skills.

Math—If you choose to start with the math program, you will probably have the best success by using your text and choosing some of your most responsible children and contracting them into the text. They can work on a number of pages for an agreed period of time. You can even arrange for these students to have access to the answer book. This way they can use part of the problems in the book as a diagnostic test, check the results, and get immediate feedback about the help they might need. If the text has unit tests, you can use the unit tests to diagnose. The child can take the unit test, check it, meet with you about problem areas, and you can teach the skill and assign some practice problems so that you can get some feedback concerning the success or failure of your teaching.

Social studies and science—If you choose to start in this area, we would suggest you take a look at the chart in chapter IV. This will give you an idea of how to organize a unit, and get some of the children involved in some independent activity. This is a good area to set up some learning stations and try to get some students involved with these. You might want to try a packet, also. The basic notion in this area is to give children an opportunity to try to do some things on their own. Give them a time limit. Perhaps groups of them could work on projects together. Remember when you begin, your first concern is to figure out a way that you can handle the program. Once you get organized you will be able to expand to other areas.

Now if you think you're up to it, try to get someone to work with you. Form a team. Try to get your next door neighbor, or try to get the principal to put the two of you in adjacent rooms. Then work together in one area until you perfect your technique. Then operate as though you've got one group of students. Try to get free movement going between the two rooms. Remember the walls are not a hindrance; there are doors. Just leave them open and use them freely. A good way to begin is to set up learning stations in each room for all the children to use, and begin by letting groups of them use them. Remember one of the first things you should discuss and agree upon are the standards. Then each of you have to try to be consistent in enforcing them.

Use the book; it will be a help. Refer to the chapters on topics you want to know more about. Most chapters tell you how to begin, so go to it, and have fun.

Children can learn individually as well as in groups.

Bibliography

Anderson, D. Carl. "Open-Plan Schools: Time for a Peek at Lady Godiva." *Education Canada.* 10:2-6. June, 1970. (Same condensed—*The Education Digest.* 36:8-10. November, 1970.)

Anderson, Ralph. "Open Learning Places, Matzke and Holbrook Schools." *Education Technology.* 10:13-15. June, 1970.

Anderson, Robert H. *Teaching in a World of Change.* New York: Harcourt, Brace & World, 1966.

Arone, Frank T. "Toward Greater Success in Team Teaching." *The Clearing House.* 45:501-2. April, 1971.

Ashton-Warner, Sylvia. "Spearpoint." *Saturday Review of Education.* 55:33-39. June 24, 1972.

Bair, Medill and Richard G. Woodward. *Team Teaching in Action.* Boston, Mass.: Houghton Mifflin, 1964.

Baker, Eva L. "Project for Research on Objective-Based Evaluation." *Educational Technology.* 10:56-59. August, 1970.

Bartel, Elaine V. "Initiating a Self-Directed Learning Program in the Classroom." *Education.* 91:247-9. February, 1971.

Barth, Roland S. "So You Want to Change to an Open Classroom." *Phi Delta Kappan.* 53:97-99. October, 1971.

Barth, Roland S. "Teaching—The Way It Is/The Way It Could Be." *Grade Teacher.* 98-101. January, 1970.

Beggs, David W. III and Edward G. Buffie (eds.). *Independent Study: Bold New Venture.* Bloomington: Indiana University Press, 1965.

Beggs, David W. III and Edward G. Buffie. *Nongraded Schools in Action: Bold New Venture.* Bloomington: Indiana University Press, 1967.

Beggs, David W. III (ed.). *Team Teaching: Bold New Venture.* Indianapolis, Ind.: Unified College Press, 1964.

Berenson, David. "How to Find Out What You've Taught Them." *Grade Teacher Magazine.* 84:130-132. April, 1967.

Berretta, Shirley. "Self-Concept Development in the Reading Program." *The Reading Teacher.* 24:232-8. December, 1970.

Berson, Minnie Perrin. "Inside the Open Classroom." *American Education.* 7:11-15. May, 1971.

Billings, Zilpha W. "Self-Selection Classroom." *Today's Education.* 59:15-16. October, 1970.

**Biscaglia, Leo. *Love.* New Jersey: Charles B. Slack, Inc., 1972.

Bishop, Lloyd K. *Individualizing Educational Systems, The Elementary and Secondary School: Implications for Curriculum, Professional Staff, and Students.* New York: Harper and Row, 1971.

Bloom, Benjamin S. (ed.). *Taxonomy of Educational Objectives, Handbook I: Cognitive Domain.* New York: David McKay Company, Inc., 1956.

Braun, Frederick G. "Changing Teacher Behavior as a Means of Enhancing Intellectual Growth in Young Children." (Bibliog.) *International Reading Association Conference Papers.* 15:134-42. 1971.

Brown, B. Frank. *The Nongraded High School.* Englewood Cliffs, New Jersey: Prentice-Hall, Inc., 1963.

*Denotes practical books with teaching ideas.
**Denotes *very* good reading.

Calabro, Hilda. "Toward a More Flexible Learning Environment." *The High School Journal.* 55:205-7. February, 1972.

Cardarelli, Sally M. "The LAP–A Feasible Vehicle of Individualization." *Educational Technology.* 23-29. March, 1972.

Carnie, George M. "Doing Your Own Thing Via Self-Determined Units." *The Science Teacher.* 37:35-37. February, 1970.

Carswell, E.M. "Moving from Graded to Nongraded Concepts." *Instructor.* April, 1972.

Carswell, Evelyn M. "The Nongraded School." *The National Elementary Principal.* 47:11-15, no. 2. November, 1967.

"Center School." *Grade Teacher.* 92-94, 104. May–June, 1968.

Cohen, Barbara. "An Open Classroom in a Traditional High School." *The Education Digest.* 38:14-16. December, 1972.

"Concerning Non-graded, Continuous-Progress Education." *The Parent's Guide to Non-graded Schools.* Wildwood and Lake Drive Schools, Mountain Lakes, New Jersey.

Cooper, Martin and Barney M. Engel. "Academic Achievement and Non-gradedness." *Journal of Experimental Education.* Winter, 1971.

Cornish, Roger N. "Open Education: The Ingredients." *The Open Education Kit.* New London, Conn.: Croft Leadership Action Folio. 46:3-16. 1972.

**Cullum, Albert. *Push Back the Desks.* New York: Citation Press, 1963.

Cutler, Marilyn H. "Wary of Open Plan High Schools? This One's Just Enough." *American School Board Journal.* 44:25-27. August, 1972.

Dell, Helen Davis. *Individualizing Instruction.* Chicago: SRA, 1972.

Dennison, George. *The Lives of Children.* New York: Random House, 1969.

Dillman, Caroline M. and Harold F. Rahmlow. "Writing Sample Test Items for Objectives." *NSPI Journal.* 9:12-19. July, 1970.

Dodd, John and Mary. "Communicating with Parents." *Academic Therapy.* Spring, 1972.

Dunbar, Howard S. "No Doors Slam Here; Open-Space Primary School at Sidney, New York." *New York State Education.* 58:34-5. November, 1970.

Eberle, Robert F. "The Open Space Schools." *The Clearing House.* 44(1):23-28. September, 1969.

Eddinger, Judith. "Report Cards . . . . Who Needs Them?" *Grade Teacher.* 68-70. January, 1969.

Eisenhardt, Catheryn T. "Individualization of Instruction." *Elementary English.* 48:341-5. March, 1971.

"Elementary School Media Programs: An Approach to Individualizing Instruction." *American Association of Elementary-Kindergarten Nursery Educators.* Washington, NEA Center, 1970. p. 32.

Featherstone, Joseph. "How Children Learn." *The New Republic.* 17-21. September 2, 1967.

Featherstone, Joseph. "Open Schools, 1: The British and Us." *The New Republic.* 20-25. September 11, 1971.

Featherstone, Joseph. *Schools Where Children Learn.* New York, N.Y.: Liveright, 1971.

Feshbach, Seymour and Howard S. Adelman. "Experimental Program of Personalized Classroom Instruction in Disadvantaged Area Schools." *Psychology in the Schools.* 8:114-20. April, 1971.

Flurry, Ruth C. "Open Education: How to Get There if You Want to Go." *Childhood Education.* 49:416-420. May, 1973.

*Forte, Imogene, Marjorie Frank and Joy MacKenzie. *Kids' Stuff Reading and Language Experiences—Intermediate-Jr. High.* Tennessee: Incentive Publications, Inc., 1973.

*Forte, Imogene, Mary Ann Pangle and Robbie Tupa. *Center Stuff for Nooks, Crannies and Corners.* Tennessee: Incentive Publications, Inc., 1973.

Frazier, Alexander. "Curriculum—A Tougher Look at Skills/A Closer Look at Children." *Grade Teacher.* 95-97. January, 1970.

"Furniture and Furnishings for the Open Plan." *School Management.* 15:16-19. March, 1971.

George, Marjorie. "The Open Classroom." *English Journal.* 61:908-912. September, 1972.

**Ginott, Haim. *Between Parent and Child.* New York, Macmillan Co., 1969

**Ginott, Haim. *Between Teacher and Child.* New York, Macmillan Co., 1970.

**Glasser, William. *Schools Without Failure.* New York: Harper and Row, 1969.

Glasser, William. "The Effect of School Failure on the Life of a Child, Part 1." *The National Elementary Principal.* 49:8-18. September, 1969.

Goodlad, John and Robert H. Anderson. *The Nongraded Elementary School.* Under the General Editorship of Willard B. Spalding. New York: Harcourt, Brace and World, 1959.

Goodlad, John and Robert H. Anderson. *The Nongraded Elementary School.* New York: Harcourt, Brace and World, 1963.

Gordon, Alice. *Games for Growth.* Palo Alto, Calif.: SRA, 1970.

Gross, Beatrice and Ronald. "A Little Bit of Chaos." *Saturday Review.* 53:71-3, 84-5. May, 1970.

Hachten, June. "New Dimension to Math." *Education.* 59:150-1. April, 1971.

Halligan, William J. and Nancy J. Pline. "Bandaids or Surgery?" *Audiovisual Instruction.* 16:40-2. November, 1971.

Hammerman, Ann and Susan Morse. "Open Teaching: Piaget in the Classroom." *Young Children.* 28:41-54. 1972.

Hapgood, Marilyn. "Open Classroom: Protect It From Its Friends." *Saturday Review.* 54:66-9+. September 18, 1971.

Hemness, L. "Operation P.O.W.; Planning Organization, Work." *Instructor.* 81:135. October, 1971.

Hillson, Maurie and Joseph Bongo. *Continuous-Progress Education.* Calif.: Science Research Asso., Inc., 1971.

Holt, John. *How Children Fail.* New York: Pitman Pub. Company, 1964.

Holt, John. *How Children Learn.* New York: Pitman Pub. Company, 1967.

Johnson, Gerald F. J. and W. C. Page. *Helping Traditional Teachers to Plan and Implement Student Centered Classrooms: Selected Classroom Project; Final Report.* New Bedford, Mass.: Project COD, 1971. pp. 3 31-32.

Johnson, Glenn R. and A. J. Lewis. "How Individualized is the Nongraded School?" *Educational Leadership.* 29:139-41. November, 1971.

Johnson, Stuart R. and Rita B. *Developing Individualized Instructor Material.* Palo Alto, Calif.: Westinghouse Learning Press, 1970.

Jones, Richard V. "Learning Activity Packages: An Approach to Individualized Instruction." *Journal of Secondary Education.* 43:178-183. April, 1968.

Kapfer, Philip G. "Practical Approaches to Individualizing Instruction." *Educational Screen and Audiovisual Guide.* 47:14-16. May, 1968.

Killough, Day. "Open-Plan School." *The Instructor.* 80:75-6. August, 1970.

Kirschenbaum, Howard. *Wad—Ja—Get? The Grading Game in American Education.* Hart Publishing Company.

**Kline, Lloyd W. "Five Sites in Search of the Word." *Journal of Reading.* 17:288-296, no. 4. January, 1974.

Kohl, Herbert. "A School Within a School." *Grade Teacher.* 87-12-14. September, 1969.

Kohl, Herbert. "A School Within a School, Part 2." *Grade Teacher.* 87:11-13. October, 1969.

Kohl, Herbert. *The Open Classroom: A Practical Guide to a New Way of Teaching.* New York: New York Review, 1969.

**Kohl, Herbert R. *The Open Classroom.* New York: Random House, 1970.

Kozol, Jonathan. "The Open Schoolroom: New Words for Old Deceptions." *Ramparts.* 38-41.

Kreamer, Ralph. "Schools Open Up." *Pennsylvania Education.* 3:24-29. March-April, 1972.

"Lake Normandy School." *Grade Teacher.* 85-91. May-June, 1968.

Lambek, Marcia and Maude Lorentzen. "Learning Resource Centers in Every Classroom." *Instructor.* 81:88. October, 1971.

Learning Centers: Children on Their Own. Virginia Rapport, Associate Editor. Washington: Association for Childhood Education International, 1970.

Lewis, Bill Ray. "An Innovative High School in a Midwestern Suburb." *Phi Delta Kappan.* 53:105-107. October, 1971.

Lewis, James. *A Contemporary Approach to Nongraded Education.* West Nyack, N.Y.: Parker Publishing Co., 1969.

*Lorton, Mary. *Workjobs.* Addison-Wesley Publishing Co., 1972.

Mack, Don and Kay Kemp. "Everything You Ever Wanted to Know About Open Education*—*and Never Knew Whom to Ask." *Grade Teacher.* 66-70, 72, 111-118. April, 1972.

Mager, Robert F. *Developing Attitude Toward Learning.* Palo Alto, Calif.: Fearon Publishers, 1968.

Mager, Robert F. *Preparing Instructional Objectives.* Palo Alto, Calif.: Fearon Publishers, 1962.

*Margrabe, Mary. *The Now Library—A Stations Approach-Media Center Teaching Kit.* Washington, D.C.: Acropolis Books Ltd., 1973.

McNally, Lawrence and Glenn Fleming. "Quest for an Alternative." *Educational Leadership.* 28:490-3. February, 1971.

Melton, Joseph. "Arithmetic for Individuals." *School Science and Mathematics.* 71:298-302. April, 1971.

Messick, Samuel. "Educational Evaluation as Research for Program Improvement." *Childhood Education.* 46:413-414. May, 1970.

Mills, Lester C. and Peter M. Dean. *Problem-Solving Methods in Science Teaching.* New York: Bureau of Publications. Teachers College, Columbia University, 1960.

Mitchell, Joy and Richard Zoffness. "Multi-age Classroom." *Grade Teacher.* 55-58, 60-61. March, 1971.

Moran, P. R. "The Integrated Day." *Educational Research.* 14:65-69. November, 1971.

Moxley, Roy A. "A Source of Disorder in the Schools and a Way to Reduce It: Two Kinds of Tests." *Educational Technology.* 10:S3-S6. March, 1970.

Muck, Ruth E. S. "Nongraded Classrooms: A Hope for Better Education." *Delta Kappa Gamma Bulletin.* 37:22-7. Summer. 1971.

Myers, R. E. "Comparison of the Perceptions of Elementary School Children in Open Area and Self-Contained Classrooms in British Columbia." *Journal of Research and Development in Education.* 4:100-6. Spring, 1971.

Neil, A. S. *Freedom-Not License.* New York: Hart Publishing Company, 1966.

Neil, A. S. *Summerhill.* New York: Hart Publishing Company, 1966.

Nyquist, Ewald B. "Open Education: It's Philosophy, Historical Perspectives, and Implications." *The Science Teacher.* 38:25-8. September, 1971. (Same condensed—*Education Digest.* 37:9-12. November, 1971.)

Ogletree, Earl J. "The Open Classroom: Does it Work?" *Education.* 93:66-7. September—October, 1972.

"One Room Schoolhouse 1972 Style, Middle Island School District, New York." *School Management.* 15:17-20. April, 1971.

"Open Education: Can British School Reforms Work Here? Special Report." (Bibliog.) *Nation's Schools.* 87:47-61. May, 1971.

"Open Education: Too Much Too Soon?" *Education U.S.A.* November 13, 1972.

"Open Plan." *School Management.* 15:8-17. August, 1971.

O'Reilly, Robert P. and Gregory J. Illenberg. "Relationship of Classroom Grouping Practices to Diffusion of Students' Sociometric Choices and Diffusion of Students' Perception of Sociometric Choice." *The Journal of Education Research.* 22:104-14. May, 1971.

Palmer, Constance and Sue Kent. "Helping Parents Understand the Flexible Classroom." *Independent School Bulletin.* 31:35-7. October, 1971.

Peterson, Carl H. *Effective Team Teaching: The Easton Area High School Program.* New York: Parker Publishing Co., 1966.

Petrequin, Gaynor. *Individualizing Learning Through Modular-Flexible Programming.* New York: McGraw-Hill, 1968.

Polos, Nicholas C. *The Dynamics of Team Teaching.* Dubuque, Iowa: W. C. Brown Co., 1965.

Postman, Neil and Charles Weingartner. *Teaching as a Subversive Activity.* New York: Delacorte Press, 1969.

"Projects on Individualizing Instruction." *The Arithmetic Teacher.* 18:161-3. March, 1971.

Pryke, David. "On Team Teaching." *Childhood Education.* 48:85-9. November, 1971.

"Put it all Together School; Walnut Hills School, Englewood, Colorado." *The Instructor.* 80:60-2. April, 1971.

Rathbone, Charles H. "Assessing the Alternatives." (Bibliog.). *Childhood Education.* 47:234-8. February, 1971.

Rathbone, Charles H. "Examining the Open Education Classroom." *School Review.* 80:521-549. August, 1972.

Rathbone, Charles H., editor. *Open Education: The Informal Classroom.* New York: Citation Press, 1971.

Read, Edwin A. and John K. Crnkovic. *The Continuous Progress Plan.* Prove, Utah: Brigham Young University Press, 1964.

Reeves, Harriet Ramsey. "Individual Conferences: Diagnostic Tools." *The Reading Teacher.* 24:411-15+. February, 1971.

Rogers, Vincent R. "Open Education." *Instructor.* 81:746+. August, 1971.

Sartore, Richard L. "A Principal with a New Outlook is Needed for the Open School." *The Clearing House.* 47:131-134. November, 1972.

Schatz, Esther E., editor. *Making Sure of Skill Development in Individualized Reading.* Columbus: College of Education, Ohio State University, 1965.

"School for Human Beings; Hamilton School, Newton, Mass." *The Instructor.* 80:40-2. May, 1971.

Short, Verl M. "The Open Classroom." *Education Canada.* 12:5-9. 1972.

Silberman, Arlene. "There's a Bug in the Air and It's Catching!" *Instructor.* 81:79+. October, 1971.

**Silberman, Charles E. *Crisis in the Classroom.* New York: Random House, 1973.

*Simon, Sidney B., Leland W. Howe and Howard Kirschenbaum. *Values Clarification: A Handbook of Practical Strategies for Teachers and Students.* New York: Hart Publishing Company, Inc., 1972.

Simon, Sidney B. "Wajagett?–Grades Must Go." *Pennsylvania Education.* 3:19-21, no. 5. May–June, 1972.

Simpson, Edwin L. and Nancy M. Vedral. "Team Teaching: Process for Professional Growth." *Contemporary Education.* 43:40-3. October, 1971.

Smith, Lee L. *A Practical Approach to the Non-Graded Elementary School.* West Nyack, New York: Parker Publishing Co., 1968.

Spodek, Bernard. "Alternatives to Traditional Education." *Peabody Journal of Education.* 48:140-6. January, 1971.

Staples, I. Ezra. "Open-Space Plan in Education." (Bibliog.) *Educational Leadership.* 28:458-63. February, 1971.

"Systems' Middle School, Went from Plans to Reality in Just Seven Months; School Construction Systems Development." *The American School Board Journal.* 159:26-7. July, 1971.

Tag, Herbert G. "Integrated Day: British Style." *Peabody Journal of Education.* 48:325-30. July, 1971.

Taylor, Joy. *Organizing the Open Classroom: A Teacher's Guide to the Integrated Day.* New York: Schocken Books, 1971.

Thomas, James E. "Pod Units in an Open Elementary School." *School and Community.* 57:12-13. April, 1971.

Trump and Miller. *Secondary School Curriculum Improvement: 2nd Edition.* Allyn and Bacon, 1973.

Turner, William E. "Individualizing Spelling with 600 Students." *The Instructor.* 80:142. August, 1970.

"Using Media in our Teaching: Discussion." *The Instructor.* 80:58-59.

*Voight, Ralph Claude. *Invitation to Learning.* Washington, D.C.: Acropolis Books Ltd., 1972.

**Warner, Sylvia Ashton. *Teacher.* New York: Bantam Books, 1963.

Watson, Carlos M. and others. "Continuous Progress: An Idea, a Method, an Organization." *Contemporary Education.* 42:247-50. April, 1971.

Wentz, Frederick Henry. *An Investigation of Learning Centers in the Elementary School.* Millersville, Pa.: State College, 1970.

Wheller, Alan H. "Creating a Climate for Individualizing Instruction." *Young Children.* 27:12-16. October, 1971.

Wilhelms, Fred T., editor. *Evaluation as Feedback and Guide.* Washington, D.C.: Association for Supervision and Curriculum Development, NEA, 1967.

Windley, Vivian D. "A New Look at Teacher Education." *Urban Review.* 514:3-11. March, 1972.

Wing, R. Cliff and Patricia H. Mack. "Wide Open for Learning; Project Solve, N. H." *American Education.* 6:13-15. November, 1970. (Same condensed—*The Education Digest.* 36:19-21. February, 1971.)

Wright, Dorothy. "Try a Quest." *English Journal.* 59:131-133, 143. January, 1970.

Learning can be fun.

Epilogue

We think this part of a book is usually used for things authors have forgotten to include in the body of the text. And, in a sense we'll use the epilogue for that too.

First, if you have any questions about the material in the book, we might be able to help; perhaps we've encountered something similar at our school or in schools where we've conducted in-service workshops. You can send your questions to either of us, Stayer Research and Learning Center, Millersville State College, Millersville, Pennsylvania 17551.

Second, if you would like to come and visit our school for one day or several days, please feel free to call or write to give the date of your visit to: Mr. John Pflum, Director, Elizabeth Jenkins School for Children, Stayer Research and Learning Center, Millersville State College, Millersville, Pennsylvania 17551.

And last, we want to thank you for buying the book, because our goal in writing it was to introduce our workable system of open education to anyone who is interested. We think if you've become interested, you'll try our program, see how beautifully it works, and become a believer. And you know what believers do? They go out and try to help other people become believers, so we hope you can help us do that. As we said in the book, come join us, let's change our present systems, let's get our behavior matching our elusive but worthwhile goals by providing kids with the opportunities to learn—to feel good about themselves, to make decisions, and to be responsible for themselves.

Index

Contents

PART TWO

The teaching materials in this part of OPEN EDUCATION have also been reproduced separately as a Teaching Materials Kit for individual classroom use. Although the two parts were meant to be sold together, the kit may be ordered separately from Part One by a school district, for instance, for each teacher, or even for each child. Copies are also available from the publisher, Acropolis Books Ltd., 2400 17th Street, N.W., Washington, D.C. 20009 at $5.95 per copy. The materials in Part Two are organized according to the chapters in Part One.

ACTIVITIES FOR INDIVIDUALIZED READING

1. Describe the main character(s).
   a.   What he looks like
   b.   What is he like, is he real or not?
   c.   What do you think of him? Why?

2. Describe the setting.
   a.   Time
   b.   Place

3. Draw a series of cartoons showing the plot of the story.

4. Draw a picture or map of the place in which the story took place (setting). Label to show what happened in each place.

5. Why did the author write the book or story? Pick one point below as the reason and write a paragraph or two about it?
   a.   To share an experience
   b.   To give information
   c.   To give an opinion

6. Describe the most exciting part of the story.

7. Describe the most beautiful part of the story, the most humorous, the saddest.

8. Could this be a true story? Why or why not? Give your reasons in paragraph form.

9. Make a poster to advertise a book you liked very much.

10. Write an original story, using the same characters as the book.

11. Write an original story using the same setting as the book.

12. Write another ending for the story.

13. Write a biography of the author of the book. Include a list of the other books written by the same author.

14. Write a short summary of the story.

15. Write a review of the book telling why you liked or disliked it; give good reasons for your views.

16. Why did you choose this book? Give your answer in paragraph form.

17. After reading two or more biographies, write a biography of yourself.

18. List the events of the story in order of time.

19. Make a book jacket and write a blurb to accompany it.

20. Create a series of original illustrations for a story.

21. Write a movie script for a good story.

22. Make a list of new, unusual words and expressions.

23. Act out a pantomine about the story.

24. Write a letter to a friend recommending a book.

25. Using information in a book or books, make a scrapbook about a subject.

26. Use puppets to retell a story.

27. Makes a map or pictorial time line for a historical book.

28. Write a set of questions which other children can answer after reading the book.

29. Broadcast a book review to a radio audience.

30. Prepare a book review to present to a class at a lower level.

31. Write a letter to the author about the book.

32. Model an illustration for a book from clay or soap.

33. Construct a diorama to represent a scene from the story.

34. Using paper, cardboard, wire, rag or pipe cleaners make a character from a story.

35. Tell the class about the book using chalk sketches on the blackboard.

36. Create a colorful mural on paper.

37. Compare a book with a similar one read or compare books by the same author.

38. Write a poem to accompany a story.

39. Add an original stanza to a poem.

40. Write a book report to hang on a line captioned "A Line of Good Books" (A cord is stretched between two points in the room).

41. Write and draw a rebus for a story.

42. Perform a science experiment for the class after having read about it.

43. Dramatize a story using stick puppets.

44. Dramatize a story using flannel board figures.

45. Make a pie plate movie. (A paper pie plate divided into four parts has a part of a scene from the story. A second pie plate with 1/4 cut out is attached to a fastener to the illustrated pie plate. The top pie plate is revolved to show one scene at a time.)

46. Write a book teaser to be displayed with a picture on the bulletin board. (ex. I'm as little as a thumb. I came out of a tulip. A frog wanted me for his wife. When it was winter, I was very cold. Do you want to know about me? If you do, read the book called *Thumbelina.*)

47. Give an illustrated lecture for travel book read.

48. Pretend you are the author. Explain why you wrote this book or what you were trying to show the readers.

49. Imagine you are the main character. Tell how you feel about one or two other characters in the story.

50. Make a mobile using the book characters.

51. Do a soap or clay model of animals in the story.

52. Demonstrate an experiment explained in the book.

53. Compose a telegram trying to find the essence of a book in 15 words. Then expand it into 100-word "over-night telegrams."

54. Have a friend who has read the story stump you with questions.

55. After reading a book of poems, learn verse, or read one to the class.

WILD AND WACKY IDEAS FOR CREATIVE WRITING

1. How would you feel if it rained ice cream?
2. How would it feel to live in a walnut shell?
3. What is Excedrin Headache #56?
4. What if everyone wrote backwards?
5. Spray on clothes.
6. What would you do with another hand?
7. If I were a germ!
8. Design a new person.
9. The Day the Fleezle Schoofed!
10. How would you like to have gills?
11. What would it feel like to be an umbrella?
12. Would you like to be swallowed? If so, by whom or what?
13. What would you do if someone sat on you?
14. Where is the freeazort in your car?
15. The Day the Rain Fell Up.
16. Who put glue in the toothpaste?
17. The Dog Who Lost His Bark!
18. What kind of sandwich would you like to be?
19. Who tied knots in my pajamas?
20. How did you feel the day you opened the door and found a six foot pink rabbit?
21. What would you do it you were shut up in a box by yourself for three days?
22. How would it feel to be a bouncing ball?
23. What do ants think about?
24. A Day Without Gravity!
25. How would you wash an elephant in your bath tub?
26. How did the leopard get his spots?
27. The Adventures of a Turtle on his Way to New York City!
28. What would you do if it snowed purple?
29. Who is McDoogle?
30. What would you do if you didn't have to go to bed every night?
31. What is in a magician's hat?
32. Describe a day of living without water.
33. Exchange places with your parents for a day.
34. How would you feel if you were a dog about to be hit?
35. What would you do for recreation if you lived underground?
36. Whose wacky idea was this?
37. What if Columbus hadn't discovered America?
38. What is over the hill behind your house?
39. What would happen if some people had no gravity?
40. What would you do if you didn't have to go to school every day?
41. Pretend a rich old woman died and left you with $1,000,000 to take care of her cat. What would you do?
42. Where do freckles come from?
43. How big is the largest person?
44. What would you do if your bed caved in?
45. Where does the white go when the snow melts?
46. How would it feel to be the sun?

LIST OF KITS AND MATERIALS

Charles E. Merrill Publishing Company
1300 Alum Creek Drive
Columbus, Ohio 43216

    #7309 Mathematics Skill Tapes
        Complete set of 40 cassettes
        (includes 10 each of 9 student study booklets and teacher's
        guide) $295.00

Cassette system with student study sheets—self correcting

* * * * * * * * * * * * * * *

Prentice Hall, Inc.
Department 121
Educational Book Division
Englewood Cliffs, New Jersey 07632

    One to One Reading Program   185.00

Individualized approach to reading, grades 4 to 8. Contains activity cards
for specific books found in most libraries and also cards for general topics
found in any library.

* * * * * * * * * * * * * * *

Charles E. Merrill Publishing Company
1300 Alum Creek Drive
Columbus, Ohio 43216

    Spoken Arts Cassette Libraries
        0900 Library for Young Listeners   275.00
        0901 Library for Intermediate Listeners   375.00

Cassettes—masterpieces in literature, poetry, speeches, etc.

* * * * * * * * * * * * * * *

Educational Progress Corporation
4900 South Lewis Avenue
Tulsa, Oklahoma 74145

    Continuous Progress Laboratories
      Social Studies:
          Series 300 (Grade 3) Complete Program-Cassette   112.50
          Series 400 (Grade 4) Complete Program-Cassette   112.50
          Series 500 (Grade 5) Complete Program-Cassette   112.50

      Science:
          Series numbers same as above   112.50

A social studies individualized kit covering a large variety of subjects.
It ties in with different basals for reference learning—pre-test—post-test,
etc. (Science kits also available)

Imperial Intermediate Reading Program
Kankakee, Illinois 60901

R-456-C	Intermediate Reading Program	395.00
R456SB	Add'n pupil workbooks	1.95

Cassette diagnostic system in reading. Activity book for children—self correcting, reading card to go with tapes, etc.

* * * * * * * * * * * * * *

Economy Company
Drawer A
5811 West Minnesota
Indianapolis, Indiana 46241

325-X	Continuous Progress in Spelling (Int. kit) Kit includes teacher's ed.	95.50
326-8	Continuous Progress in Spelling Int. pupil's workbook	1.29
327-6	Continuous Progress in Spelling Int. Teacher's Ed.	1.29

Spelling program where child is put on correct level and works with a small group or a "buddy."

* * * * * * * * * * * * * *

Harcourt Brace Jovanovich, Inc.
757 Third Avenue
New York, New York 10017

366115-1	On My Own—Green (Level 3)	78.00
366125-9	On My Own—Orange (Level 4)	78.00
366134-8	On My Own—Purple (Level 5)	78.00
366143-7	On My Own—Brown (Level 6)	78.00

Individual kit in science—can be used individually in small group or large group.

* * * * * * * * * * * * * *

American Guidance Service, Inc.
Publishers Building
Circle Pines, Minnesota

C-134	Complete Key Math Test Kit (25 students)	21.00
R-136	Diagnostic Records	4.25
M-137	Manual (if ordered separately)	2.25

A diagnostic math test—individually administered to find proficiency levels in content, operations, and applications—good for individual diagnostic help.

Science Research Association
259 East Erie Street
Chicago, Illinois

    3-545   Math Applications Kit
            A kit that allows children to use computational skills and
            apply them to science, social studies, everyday things, etc.   54.50
    3-3350 Computational Skills Development Kit
            Practice in addition, subtraction, multiplication, etc.
            self correcting.   72.50
    3-520   Arithmetic Fact Kit
            Practice kit in addition, multiplication, subtraction,
            division with automatic "fact pacer"   54.95

                    * * * * * * * * * * * * * *

Language Experiences in Early Childhood
    #59462   Teacher's resource book, including one set of 30 pupil-
              parent leaflets.   18.50

                    * * * * * * * * * * * * * *

Language Experiences in Reading

    Level 1 Pupil books:
            59410—Units 1-2
            59411—Units 3-4
            59412—Units 5-6
    Level I Teachers Resource Book
            59414
    Level II Teacher Resource Book
    Level III Teacher Resource Book
            59453

A teachers manual for unit ideas in a Language Experience Approach to
Reading. A big help in individualizing programs. All levels $8.25 per book.

                    * * * * * * * * * * * * * *

Botell Reading Inventory
Follet Educational Corporation

A testing system that measures instructional level, frustration level, free
reading level, word attack skills, common spelling problems, etc.

    Examiner's Kit (essential)   4.00
    Scoring sheets (per pack of 35)   2.00

                    * * * * * * * * * * * * * *

Scott Foresman & Company
99 Bauer Drive
Oakland, New Jersey 07436

    Reading Systems Context Puzzles and Dictionary Puzzles
    Primary grades:

    Context Puzzles:
        Set 1, Level 5   2.25   227

Set 2, Level 6	3.36
Set 3, Level 7	3.36
Dictionary Puzzles:	
Set 1, Level 8	3.36
Set 2, Level 9	3.36
Dictionary Puzzles:	
Set 3, Level 10	2.25
Set 4, Level 11	2.25
Set 5, Level 12	2.25

These are self correction games that children can use independently to practice reading skills.

* * * * * * * * * * * * * *

Xerox Education Center
Columbus, Ohio 43216

Personalized Reading Center

An individualized kit of 100 books. It includes a child placement test, cards for vocabulary and comprehension for each book, creative follow-up activities for each book, and questions a teacher can ask at conference time. This is for intermediate children only.   No cost available

COMMUNICATION SKILLS SEQUENCE

LEVEL O

AUDITORY DISCRIMINATION

1. Identifies sound intensity by discriminating between loud and soft sounds.
2. Identifies pitch by discriminating between high and low sounds.
3. Identifies quality of sounds through their distinguishing characteristics.
4. Compares many sounds to determine variations in duration.
5. Identifies the sequence of sounds.
6. Identifies word pairs that are the same and word pairs that are different.
7. Identifies words which rhyme.
8. Identifies alliteration in oral discourse.
9. Distinguishes likenesses and differences in initial consonant sounds.

VISUAL DISCRIMINATION

1. Discriminates size differentials, e.g., big-little; tall-short; fat-thin.
2. Discriminates shape differentials.
3. Identifies position of an object in a series.
4. Identifies internal details of a picture.
5. Identifies colors.
6. Identifies first name in manuscript form.
7. Identifies likenesses and differences in words.
8. Identifies words and spaces in written language.

VISUAL-MOTOR COORDINATION

1. Demonstrates effective big muscle control.
2. Demonstrates effective hand-muscle control.
3. Demonstrates effective eye-hand coordination.
4. Distinguishes between right and left.
5. Demonstrates left-to-right eye movement with return sweep in identifying objects, letters, words, etc.
6. Demonstrates ability to focus on close work.
7. Demonstrates top-to-bottom eye movement.
8. Demonstrates left-to-right, front-to-back progression.

LISTENING SKILLS

1. Demonstrates ability to listen and form associations with related items from one's own experience.
2. Demonstrates ability to listen closely enough to oral discourse to identify the organization.
3. Demonstrates ability to follow directions.

229

4. Demonstrates ability to listen critically.
5. Demonstrates ability to listen appreciatively and creatively, with mental and emotional participation.

ORAL LANGUAGE DEVELOPMENT

1. Demonstrates quality of ideas through expressive language.
2. Defines words as a clue to the quality of language development.
3. Demonstrates ability to verbalize ideas.
4. Demonstrates ability to master English sentence structure.

CONCEPT DEVELOPMENT

1. Associates meaning with words based on experiences.

LETTERS OF THE ALPHABET

1. Matches letters to other letters (Matching).
2. Discriminates a letter in a series after a stimulus letter has been shown and removed (Recognition).
3. Names and letter (Identification).
4. Names and differentiates capital and lower case letters.
5. Matches each capital letter to its lower case form.

INTEREST IN READING

1. Demonstrates ability to listen and respond in concrete and creative ways to a wide variety of literary forms, styles, and moods.
2. Demonstrates interest in reading material through exploration of books, pictures, and other literary media.

SOCIAL-EMOTIONAL DEVELOPMENT

1. Demonstrates ability to work and play with a group and with individuals.
2. States reasons for things happening as they do.
3. Acquires and applies the operations necessary for carrying out classroom routine.

HANDWRITING

1. Demonstrates mastery of skills in visual-motor coordination.
2. Demonstrates correct position of body, hand, and writing tools.
3. Draws familiar objects with a free-full arm movement using basic manuscript strokes.

LEVEL 1—ESTABLISHING BASIC SIGHT VOCABULARY

SIGHT VOCABULARY

1. States orally experience stories at the concrete level.
2. States orally experience stories at the semi-concrete level.
3. States orally experience stories at the abstract level.
4. Identifies words by using picture clues.
5. Identifies words by using context clues.
6. Identifies words through labels and signs.
7. Identifies words by applying word recognition clues.
8. Acquires basic sight vocabulary.

PHONIC ANALYSIS

1. Matches initial consonant sounds with their corresponding symbols.
   (b,c [hard] or k,d,f,g [hard] , h,j,l,m,n,p,r,s,t,v,w,y,z)
2. Identifies words which rhyme and states additional rhyming words.

STRUCTURAL ANALYSIS

1. Identifies contractions as they appear in pre-primer or child's oral discourse.
2. Identifies compound words.
3. Identifies the morpheme "s" signaling plurality.
4. Demonstrates sensitivity to syllables in polysyllabic words.

ORAL LANGUAGE DEVELOPMENT

1. Demonstrates effective oral interpretation of printed text by achieving intonation and inflection through punctuation cues.
2. Demonstrates emotional overtones and meaningful expression through oral language.
3. Applies the skills in oral language development introduced in the readiness period.

WRITTEN LANGUAGE DEVELOPMENT

1. Constructs lists, records, and memoranda.
2. Constructs news reports.
3. Writes labels.
4. Writes picture captions.
5. Constructs sentences using a capital letter to begin the first word.
6. Makes a period at the end of a sentence.
7. Makes a question mark at the end of a group of words that ask a question.

COMPREHENSION

1. Builds and applies literal comprehension skills.

Specific information

Sequence

2. Builds and applies interpretive comprehension skills.

Main idea and supporting details

Relationships

Figurative and special language

Inferences

3. Builds and applies critical-evaluative comprehension skills.

Prediction of outcomes

Evaluation of accuracy

Literary forms and author techniques

Characterization

4. Applies comprehension skills stated above to listening activities.

STUDY SKILLS

1. Demonstrates ability to follow written directions.
2. Demonstrates ability to attend to silent reading assignment.
3. Demonstrates ability to use table of contents.
4. Demonstrates ability to use alphabetical order.
5. Demonstrates ability to use a picture dictionary.
6. Demonstrates independence in study through self-selection techniques.
7. Demonstrates ability to organize and record information.
8. Demonstrates ability to organize material.
9. Demonstrates ability to summarize.

HANDWRITING

1. Demonstrates correct position of body, feet, hands, paper, crayon, pencil, and chalk at desk and at chalkboard while making basic manuscript strokes.
2. Differentiates and makes all upper- and lower-case letters.
3. Forms the numerals 1 - 10.
4. Identifies and forms the math symbols common to first-year math programs.
5. Identifies and makes punctuation marks used in first-year reading and writing activities.
6. Demonstrates ability to write letters and words observing proper spacing.
7. Demonstrates ability to use the following terminology:

movement	tail letters
horizontal	space
vertical	spacing
slant	mid-line
circle	form
evaluation	rhythm
manuscript	baseline
clockwise	headline
counterclockwise	headroom

Note: All of these behaviors are not expected to be acquired at Level 1. The first evaluation will be made at the completion of Level 3. Results of the evaluation will indicate whether student makes transition to cursive writing included in the Continuum at Level 4 or remains on skill development program outlined in Level 1.

LEVEL 2

PHONIC ANALYSIS

1. Demonstrates mastery of initial consonant sounds with their corresponding symbols. (b, c, [hard] k, d, f, g, [hard], h, j, l, m, n, p, r, s, t, v, w, y, z)
2. Matches the sound and letter for final consonants. (b, hard c or k, d, f, g [hard], j, l, m, n, p, r, s, t, v, z)
3. Matches the sound and letter for consonant digraphs in initial position. (ch,sh, th, wh)
4. Demonstrates ability to substitute consonants in the initial position using the following rhyming parts: ake- all- an- at- ay- en- et, ill, it, ook, ot, own, un.
5. Demonstrates ability to substitute consonant digraphs in the initial position.
6. Identifies letters which are vowels.
7. Discriminates between consonants and vowels and matches the terms *consonant* and *vowel* to the appropriate symbols.

STRUCTURAL ANALYSIS

1. Forms compound words from two known words.
2. Identifies the word endings *s, d, ed,* and *ing.*
3. Identifies number of syllables in a word at the auditory level.

ORAL LANGUAGE DEVELOPMENT

1. Demonstrates ability to apply skills introduced at Levels 0 and 1.
2. Chooses standard English forms of usage in oral expression.
3. Identifies large thought units and word groups in oral reading.

WRITTEN LANGUAGE DEVELOPMENT

1. Demonstrates ability to apply skills introduced at Levels 0 and 1.
2. Identifies and constructs proper nouns.
3. Identifies *I* as a word and writes it with a capital letter.
4. Makes an exclamation point at the end of a sentence showing surprise or strong emotion.
5. Demonstrates ability to use language creatively through composition.

VOCABULARY DEVELOPMENT

1. Builds additional developmental vocabulary through formal and incidental experiences.
2. Identifies the relationship in simple analogies.

COMPREHENSION

1. Builds and applies skills introduced at Level 1 under literal, interpretive, and critical-evaluative comprehension using the Directed Reading-Thinking Activity.

STUDY SKILLS

1. Builds and applies skills described under Study Skill Category at Level 1.

HANDWRITING

1. Same as Level 1.

LEVEL 3

PHONIC ANALYSIS

1. Demonstrates ability to substitute consonants in the final position.
2. Matches the sound and letters for final consonant digraphs (sh, ch, th, nk, ng, ck).
3. Demonstrates ability to substitute consonant digraphs in the initial position.
4. Demonstrates ability to substitute consonant digraphs in the final position.
5. Matches the sound and letters for initial consonant blends.
   (br, cr, dr, fr, gr, pr, tr, bl, cl, fl, gl, pl, sl, sc, sk, sm, sn, sp, st, sw, qu [kw]).
6. Demonstrates ability to substitute consonant blends in the initial position.
7. Matches the sounds and letters for final consonant blends.
   (sk, sp, st, nt, nd)
8. Demonstrates ability to substitute consonant blends in the final position.
9. Identifies following rhyming parts: ack - ell, ight, ing; old, ark, ate.

STRUCTURAL ANALYSIS

1. Identifies number of syllables heard in a word.
2. Identifies compound words when made from one known and one unknown word.
3. Identifies by naming the structural parts—"root" or "base" word and "word endings". (s, d, ed, ing)
4. Identifies contractions.
5. Identifies the singular possessive and distinguishes between the plural form and the singular possessive of words.

ORAL LANGUAGE DEVELOPMENT

1. Demonstrates ability to maintain and refine skills introduced at Levels 0-2.
2. Demonstrates effective oral interpretation of printed text in identification of quotation marks.
3. Demonstrates emotional overtones through stress and pitch.

WRITTEN LANGUAGE DEVELOPMENT

1. Demonstrates ability to apply skills introduced at Levels 0-2.
2. Identifies titles and distinguishes words in titles that are to be written with capital letters.
3. Writes names of days and months with a beginning capital letter.
4. Discriminates among Mr., Mrs., Miss and writes them correctly.
5. Writes dates demonstrating correct form as to capitalization and punctuation including the new term "comma."
6. Constructs simple friendly letters and identifies the heading, greeting, body, closing, name, and the terms "indent" and "comma."

STRUCTURE OF LANGUAGE

1. Orders letters of the alphabet sequentially.
2. Classifies letters of alphabet by consonants and vowels.
3. Classifies words according to simple parts of speech.
      naming words
      action words
      descriptive words
4. Identifies phrases.
5. Identifies a sentence as a group of words which expresses a complete thought.
6. Identifies the terms "paragraph" and "ident."
7. Identifies antecedents of personal pronouns.

VOCABULARY DEVELOPMENT

1. Builds additional developmental vocabulary.
2. Demonstrates skill in selecting word opposites.
3. Identifies words with multiple meanings.
4. Builds additional vocabulary through formal and incidental means.

COMPREHENSION

1. Builds and applies skills introduced at preceding levels in literal, interpretive, and critical-evaluative comprehension using the Directed Reading-Thinking Activity.

Note: The material at a first reader level should permit the development of all the comprehension skills listed at Level 1. Success in the development of these abilities rests on the qualities of the questions asked during the Directed Reading-Thinking Activity.

SELF SELECTION

1. Demonstrates ability to select trade books in terms of interset and reading level.
2. Identifies needs in teacher-pupil conferences or teacher-group sessions.
3. Demonstrates ability to transfer and reinforce the basic reading skills to trade books.
4. Identifies the major skills in literary analysis and demonstrates ability to apply them to self-selected trade books during sharing sessions.
5. Demonstrates ability to extend and refine reading skills that promise independence in reading.

STUDY SKILLS

1. Demonstrates ability to maintain and refine skills listed under this category in preceding levels.
2. Demonstrates ability to state and apply the strategy for recognizing new words.

HANDWRITING

1. Demonstrates ability to apply handwriting skills listed at Level 1 completing the instructional program in manuscript.

Note: Students may move to Level 4 in other categories on the continuum even though failing to reach the competency level required in the handwriting category. However, instruction in handwriting must continue to be given in the skills identified for Levels 0-3 until competency has been obtained. Since Level 4 moves into cursive writing, it is imperative that children who move to this level in some categories, but are continuing to use manuscript, receive written directions, board work, follow-up activities, etc. in manuscript form.

LEVEL 4

PHONIC SKILLS

1. Matches long vowel sounds with their corresponding symbols. (a,e,i,o,u)
2. Matches short vowel sounds with their corresponding symbols. (a, e, i, o, u)
3. Demonstrates ability to apply vowel generalizations in attacking unfamiliar words.

STRUCTURAL ANALYSIS

1. Identifies and applies meaning to new words formed when the following suffixes have been added to root words: *er* of agent, *er* of comparision, *est*.

2. Demonstrates ability to add endings to root words that necessitate structural changes in the root words:
   a. Doubling the final consonant when adding *ed* and *ing*
   b. Changing *y* to *i* when adding certain endings
   c. Dropping final *e* when adding *ing*
3. Identifies number of syllables and the accented syllable in polysyllabic words.
4. Constructs and identifies the following contractions:

didn't	don't
let's	hadn't
doesn't	haven't
aren't	I'd
can't	I'll
couldn't	I'm
won't	wouldn't
you're	isn't
it's	I've
o'clock	that's
wasn't	you'll

5. Identifies the plural possessive and discriminates between singular and plural possessives.

ORAL LANGUAGE DEVELOPMENT

1. Demonstrates improvement in phrase reading and in interpretation of printed text by using stress and voice pitch.
2. Demonstrates improvement in expressive language by choosing from among the following words the form which represents standard English language patterns to express ideas:

did-done	doesn't-don't
saw-seen	gave-given
was-were	ran-run
went-gone	ate-eaten
come-came	is-are
has gone-have gone	we-us
I-me	she-her
he-him	broke-broken
took-taken	
Double negatives	

WRITTEN LANGUAGE DEVELOPMENT

1. Applies the following skills of capitalization and punctuation in written work:
   First word of sentence
   Proper nouns
   Personal pronoun *I*

Mr., Miss, Mrs.
Months
Days
First word in the greeting and closing of a letter
First word and all important words in titles
Period
Question Mark
Exclamation point
Comma (dates—letter writing)

2. Demonstrates ability to transfer mechanics of composition and usage to creative writing activities.

STRUCTURE OF LANGUAGE

1. Orders sequentially a list of words by noting the first letter.
2. Identifies words or phrases within sentences that tell who, what, when, where, why, how.
3. Writes sentences expressing complete thoughts using naming, action, and descriptive words.
4. Demonstrates ability to transform statements into questions and questions into statements.
5. Identifies a paragraph as a group of sentences that tells about one thing.
6. Identifies multiple pronoun antecedents.

VOCABULARY DEVELOPMENT

1. Builds additional developmental vocabulary.
2. Selects word opposites and identifies them as antonyms.
3. Identifies the concept of synonymous ideas.
4. Identifies homonyms.
5. Demonstrates continuing ability to identify and use words with multiple meanings.
6. Identifies the relationship in simple analogies.

COMPREHENSION

1. Demonstrates increasing skill in interpreting printed material.
2. Demonstrates ability to expand literal comprehension skills:
    Specific information
    Sequence
3. Demonstrates ability to expand interpretive comprehension skills:
    Main idea and supporting details
    Relationships
    Figurative and special language
    Inferences
4. Demonstrates ability to expand critical-evaluative comprehension skills:
    Prediction of outcomes

Evaluation of accuracy
Literary forms and author techniques
Characterization

SELF-SELECTION

1. Demonstrates increasing ability to select and read literary materials (trade books) with interest, comprehension, and appreciation.
2. Demonstrates ability to identify and evaluate literary forms and author techniques.

STUDY SKILLS

1. Demonstrates ability to maintain and refine skills listed under this category in preceding levels.
2. Demonstrates ability to follow two-step oral and written directions.
3. Demonstrates ability to attend to assigned tasks until completed.
4. Identifies the following items in the Table of Contents:
   Titles
   Unit Titles
   Subtitles
   Authors
   Page Numbers
5. Identifies kind and content of story through clues in the title and/or subtitle.
6. Demonstrates proficiency in using a simplified dictionary.
7. Demonstrates ability to interpret charts, maps, and globes.
8. Demonstrates ability to use multiple sources for investigation of a topic.
9. Demonstrates ability to organize material according to main idea and details.

HANDWRITING

Students may make the transition to cursive writing in either their second year (levels 4 and 5) or third year (levels 6 and 7) of school. The decision as to the time of transition will be based on the child's competency on the handwriting evaluation given at the completion of Level 3.

At the conclusion of either sequence, all children should be doing cursive writing. For those students who are still unable to meet the competency requirements for manuscript, it seems wiser to let them move on in to cursive writing. These children will need continuing reinforcement to improve their proficiency.

SPELLING

1. Demonstrates ability to spell words correctly which contain elements previously taught under the categories of Phonic Analysis, Structural Analysis, and Written Language Development both on formal spelling lists and in all written productions.

239

2. Demonstrates ability to master words needed in functional writing that do not conform to phonic or structural regularities.

Note: Spelling skills are the same as word recognition skills. A student may be constructing spelling lists from his written work, his independent reading, or from a conventional speller. Regardless of the source, spelling, like writing, must be considered as a procedure for reinforcing word recognition skills.

LEVEL 5

PHONIC ANALYSIS

1. Matches three-letter consonant blends with their corresponding symbols (scr, spl, spr, squ, str, thr).
2. Demonstrates ability to substitute three-letter blends in the initial position.
3. Matches vowel digraphs with their corresponding symbols. (ee, oa, ai, ea)
4. Matches vowel diphthongs with their corresponding symbols. (oi, oy, ou, ow as in cow, au, aw, ew)
5. Distinguishes between the hard and soft sounds for *c* and *g*.
6. Identifies the common exceptions to the vowel generalization covering the sound of a vowel in the medial or initial position.
    o followed by ld (old, cold)
    i followed by nd (find, kind)
    i followed by gh (high, right)
    i followed by ld (wild, child)
7. Identifies vowel sounds affected by the letter *r* as in:

| car | her | corn | fir | fur |
| farm | serve | north | bird | turn |

8. Identifies the sound of the vowel *a* when followed by the letters *l* and *ll* as in *talk, salt, call,* and *ball.*
9. Distinguishes between the diphtong *ow* as in cow and the long *o* sound of *ow* as in *snow.*
10. Identifies the two sounds of the letter combination *oo* and distinguishes between the two sounds when attacking new words.
11. Identifies the conditions under which the letter *y* functions as a vowel.
12. Identifies silent consonants in words.

STRUCTURAL ANALYSIS

1. Identifies the conditions under which the plural of a noun is formed by adding *es.*
2. Forms plurals of words ending in *y.*
3. Identifies the structural changes involved when suffixes are added to root words ending in *y* or silent *e.*

ORAL LANGUAGE DEVELOPMENT

1. Demonstrates growth in oral language by extending and refining expressional skills through:
   - Discussions
   - Story telling
   - Dramatization
   - Oral reading
   - Dramatic play
   - Oral descriptions
   - Oral planning
   - Sharing experiences
   - Reporting
   - Conversations
   - Summarizing

Note: Mastery is not expected in this category. Facility in oral language is a developmental process. The emphasis at all levels is on providing fertile experiences which stimulate and promote oral language development.

2. Demonstrates continuing growth in phrase reading, fluency, and in interpretation of the printed text through stress and voice pitch.
3. Demonstrates continued improvement in selecting the correct form when using the following words in spontaneous conversation, informal, and formal oral productions:

did-done	doesn't-don't
saw-seen	gave-given
was-were	ran-run
went-gone	ate-eaten
come-came	is-are
has gone-have gone	we-us
I-me	she-her
he-him	broke-broken
took-taken	Double negatives

Avoidance of *he, she, it, we, they* following a stated subject, i.e., "Mary, she went to the store."

Avoidance of *here* and *there* following *this, that, these, those.*

4. States directions accurately.

WRITTEN LANGUAGE DEVELOPMENT

1. Demonstrates mastery in the following skills of capitalization and punctuation in written work:

241

Capitalization
- First word of sentences
- Proper nouns
- Pronoun *I*
- Titles: Miss, Mrs., Mr.
- Days and months
- Greeting and close of letter
- Titles of stories and books

Punctuation
- Abbreviations: Mr., Mrs.
- End of sentence (.-?-!)
- Greeting and close of letter
- Writing dates
- Comma in dates

2. Demonstrates continued improvement in selecting the correct form when using the following words in written productions:

did-done	doesn't-don't
saw-seen	gave-given
was-were	ran-run
went-gone	ate-eaten
come-came	is-are
has gone-have gone	we-us
I-me	she-her
he-him	broke-broken
took-taken	Double negatives

Avoidance of *he, she, it, we, they* following a stated subject, i.e., "Mary, *she* sent to the store."

Avoidance of *here* and *there* following *this, that, these, those.*

3. Demonstrates ability to write personal address in correct form.
4. Writes other addresses in correct form.
5. Demonstrates ability to transfer mechanics of composition and usage to creative writing activities.

STRUCTURE OF LANGUAGE

1. Demonstrates ability to extend and refine the skills identified in this category at the previous levels.

VOCABULARY DEVELOPMENT

1. Builds additional developmental vocabulary.
2. Builds additional listening, speaking, reading, and writing vocabulary and associates meaning to new words acquired.

COMPREHENSION

1. Demonstrates ability to read increasingly longer units of material and apply the comprehension skills identified at Level 1 and expanded at Level 4.

SELF-SELECTION

1. Selects and reads trade books and other printed material in order to gain information and to satisfy personal needs.
2. Demonstrates ability to identify and evaluate literary forms and author techniques while developing a positive attitude toward reading and an appreciation for books.

STUDY SKILLS

1. Demonstrates ability to maintain, refine, and extend the study skills identified at Level 4. (Mastery of study skills is not attained at any one level, consequently, instruction continues through various levels. No new study skill is introduced at this level.)

HANDWRITING

1. Refer to Level 4.

SPELLING

1. Refer to Level 4.

LEVEL 6

PHONIC ANALYSIS (Reinforcement of all preceding skills) (No new skill introduced)

1. Demonstrates increasing ability to identify the following phonetic properties as an aid to recognition:
    a. Single consonants in initial, final, and medial position.
    b. Consonant blends in initial and final position.
    c. Consonant digraphs.
    d. Rhyming parts (constructing words through substituting initial sounds).
    e. Consonant irregularities.
    f. Silent consonants in specific combinations.
    g. Long and short vowel sounds.
    h. Vowel digraphs.
    i. Vowel generalizations.
    j. Exceptions to generalizations.
    k. Vowel sounds affected by *r*.
    l. Vowel *a* followed by *l* and *ll*.
    m. The *oo* sounds.

243

n. Diphthongs.

o. Two sounds of *ow.*

STRUCTURAL ANALYSIS

1. Demonstrates increasing ability to identify structural elements of words as an aid to word recognition.
2. Identifies common prefixes affixed to root words:

   dis-

   en-

   in-

   re-

   un-
3. Identifies common suffixes affixed to root words:

   -er (of agent)

   -er (of comparison)

   -est

   -ful

   -ish

   -less

   -ly

   -ness

   -y
4. Forms plurals of words ending in *f* or *fe.*
5. Identifies the generalization that a word has as many syllables as it has vowel sounds.
6. Identifies *a* and *be* as common syllabic units.
7. Identifies prefixes and suffixes previously taught as syllabic units.
8. Identifies the vowel-consonant-consonant-vowel pattern (v-c-c-v) in words and uses it to divide words into syllables.

ORAL LANGUAGE DEVELOPMENT

1. Demonstrates continued growth in expressional skills through:

   Discussions

   Story telling

   Dramatization

   Oral reading

   Dramatic play

   Oral descriptions

   Oral planning

   Sharing experiences

   Reporting

   Conversations

   Summarizing

2. Demonstrates continuing growth in oral reading in fluency, eye-voice span, and interpretation of the printed text through stress, pitch, and identification of punctuation clues.

3. Identifies the correct form when using the following words in spontaneous conversation, informal and formal oral productions:

a-an	we-us
ate-eat-eaten	I-me
broke-broken	is-are
came-come	run-ran
do-did-done	see-saw-seen
doesn't-don't	she-her
gave-give-given	took-taken
has gone-have gone	was-were
he-him	went-gone

Avoidance of *he, she, it, we, they* following a stated subject, i.e., "Mary, *she* went to the store."

Avoidance of *here* and *there* following *this, that, these, those.*

4. Demonstrates correct telephone behavior.
5. Demonstrates ability to make introductions.
6. Demonstrates ability to give a simple book talk.
7. Demonstrates ability to state simple oral reports.
8. Constructs stories from experiences and states them in story form.
9. States directions accurately and follows them carefully.

WRITTEN LANGUAGE DEVELOPMENT

1. Demonstrates ability to use the following skills of capitalization and punctuation in written work:

Capital Letters

—To begin the first word in a sentence
—To begin the names of people and pets
—To begin the names of streets and roads
—To begin the name of a school, city, town, and state
—To begin the first word and all important words in the title of a book, story, or report
—To write the word *I*
—To write initials
—To begin titles—Mr., Mrs., Miss
—To begin the names of days of the week and months of the year and their abbreviations
—To begin the names of holidays and special events
—To begin the first word in the greeting and in the closing of a letter
—Usually to begin the first word in each line of poetry

Periods

—At the end of a statement

245

—After each initial

—After an abbreviation

Question Mark

—At the end of a question

Exclamation Mark

—At the end of a telling sentence if the sentence shows strong feeling or surprise.

Apostrophes

—In a contraction to show omission of a letter or letters

—Before or after *s* at the end of a word to show possession

Commas

—Between the name of a city and a state

—Between the day and the year when writing a date

—After the greeting of a letter

—After the closing of a letter

2. Constructs paragraphs identifying indentation and margins.
3. Demonstrates ability to proofread written work.
4. Demonstrates increasing ability to transfer mechanics of composition and usage to functional and creative writing.
5. Demonstrates ability to select the correct form of the following words in written work:

a-an	I-me
ate-eat-eaten	is-are
broke-broken	run-ran
came-come	see-saw-seen
do-did-done	took-taken
doesn't-don't	she-her
gave-give-given	was-were
he-him	we-us
Double negatives	went-gone

Avoidance of *he, she, it, we, they,* following a stated subject, i.e., "Mary, *she* went to the store."

Avoidance of *here* and *there,* following *this, that, these, those.*

6. Writes correctly a friendly letter.
7. Writes the addresses on envelopes using correct capitalization, punctuation, and form.

STRUCTURE OF LANGUAGE

1. Identifies three basic sentence types and their end punctuation:
   Telling or declarative
   Asking or interrogative
   Exclamatory

2. Demonstrates continuing ability to identify the structural elements of the English language:

Letters

Words

Phrases

Sentences

Paragraphs

3. Demonstrates ability to identify the main idea in a paragraph.

VOCABULARY DEVELOPMENT

1. Builds additional developmental vocabulary.
2. Builds additional listening, speaking, reading, and writing vocabulary and associates meaning to new words acquired.

COMPREHENSION

1. Demonstrates ability to read increasingly longer units of material with accuracy and comprehension and with less guidance.
2. Demonstrates ability to expand literal comprehension skills:

Specific information

Sequence

3. Demonstrates ability to expand interpretive comprehension skills:

Main idea and supporting details

Relationships

Figurative and special language

Inferences

4. Demonstrates ability to expand critical-evaluative comprehension skills:

Prediction of outcomes

Evaluation of accuracy

Literary forms and author techniques

Characterization

SELF-SELECTION

1. Demonstrates continuing ability to select and read trade books and other printed material in terms of interest and needs.
2. Demonstrates continuing ability to identify and evaluate literary forms and author techniques while developing a positive attitude toward reading and an appreciation for books.

STUDY SKILLS

1. Demonstrates ability to maintain and refine the study skills identified at Level 4.
2. Demonstrates ability to follow multiple steps in oral and written directions.
3. Demonstrates ability to adjust silent reading rate to type of material and purposes.
4. Demonstrates ability to alphabetize words to the second letter. 247

5. Demonstrates ability to use a primary dictionary.
6. Demonstrates ability to use an encyclopedia.
7. Demonstrates ability to apply simple map and globe skills.
8. Demonstrates ability to interpret a diagram.
9. Constructs simple outlines.
10. Demonstrates ability to utilize note-taking techniques in preparing an outline for a summary.

HANDWRITING

1. Demonstrates correct position of body, feet, hands, paper, crayon, pencil, and chalk at desk and at chalkboard while making basic cursive strokes.
2. Differentiates and makes all upper- and lower-case letters of the cursive alphabet.
3. Forms the numerals 1-10 with cursive slant.
4. Demonstrates ability to write words and sentences observing proper spacing.
5. Identifies the following terminology related to cursive writing:

Beginning stroke	Ending stroke
Cane-stem letter	Loop
Check-stroke	Oval
Compound curve	Overcurve
Connecting stroke	Retrace
Cursive	Slant
Downcurve	Undercurve
Downstroke	

SPELLING

1. Refer to Level 4

LEVEL 7

PHONIC ANALYSIS

1. Demonstrates ability to maintain and apply all phonetic skills introduced in this category at preceding levels.
2. Identifies consonant irregularities as an aid to word recognition.
3. Identifies irregular vowel digraphs as an aid to word recognition.
4. Identifies the diacritical marks—breve and macron.

STRUCTURAL ANALYSIS (Reinforcement of all preceding skills; extension of syllabication principles)

1. Demonstrates increasing ability to identify the following structural properties of words as an aid to recognition:
    a. Inflectional endings (s, d, ed, ing, es)
    b. Compound words

    c.   Contractions
    d.   Root words
    e.   Suffixes (er, est, ly, ful, ish, less, y, ness)
    f.   Verbs which double the final consonant before *ed, ing, er, est*
    g.   Verbs which drop the final *e* before *ing*
    h.   Plurals formed by adding *es* to words ending in *s, ss, ch, sh, x*
    i.   Plurals of words ending in *y*
    j.   Suffixes added to words ending in *y* or silent *e*
    k.   Possessives *'s, s'*
    l.   Hearing syllables
    m.   Hearing accent
    n.   Each syllable usually has one vowel sound
    o.   Dividing words into syllables in v-c-c-v words
    p.   Prefixes
    q.   Forming plurals of words ending in *f* or *fe*
    r.   Common syllables *a, be*

2. Identifies *ed* as a syllable when added to root words ending in *d* or *t.*
3. Identifies the vowel-consonant-vowel pattern (v-c-v) in words and uses it to divide words into syllables.
4. Identifies the common syllable at the end of words made of *le* and the consonant immediately preceding the *le.*
5. Notes that, as a general rule, words are not divided between consonant digraphs and consonant blends.
6. Notes that prefixes and suffixes generally form separate syllables.
7. Applies vowel generalizations to accented syllables.
8. Discriminates between solid and hyphenated compound words and divides them into syllables.

ORAL LANGUAGE DEVELOPMENT

1. See Level 6.

Note: Add the following words to Item 3.

are-aren't	to-too-two
bring-brought	them-this-those
feed-fed	write-wrote-written
get-got	No words and Not words
hasn't any	

(Not words are contractions made by adding the short form of not-n't to other words. No words are words such as never, no, none, nobody, no one, nowhere, nothing. No words and not words are never used together in a sentence.)

WRITTEN LANGUAGE DEVELOPMENT

1. Demonstrates ability to maintain and apply skills from previous levels.   249

2. Discriminates between an apostrophe used in a contraction and an apostrophe used to show possession.
3. Demonstrates ability to write answers to comprehension questions.
4. Indicates titles by underlining.
5. See Level 6

Note: Add the following words to Item 5:

are-aren't	to-too-two
bring-brought	them-this-those
feed-fed	write-wrote-written
get-got	No words and Not words
hasn't any	

6. Demonstrates ability to write a simple book report.

STRUCTURE OF LANGUAGE

1. Demonstrates ability to maintain and apply skills from previous levels.
2. Identifies nouns, verbs, and adjectives as word form classes and classifies words into these categories.
3. Identifies comparative and superlative degree of adjectives.
4. Identifies the command as a sentence type.

VOCABULARY DEVELOPMENT

1. Builds additional developmental vocabulary.
2. Builds additional listening, speaking, reading, and writing vocabulary and associates meaning to new words acquired.
3. Constructs simple analogies.

COMPREHENSION

1. See Level 6.

SELF-SELECTION

1. See Level 6.

STUDY SKILLS

1. Demonstrates ability to maintain and refine study skills from previous levels.
2. Demonstrates ability to state and apply the strategy for recognizing new words.
3. Demonstrates ability to alphabetize words to the third letter.
4. Locates information by using guide words.

HANDWRITING

250 1. Refer to Level 6.

SPELLING

1. Refer to Level 4.

LEVEL 8

PHONIC ANALYSIS

1. Demonstrates ability to apply the following skills of phonic analysis in decoding new words in basal readers, trade books, and content material at a 4^1 level of difficulty:
   a. Single consonants in initial, final, and medial position
   b. Consonant blends in initial and final position
   c. Consonant digraphs
   d. Rhyming parts (constructing words through substituting initial sounds)
   e. Long and short vowel sounds
   f. Vowel digraphs
   g. Exceptions to vowel generalizations
   h. Vowel sounds affected by *r*
   i. Vowel *a* followed by *l* or *ll*
   j. The *oo* sounds
   k. Diphthongs
   !. Two sounds of *ow*
2. Applies the sounds produced by consonant irregularities as an aid to word recognition.
3. Demonstrates ability to decode words containing silent consonants.
4. Identifies the schwa sound in unaccented syllables.

STRUCTURAL ANALYSIS

1. Demonstrates ability to apply the following structural skills in decoding new words in basal readers, trade books, and content material at a 4^1 level of difficulty:
   a. Identifies syllables
   b. Identifies accent
   c. Divides words into syllables in v-c-c-v words
   d. Divides words into syllables in v-c-v words
   e. Identifies prefixes and suffixes as separate syllables
   f. Divides words with consonant digraphs and consonant blends
   g. Identifies open and closed syllables
2. Identifies the word endings *s, d, ed,* and *ing.*
3. Identifies compound words when made from one known and one unknown word.
4. Constructs and identifies contractions.
5. Identifies and names the structural parts of a word—"root" or "base" word and "affixes."
6. Demonstrates ability to add endings to root words that necessitate structural changes in the root word.

7. Identifies irregular plurals.
8. Identifies the plural possessive and discriminates between singular and plural possessives.
9. Identifies *a* and *be* as common syllabic units.
10. Identifies *ed* as a syllable when added to root words ending in *d* or *t.*
11. Identifies the common syllable at the end of words made of *le* and the consonant immediately preceding the *le.*
12. Discriminates between solid and hyphenated compound words and divides them into syllables.
13. Applies the principles of syllabication to polysyllabic words.
14. Identifies exceptions to syllabic generalizations.
15. Applies the rule requiring the use of a hyphen when separating a word at the end of a line.
16. Identifies the following prefixes added to root words:

non-	fore-
mis-	ante-
post-	trans-
anti-	pre-
semi-	im-
de-	micro-
ex-	under-
super-	inter-

17. Identifies the following suffixes added to root words:

-or	-n
-hood	-self
-like	-fully
-able	-lessly
-en	-ous
-ive	-tion
-ion	-al
-ment	-ation
-ess	-ship
-ward	-ty
-tween	-sion

Note: In teaching both prefixes and suffixes, teach only those from above list that appear in content being used.

ORAL LANGUAGE DEVELOPMENT

1. Demonstrates continued growth in expressional skills through:

Discussions	Oral planning
Story telling	Sharing experiences
Dramatization	Reporting
Oral reading	Conversations
Dramatic play	Summarizing
Oral descriptions	Choral Speaking

2. Demonstrates continuing growth in oral reading in fluency, increased eye-voice span, and interpretation of the printed text through use of intonation, inflection, pitch, rhythm, and the identification of punctuation clues.
3. Identifies the correct form when using the following words in spontaneous conversation, informal, and formal oral productions:

a-an	are-aren't	doesn't-don't
ate-eat-eaten	bring-brought	gave-give-given
broke-broken	feed-fed	has gone-have gone
came-come	get-got	see-saw-seen
do-did-done	hasn't any	to-too-two
he-him	I-me	them-this-those
is-are	run-ran	write-wrote-written
she-her	took-taken	good-better-best
was-were	we-us	bad-worse-worst
went-gone	let-leave	No words and Not words
good-well	sit-set	
teach-learn	they-them	

(*Not-words* are contractions made by adding the short form of not-n't to other words. *No-words* are words such as never, no, none, nobody, no one, nowhere, nothing. *No-words* and *not-words* are never used together in a sentence.)

Avoidance of *he, she, it, we, they* following a stated subject, i.e., "Mary, *she* went to the store."

Avoidance of *here* and *there* following *this, that, these, those.*

4. Demonstrates ability to state simple oral reports.
5. Constructs stories and states them in story form.
6. States multiple-step directions accurately and follows them carefully.

WRITTEN LANGUAGE DEVELOPMENT

1. Demonstrates ability to apply written language skills identified at Levels 6 and 7.
2. Demonstrates ability to select the correct form of the following words in written work:

a-an	took-taken	good-well
he-him	we-us	let-leave
I-me	went-gone	teach-learn
is-are	ate-eat-eaten	here is-here are
she-her	broke-broken	where is-where are
was-were	came-come	bring-brought
sit-set	do-did-done	hasn't any
are-aren't	doesn't-don't	to-too-two
feed-fed	gave-give-given	them-this-those
get-got	has gone-have gone	write-wrote-written
run-ran	see-saw-seen	No-words and Not-words

(*Not-words* are contractions made by adding the short form of not-n't to other words. *No-words* are words such as never, no, none, nobody, no one, nowhere, nothing. *No-words* and *not-words* are never used together in a sentence.) 253

they-them
good-better-best
bad-worse-worst

Avoidance of *here* and *there* following *this, that, these* and *those*. Avoidance of *he, she, it, we, they* following a stated subject, i.e., "Mary, *she* went to the store."

3. Selects closings for friendly letters that are appropriate for the person to whom the letter is written such as:

Sincerely	Love	Your loving nephew
Respectfully	Your grandaughter	Affectionately
Your friend		

4. Writes correctly a "thank-you" letter.
5. Writes correctly an invitation.
6. Constructs a book list.
7. Demonstrates increasing proficiency in transferring mechanics of composition and usage to functional and creative writing.

STRUCTURE OF LANGUAGE

1. Demonstrates continuing ability to identify the structural elements of the English language at a 4^1 level of difficulty
   a. Letters
   b. Words
   c. Phrases
   d. Sentences
   e. Paragraphs
   f. Parts of speech

2. Student writes an imperative sentence.
3. Identifies the two major parts of a sentence.

   Subject and predicate both simple and complete (noun phrase and verb phrase)

4. Identifies the topic sentence of a paragraph.
5. Writes a good paragraph built around a topic sentence.

VOCABULARY DEVELOPMENT

1. Builds additional developmental vocabulary.
2. Builds additional listening, speaking, reading, and writing vocabulary and associates meaning with new words acquired.
3. Acquires specialized vocabulary indigenous to different subject areas.
4. Differentiates meanings for words claimed in two subject fields.
5. Selects the correct meaning for polysemantic words used in different subject contexts.

COMPREHENSION

1. Demonstrates ability to read increasingly longer units of material at a 4^1 level of difficulty in various literary forms and content material and apply skills of literal, interpretive, and critical-evaluative comprehension.
2. Demonstrates ability to expand interpretive comprehension skills.
   Main idea and supporting details
   Relationships
   Figurative and special language
   Inferences
3. Demonstrates ability to expand critical-evaluative comprehension skills.
   Prediction of outcomes
   Evaluation of accuracy
   Literary forms and author
   Techniques
   Characterization
4. Identifies major patterns found in science content, adjusts reading rate to the specific pattern, and applies both the comprehension and study skills necessary in working with the pattern.
5. Identifies major patterns found in social studies content, adjusts reading rate to the specific pattern, and applies both the comprehension and study skills necessary in working with the pattern.
6. Identifies major patterns found in mathematics content, adjusts reading rate to the specific pattern, and applies both the comprehension and study skills necessary in working with the pattern.
7. Applies comprehension skills stated above to listening activities.

SELF-SELECTION

1. See Levels 3 and 6 under Self-Selection Category.

STUDY SKILLS

1. Demonstrates ability to maintain and refine study skills from previous levels.
2. Constructs a strategy for following written directions.
3. Locates specific information through use of a table of contents.
4. Demonstrates ability to alphabetize words to the fourth letter and beyond.
5. Demonstrates ability to use alphabetical order to locate information in reference books.
6. Locates information by using guide words.
7. Selects and verifies word meanings in relation to context.
8. Demonstrates ability to use a pronunciation key to interpret dictionary respellings.
9. Identifies and discriminates primary and secondary accent.
10. Selects the volume in which to look for a given topic and locates the pages on which the given matter is treated.

11. Demonstrates ability to read maps and globes for information.
12. Demonstrates ability to read graphs for information.
   Pictorial
   Bar
   Line
   Circle

HANDWRITING

1. Demonstrates increasing proficiency and refinement of skills in cursive handwriting.
2. Demonstrates ability to maintain manuscript form for:
   Charts
   Application Forms
   Class Record Lists
   Special Needs

SPELLING

1. Refer to Level 4.

LEVEL 9

PHONIC ANALYSIS

1. Demonstrates ability to maintain and refine all previous skills in phonic analysis:
   a. Single consonants in initial, final, and medial position
   b. Consonant blends in initial and final position
   c. Consonant digraphs
   d. Rhyming parts (Constructing words through substituting initial sounds)
   e. Consonant irregularities
   f. Silent consonants in specific combinations
   g. Long and short vowel sounds
   h. Vowel digraphs
   i. Vowel generalizations
   j. Exceptions to generalizations
   k. Vowel sounds affected by *r*
   l. Vowel *a* followed by *l* and *ll*
   m. The *oo* sound
   n. Diphthongs
   o. Two sounds of *ow*
   p. Irregular vowel digraphs
   q. Diacritical marks
   r. Schwa

STRUCTURAL ANALYSIS

1. Demonstrates ability to maintain and refine all previous skills in structural analysis:
   a. Inflectional endings (s, d, ed, ing, es)
   b. Compound words
   c. Contractions
   d. Root words
   e. Suffixes (er, est, ly, ful, ish, less, y, ness)
   f. Verbs which double the final consonant before *ed, ing, er, est*
   g. Verbs which drop the final *e* before *ing*
   h. Plurals formed by adding *es* to words ending in *s, ss, ch, sh, x*
   i. Plurals of words ending in *y*
   j. Suffixes added to words ending in *y* or silent *e*
   k. Possessives *'s, s'*
   l. Identifying syllables
   m. Hearing accent
   n. Dividing words into syllables in v-c-c-v words
   o. Prefixes (dis, en, in, re, un)
   p. Forming plurals of words ending in *f* or *fe*
   q. Common syllables *a, be*
   r. The syllable *ed*
   s. Dividing words into syllables in v-c-v words
   t. The consonant plus *le* syllable
   u. Prefixes and suffixes as separate syllables
   v. Syllabicating words containing consonant blends and digraphs
   w. Open and closed syllables
   x. Solid and hyphenated compound words

ORAL LANGUAGE DEVELOPMENT

1. See Level 8.

Note: Skills identified at Level 8 are to be extended and refined.

2. Demonstrates correct telephone behavior.

WRITTEN LANGUAGE DEVELOPMENT

1. See Level 8.

Note: Skills identified at Level 8 are to be extended and refined at a 4^2 level of difficulty.

2. Demonstrates the ability to write a friendly letter independently.
3. Writes correctly a business letter applying the following rules:
   a. A business letter must have a purpose.
   b. It must be brief as well as complete.
   c. It must be neat and clearly written.
   d. Punctuation and form must be correct.

257

4. Identifies written format of a poem.
5. Constructs written book reports.
6. Constructs a written story.
7. Writes direct quotations applying rules of capitalization and punctuation.

STRUCTURE OF LANGUAGE

1. Refer to Level 8.

Note: Skills identified at Level 8 are to be extended at a 4^2 level of difficulty.

2. Identifies parts of speech.

VOCABULARY DEVELOPMENT

1. Builds additional developmental vocabulary.
2. Refer to Level 8.

Note: Skills 2-5 identified at Level 8 are to be extended and refined at a 4^2 level of difficulty.

COMPREHENSION

1. Demonstrates ability to read increasingly longer units of material at a 4^2 level of difficulty in various literary forms and apply the skills of literal, interpretive, and critical-evaluative comprehension.
2. Demonstrates increasing proficiency in identifying major patterns in content area reading, in adjusting reading rate to specific pattern, and in applying comprehension and study skills necessary in working with the pattern.
3. Applies comprehension skills to listening activities.

SELF-SELECTION

1. See Levels 3 and 6 under self-selection category.

STUDY SKILLS

1. Demonstrates ability to maintain and refine study skills from previous levels.
2. Demonstrates ability to follow the SQ3R study plan.
3. Locates specific information in reference material by using the index.
4. Demonstrates ability to locate information by using the following parts of a book:
   Preface
   Table of Contents
   Glossary
   Index
   Title Page
   Copyright Date
5. Identifies key words in topic sentences and locates information in an index by the key word.

6. Demonstrates ability to read tables.
7. Demonstrates ability to locate and organize material for a written report.
8. Demonstrates ability to organize material for an oral report.

(Note: The above study skills should be developed during directed reading activities in content material. Most directed reading at this and following levels should be in content books with the primary purpose of developing study skills. Basal readers may be used periodically to refine and extend comprehension skills and for any re-teaching necessary in phonic and structural analysis.)

HANDWRITING

1. Refer to Level 8.

SPELLING

1. Refer to Level 4.

LEVEL 10

PHONIC ANALYSIS

1. Refer to Level 8.

STRUCTURAL ANALYSIS

1. Refer to Level 8 adding the following prefixes and suffixes:

Prefixes

mono-	dis-
uni-	mal-
bi-	mid-
tri-	mis-
deca-	un-
omni-	auto-
pan-	bio-
para-	hydro-
circum-	lith-
com-, con-	phono-
extra-	photo-
intra-	tele-
sub-	

Suffixes

-eer	-meter
-ier	-ology
-ster	-phobia
-ist	-scope

259

-arium	-most
-cide	-ic
-ee	-al
-gram	

Note: Some of these suffixes are used to form nouns and adjectives causing base words to change parts of speech, i.e., "employ"—"employee."

2. Identifies exceptions to syllabic generalizations.
3. Applies the rule requiring the use of a hyphen when separating a word at the end of a line.

ORAL LANGUAGE DEVELOPMENT

1. Demonstrates the human need to communicate through continued growth in expressional skills in:

Discussions	Sharing experiences
Story telling	Reporting
Dramatization	Conversations
Oral reading	Summarizing
Dramatic play	Choral speaking
Oral descriptions	Telephone behavior
Oral planning	

2. Demonstrates continuing growth in oral reading in fluency, increased eye-voice span, and interpretation of the printed text through use of intonation, inflection, pitch, rhythm, and the identification of punctuation clues.
3. Selects correct word forms in spontaneous conversation, informal, and formal oral productions. See Level 8, Skill 3 and add the following words:

began-begun	sang-sung
drank-drunk	spoke-spoken
chose-chosen	threw-thrown
fell-fallen	wrote-written
grew-grown	rode-ridden
knew-known	stole-stolen
rang-rung	

4. Demonstrates ability to state oral reports.
5. Constructs stories and states them in story form.
6. States multiple-step directions accurately and follows them carefully.
7. Demonstrates ability to make introductions with poise.
8. Demonstrates ability to extend and refine ability to handle introductions.
9. Demonstrates ability to give a book talk.

WRITTEN LANGUAGE DEVELOPMENT

1. Demonstrates ability to apply written language skills identified at levels 6, 7, 8, and 9. Note: Add the following words to Level 8, Skill 2:

began-begun	sang-sung
drank-drunk	spoke-spoken

chose-chosen	threw-thrown
fell-fallen	wrote-written
grew-grown	rode-ridden
knew-known	stole-stolen
rang-rung	

2. Identifies proper adjectives formed from proper nouns and capitalizes each one.
3. Applies the following rules for using commas:
   a. To separate the day of the month from the year, and after the year if the date appears in the middle of the sentence.
   b. To separate the name of a city from the name of the state and country in which it is located
   c. To set off the name of a person spoken to or about
   d. After the word "yes," "no," or "well" when a pause follows
   e. To set apart words in a series
   f. To separate words like "he said" from a direct quotation
   g. After the greeting of a friendly letter and the closing of any letter
   h. When "and," "but," and "or" are used to combine two sentences into one, place a comma before these connective words

4. Identifies and interprets the purpose of varying type style and punctuation in written language

Ellipsis	Quotation marks
Dash	Comma
Italics	Semi-colon
Period	Apostrophe
Colon	Parenthesis

Exclamation point
Question mark

5. Writes answers to invitations.

STRUCTURE OF LANGUAGE

1. Demonstrates continuing ability to identify the structural elements of the English language at a 5^1 level of difficulty.
   a. Letters
   b. Words
   c. Phrases
   d. Sentences
   e. Paragraphs
   f. Parts of speech

2. Identifies a topic sentence regardless of its position in a paragraph.
3. Discriminates between "its" as a possessive pronoun and "it's" as a contraction of the pronoun "it" and the verb "is."
4. Identifies adjectives by position in sentence, differentiating between those coming before a noun and those that follow verbs like *am, are, is, was, will be, were, became, grew, looked, felt*, and *seemed*.

5. Demonstrates ability to use the correct form of the verb "to be."

VOCABULARY DEVELOPMENT

1. Builds additional developmental vocabulary.
2. Refer to Level 8, Skills 2,3,4, and 5 and maintain and refine these skills at a 5^1 level of complexity.
3. Demonstrates ability to make word analogies.

COMPREHENSION

1. Demonstrates ability to read increasingly longer units of material at a 5^1 level of difficulty in various literary forms and content material and apply the skills of literal, interpretive, and critical-evaluative comprehension.
2. Demonstrates increasing proficiency in identifying major patterns in content area reading, in adjusting reading rate to specific patterns, and in applying comprehension and study skills necessary in working with the patterns.
3. Applies comprehension skills to listening activities.

SELF-SELECTION

1. See Levels 3 and 6 under Self-Selection Category.

STUDY SKILLS

1. Demonstrates ability to maintain and refine study skills from previous levels adjusting to a 5^1 level of difficulty.
2. Demonstrates ability to locate fiction books in the library through their alphabetical arrangement according to the last names of the authors.
3. Demonstrates ability to locate non-fiction books by the ten main categories of the Dewey Decimal System.
4. Demonstrates ability to locate a biography by its call letters.
5. Demonstrates ability to use the card catalogue in locating the call number or call letters of a book.
6. Locates material by using a cross-reference.
7. Demonstrates ability to use a dictionary to identify word origins and the part of speech of the entry word.
8. Locates information about important persons, places, and historical events in dictionaries.
9. Demonstrates ability to read diagrams.

HANDWRITING

1. Demonstrates increasing proficiency and refinement of skills in cursive handwriting.

2. Demonstrates ability to maintain manuscript form for:
    —Charts
    —Application Forms
    —Class Record Lists
    —Special Needs

SPELLING

1. Refer to Level 4

LEVEL 11

PHONIC ANALYSIS

1. Refer to Level 9.

STRUCTURAL ANALYSIS

1. Refer to Levels 9 and 10 adjusting material to a 5^2 level of difficulty.

ORAL LANGUAGE DEVELOPMENT

1. See Level 10

Note: Skills identified at Level 10 are to be extended and refined.

2. Demonstrates ability to conduct a personal interview.
3. Demonstrates ability to initiate, continue, and conclude a conversation.

WRITTEN LANGUAGE DEVELOPMENT

1. Demonstrates ability to maintain and refine the written language skills identified at Levels 6, 7, 8, 9, and 10 by applying them to written composition.
2. Writes titles and authors correctly.
3. Identifies meaning, correct spelling, and punctuation of various abbreviations met in a variety of contexts. (Those listed are only suggestive; teach what the pupil meets and needs.)
    —Days of the week
    —Months of the year
    —States
    —Titles of people
    —Parts of speech
    —Measurement
    —Common abbreviations used in address (st., blvd., rd.)
    —Others such as: a.m., p.m., Co., Inc. Mt., R.R., C.O.D., P.O.
4. Chooses from the following a courteous and business-like closing for a business letter:

263

Yours sincerely,
Sincerely yours,
Very sincerely yours,
Yours truly,
Yours very truly,
Very truly yours,

STRUCTURE OF LANGUAGE

1. Refer to Level 10

Note: Skills identified at Level 10 are to be extended and refined at a 5^2 level of difficulty.

2. Identifies adverbs and discriminates the meaning they add to verbs by giving time (when), place (where), and manner (how).

VOCABULARY DEVELOPMENT

1. Builds additional developmental vocabulary.
2. Maintains and refines at a 5^2 level of difficulty skills identified at Levels 8 and 10.

COMPREHENSION

1. Demonstrates ability to read increasingly longer units of material at a 5^2 level of difficulty in various literary forms and applies the skills of literal, interpretative, and critical-evaluative comprehension.
2. Demonstrates increasing proficiency in identifying major patterns in content area reading, in adjusting reading rate to specific pattern, and in applying comprehension and study skills necessary in working with the pattern.
3. Applies comprehension skills to listening activities.

SELF-SELECTION

1. See Levels 3 and 6 under Self-Selection category.

STUDY SKILLS

1. Demonstrates ability to maintain and refine study skills from previous levels adjusting material to a 5^2 level of difficulty.
2. Writes a three step outline.

HANDWRITING

1. Refer to Level 10.

SPELLING

264   1. Refer to Level 4.

LEVEL 12

PHONIC ANALYSIS

1. Refer to Level 8.

STRUCTURAL ANALYSIS

1. Refer to Levels 8 and 10 adding the following prefixes and suffixes if they are encountered in content being used for instructional purposes.

Prefixes

pro-	em-
out-	ill-
self-	ir-
enter-	col-
cor-	co-
mal-	

Suffixes

-ary	-ant
-ure	-ence
-ative	-wise
-let	-fold
-archy	-itis
-ity	-ance
-ible	

ORAL LANGUAGE DEVELOPMENT

1. Demonstrates continuing growth and proficiency in applying skills identified at Levels 10 and 11.
2. Constructs a panel discussion observing the following guide:
   a. Be prepared to talk intelligently by thinking, reading, asking questions, and by researching the topic
   b. Discuss only the topic; avoid irrelevancies
   c. Listen to and think about contributions of other panel members
   d. Make your statements as brief as possible
   e. Do not interrupt other speakers under any circumstances

WRITTEN LANGUAGE DEVELOPMENT

1. Demonstrates ability to apply written language skills identified at Levels 6, 7, 8, 9, 10 and 11 substituting 6[1] level material for instructional tasks.
2. Writes first letter of names of races, religions, nationalities and language with capital letter.
3. Writes the first letter of the names of clubs, organizations, and business firms with capital letters.

4. Demonstrates ability to capitalize and punctuate sentences containing broken quotations.
5. Applies the following rules for using a colon:
   a. After the salutation of a business letter
   b. To separate hours from minutes in telling time
   c. To introduce a list except when the list directly follows a verb or preposition
6. Applies the following rules for using a semicolon:
   a. In place of a conjunction between two closely related independent clauses
   b. Before connecting words like *besides, however, moreover, nevertheless, then, therefore*
   c. Between items in a series if the series contains commas

STRUCTURE OF LANGUAGE

1. Demonstrates continuing ability to identify the structural elements of the English language at a 6^1 level of difficulty.
   a. Letters
   b. Words
   c. Phrases
   d. Sentences
   e. Paragraphs
   f. Parts of speech
2. Identifies transitional words and phrases in paragraphs by applying the technique of asking "What word or words in this sentence tie it to an earlier sentence?"
3. Identifies common words that signal nouns (Determiners)

Articles	*Numbers*
the	one
a	two
an	three

Demonstratives	*Indefinites*
this	every
that	many
these	any
those	several
	each
	both
	some

4. Identifies common prepositions.

of	to	at	into	between	over
in	for	on	under	down	across
by	with	from	toward	among	against

5. Identifies pronouns as parts of speech and applies the following rules relative to their usage:

   a. Pronouns take the place of nouns.

b. Pronouns can be either singular or plural.

c. These pronouns are used as the subjects of verbs: I, we, he, she, they.

d. These pronouns are used as objects of both verbs and prepositions: me, us, him, her, them.

e. When a pronoun and a noun are used as a compound subject, use a subject pronoun.

f. When a pronoun and noun are used as the subject of a verb, use a subject pronoun.

g. Use a subject pronoun after forms of the very "to be."

h. Most pronouns have two possessive forms. *My, your, her, its, ours,* and *theirs* are used only when the possessive is followed by a noun. *Mine, yours, hers, ours,* and *theirs* are used when the possessive pronoun stands alone. *His* is used either before nouns or alone.

6. Identifies the three basic functions of nouns:
   a. Subject
   b. Object of verb
   c. Object of preposition

7. Identifies compound subjects and compound predicates.

8. Identifies a compound sentence as two independent clauses joined by connectives such as *and, but,* and *or.*

9. Identifies dependent clauses through naming signal words used to introduce them.

who	that	after
which	when	before
while	where	although
why	how	since
		because

10. Constructs sentences which demonstrate agreement in number and person between subject and verb according to the following rules:
    a. In the present tense a verb is said to agree in number with its subject.
    b. In the past tense, verbs have the same form with singular or plural subjects. The only exception is *be.*
    c. In the present tense, verbs normally add *-s,* or *-es* to agree with third person singular subjects.
    d. The present tense forms of *be* are *am, is, are. Am* is used with subject *I; is* is used with a third-person singular subject; *are* is used with plural subjects and *you.*

11. Identifies the principal parts of irregular verbs. (begin-began-begun; choose, chose, choosen; go-went-gone, etc.)

VOCABULARY DEVELOPMENT

1. Builds additional developmental vocabulary.
2. Refer to Level 8, Skills 2,3,4, and 5 and Level 10, Skill 3 and maintain and refine these skills at a 6^1 level of difficulty.

COMPREHENSION

1. Demonstrates ability to read increasingly longer units of material at a 6^1 level of difficulty in various literary forms and content material and apply the skills of literal, interpretive, and critical-evaluative comprehension.
2. Demonstrates increasing proficiency in identifying major patterns in content area reading, in adjusting reading rate to specific patterns, and in applying comprehension and study skills necessary in working with the patterns.
3. Applies comprehension skills to listening activities.

SELF-SELECTION

1. See Levels 3 and 6 under Self-Selection Category.

STUDY SKILLS

1. Demonstrates ability to maintain and refine study skills from previous levels adjusting to a 6^1 level of difficulty.
2. Locates specific information in an encyclopedia by using subheadings.
3. Compares information concerning a common entry to using two encyclopedias.
4. Locates specific information in an encyclopedia by using cross references.
5. Locates the call numbers of library books by using the card catalog.
6. Locates author, subject, and title cards in the card catalog.
7. Locates bibliographic information concerning specific books by using the card catalog.
8. Locates specific information by using the key to the index of a book.
9. Selects relevant headlines for newspaper articles.
10. Locates and distinguishes between types of information in various sections of a newspaper.

HANDWRITING

1. Demonstrates increasing proficiency and refinement of skills in cursive handwriting.
2. Demonstrates ability to maintain manuscript form for:
    —Charts
    —Application Forms
    —Class Record Lists
    —Special Needs

SPELLING

1. Refer to Level 4.

LEVEL 13

PHONIC ANALYSIS

1. Refer to Level 9.

STRUCTURAL ANALYSIS

1. Refer to Levels 9, 10 and 12 adjusting material to a 6^2 level of difficulty.

ORAL LANGUAGE DEVELOPMENT

1. Demonstrates ability to maintain and refine skills identified at Levels 10, 11, and 12.

WRITTEN LANGUAGE DEVELOPMENT

1. Demonstrates ability to maintain and refine the written language skills identified at Levels 6, 7, 8, 9, 10, 11, and 12 by applying them to written composition.

STRUCTURE OF LANGUAGE

1. Refer to Level 12.

Note: Skills identified at Level 12 are to be extended and refined at a 6^2 level of difficulty.

VOCABULARY DEVELOPMENT

1. Builds additional developmental vocabulary.
2. Maintains and refines at a 6^2 level of difficulty skills identified at Levels 8 and 10.
3. Identifies the following language forms:
    a. Slang
    b. Euphemism
    c. Dialect
    d. Echoic words
    e. Archaic expressions
    f. Recently coined words
    g. Words borrowed from other languages
    h. Idioms
    i. Colloquialisms

COMPREHENSION

1. Demonstrates ability to read increasingly longer units of material at a 6^2 level of difficulty in various literary forms and applies the skills of literal, interpretative, and critical-evaluative comprehension.
2. Demonstrates increasing proficiency in identifying major patterns in content area of reading, in adjusting reading rate to specific pattern, and study skills necessary in working with the pattern.

3. Applies comprehension skills to listening activities.

SELF-SELECTION

1. See Levels 3 and 6 under Self-Selection Category.

STUDY SKILLS

1. Demonstrates ability to maintain and refine study skills from previous levels adjusting material to a 6^2 level of difficulty.
2. Compares the functions and coverage of specific magazines.
3. Locates the following information about a magazine:

Editor	Publisher
Editorials	Contents
Date of publication	

4. Compares and contrasts various types of magazines.

Sports	Science
Mechanics	Nature
News	Hobby
Fashion	Home

5. Classifies advertisements in newspapers or magazines according to type of propaganda.
6. Differentiates between the usage of the abridged and unabridged dictionaries.
7. Locates origins, histories, and meanings of words in an unabridged dictionary.
8. Demonstrates ability to use the dictionary to locate abbreviations, signs, symbols, proofreader's marks, biographical names, pronouncing gazeteer, and forms of address.
9. Selects correct source for specific reference problems from the following:
   Reader's Guide to Periodical Literature
   The World Almanac
   The Library Catalog
   Roget's Thesaurus
   Atlases
   Who's Who in America
   Subject Index to Poetry
   Other common reference materials and anthologies
10. Lists information on specific books in correct bibliographic form.

HANDWRITING

1. Refer to Level 12.

SPELLING

270   1. Refer to Level 4.

*EVALUATION INSTRUMENT—LEVEL 0

MAJOR CATEGORY: AUDITORY DISCRIMINATION

1. Given the following pairs of words stated orally by teacher, student responds orally by stating whether pairs are the same words or not:

car - car	yes - yes
dog - big	went - want
fat - vine	this - this
look - look	then - where
house - horse	thing - think
of - off	zoom - zoom
and - can	our - out

2. Given the following pairs of words stated orally by the teacher, student responds orally by stating whether the word pairs rhyme or not:

cake - lake	cold - kite
mark - feet	hill - will
plate - door	rug - rode
call - fall	sit - hit
back - cow	nest - tree
ran - fan	bad - walk
cat - sat	look - talk
duck - tack	neck - nice
may - way	not - got
night - green	down - brown
sing - hen	bell - book
ten - pen	find - sand
let - met	fun - sun

MAJOR CATEGORY: VISUAL DISCRIMINATION

3. Using the following shapes: circle, square, and rectangle, student responds orally to the following kinds of questions with correct responses:
   a. Show me something big, little, tall, short.
   b. Find something that has the same shape as this. . . , and hold up the various shapes.
   c. Line up the children at the fountain. Tell the student to touch the one that is last; the one that is first; the one in the middle.
   d. Put your finger on the door knob; on the window pane; on the waste basket.
4. Given color chips of red, orange, yellow, green, blue, purple, brown, black, student names the color of each one.
5. Given a printed list of 5 first names, student points to his own name.

*Authors' Note: Since the evaluation instrument included from Frederick County must be adapted to your district and to your materials, we have replaced the material under the Listening Skills and Comprehension categories at all levels. Instead we've given you directions on how to administer this test using your own textbooks. We've enclosed the directions in parentheses.

6. Given the following lines of letters and words written in manuscript form, the student points to the letter or word which is the same as the first letter or word.

E	E	T	F	H
l	L	l	T	F
b	d	b	p	q
P	R	D	P	B
u	v	w	y	u
l	k	j	l	t

mother	father	brother	sister	mother
kitten	mitten	little	kitten	funny
went	went	want	with	what
wet	pet	get	bet	wet
big	bag	bug	beg	big
can	cat	can	cap	car

7. Given the following sentence in manuscript writing, student identifies the visual form of a word by framing at least two words and pointing to two spaces:

The dog ran down the street.

MAJOR CATEGORY: VISUAL-MOTOR COORDINATION

8. Given an irregular shape drawn on paper, student cuts out shape without deviating from line by more than 1/8 inch.
9. Given a page of pictures (3 pictures to a row; 3 rows to the page), student names pictures in left-to-right; top-to-bottom progression.

MAJOR CATEGORY: LISTENING SKILLS

10. (For this test, get a 100 to 150 word selection from a picture book. Read this selection to the child. Ask the child about 10 to 15 questions concerning the selection. He should answer approximately 80% of these correctly. Include questions that will test the child's ability to deal with the following aspects of comprehension: (1) Detail (such as—What color was the boy's dog?); (2) Sequence (such as—Where did the boy go first, who did he talk to, and what did he do before he got home?); (3) Specific Word Meaning (as in the sentence, "Mary likes to swing." What can the word "swing" mean in the sentence?); (4) Interpreting Mood (as in the sentence, "Mary was so happy she cried." How do you think Mary really felt?); (5) Inference (such as—When people take their pets to a pet show, why does someone who has 15 cats choose his best cat to be in the show?); (6) Main Idea (such as—What is a good title for the story?).

This part of the test should be developed from materials that you have available, then duplicated and inserted in test.)

11. Given a three-part direction and the terms left and right orally by the teacher, the student follows them in sequence.

> I will read you a three part direction. Listen carefully, and then follow them in order.
>
> 1. Stand up.
> 2. Put your right hand on your nose.
> 3. Put your left hand on your ear.

MAJOR CATEGORY: ORAL LANGUAGE DEVELOPMENT

12. Given the Picture Interpretation Test, student demonstrates ability to extrapolate.

    A. *Directions*
Present a picture to the student and tell him to look at it carefully. Ask the questions below. If no response is obtained, move down the list of questions until child responds. Record the response as near verbatim as possible.

    B. *Questions*
1. What do you think will happen next?
2. What is happening in the picture?
3. What do you see in the picture?

    C. *Record response:*

    D. *Evaluation*
1. Ability to answer the first question indicates the highest level of oral language development.
(Extrapolation-prediction)
> Example: I think the boy will fall off the box before he catches the butterfly. I hope he catches it.
2. Ability to answer the second question indicates that child can interpret the "here-and-now" through language.
(Interpretation)
> Example: The boy is on the box. He is catching the butterfly.
3. Responding only to the last question, (Enumeration), or no response at all, indicates a need for many experiences that will promote language development prior to reading instruction.
> Example: house   box
>   butterfly   boy

13. Given a printed list of letters of the alphabet, or alphabet flash cards containing both upper and lower case letters, student names each letter. The following order is suggested:

```
O X A B T C L R I S P N F
E H D M K Z J Y W G Q U V

o x s c i p t m k z e w r
j y t n a h v u b d l g q
```

EVALUATION INSTRUMENT—LEVEL 1

MAJOR CATEGORY: SIGHT VOCABULARY

1a. Experience Story Approach

Given word cards from his experience stories, student names 50-75 words correctly excluding proper nouns.

1b. Basal Reader Approach

Given Level 1 of the Informal Word Recognition Inventory, student names 85% of the words correctly.

Level 1:
1. and
2. we
3. at
4. go
5. see
6. a
7. the
8. train
9. look
10. down
11. ride
12. stop
13. it
14. can
15. airplane
16. out
17. mother
18. what
19. father
20. make

MAJOR CATEGORY: PHONIC ANALYSIS

2. Given the following pairs of words stated orally by teacher, student responds orally by stating whether pairs begin with the same sound or different sounds:

most - my	late - song
dime - sand	note - mile

rat - came	book - big
cow - keep	got - good
Jim - wind	here - pay
far - first	hat - he
light - last	gave - fun
help - bed	Jack - joke
paint - pick	call - had
game - name	like - milk
bake - cook	red - ring
name - night	yard - yet
sing - soap	nose - barn
wing - long	zoo - zebra
tell - to	fish - store
tent - want	vote - very
walk - wait	down - dark

3. Given the following words stated orally by the teacher, student responds orally with a word that rhymes.

Stimulus

a. shake— _____

b. tall— _____

c. tan— _____

d. vat— _____

e. way— _____

f. den— _____

g. met— _____

h. pill— _____

i. bit— _____

j. hook— _____

k. dot— _____

l. town— _____

m. bun— _____

MAJOR CATEGORY: STRUCTURAL ANALYSIS

4. Given the following list of singular nouns or words from the student's sight vocabulary whose plurals are formed by adding *s*, student will write the plural forms and name the words formed.

1. boy   3. ball

2. car   4. cat

5. (For this test, get a 100 to 150 word selection from a picture book. Read this selection to the child. Ask the child about 10 to 15 questions concerning the selection. He should answer approximately 80% of these correctly. Include questions that will test the child's ability to deal with the following aspects of comprehension: (1) Detail (such as—What color was the boy's dog?); (2) Sequence (such as—Where did the boy go first, who did he talk to, and what did he do before he got home?); (3) Specific Word Meaning (as in the sentence, "Mary likes to swing." What can the word "swing" mean in the sentence?); (4) Interpreting Mood (as in the sentence, "Mary was so happy she cried." How do you think Mary really felt?); (5) Inference (such as—When people take their pets to a pet show, why does someone who has 15 cats choose his best cat to be in the show?); (6) Main Idea (such as—What is a good title for the story?).

    This part of the test should be developed from materials that you have available, then duplicated and inserted in test.)

EVALUATION INSTRUMENT–LEVEL 2

MAJOR CATEGORY: PHONIC ANALYSIS

1. Given the following list of words stated orally by teacher, student names or writes the letter that stands for the initial consonant sound of each word:

a.	batch	f.	deft	k.	hulk	p.	yacht
b.	foil	g.	keel	l.	nape	q.	ramp
c.	jade	h.	gape	m.	zest	r.	terse
d.	coin	i.	malt	n.	wean	s.	vague
e.	lair	j.	par	o.	soot		

2. Given the following list of words stated orally by the teacher, student names or writes the letter that stands for the final consonant sound of each word:

a.	dig	e.	roof	i.	dive	m.	steer
b.	trip	f.	dark	j.	dress	n.	peel
c.	tub	g.	from	k.	buzz	o.	shut
d.	had	h.	hen	l.	bridge		

3. Given the following list of words stated orally by the teacher, student names or writes the letter that stands for the sound of the initial digraph in each word:

a.	whale	b.	think	c.	shore	d.	churn

4. Given the following list of written words, student writes three or more words that rhyme with the stimulus word by substituting another consonant for the initial consonant in the stimulus word and names the new words written. (Accept nonsense words if child can pronounce them.)

win	look	ten
_in	_ook	_en
_in	_ook	_en
_in	_ook	_en

MAJOR CATEGORY: STRUCTURAL ANALYSIS

5. Given the following columns of words, student draws a line between the two that make compound words:

can	house
in	get
play	not
for	to

6. Given the following words and sentences, student underlines the correct word for each blank:

1. The boy ran to the tree and _____ up in it.

      jump - jumped - jumping

2. The girls can _____ in the house today.

      play - plays - played

3. Mother _____ in the house today.

      work - works - working

4. The cat is _____ at the dog.

      look - looks - looking

MAJOR CATEGORY: VOCABULARY DEVELOPMENT

7a. Experience Story Approach

Given word cards from his experience stories, student names 175-200 words correctly, excluding proper nouns

7b. Basal Reader Approach

Given Level 2 of the Informal Word Recognition Inventory, student names 85% of the words correctly.

Level 2:
1. duck
2. hill
3. did
4. may
5. they
6. soon
7. know
8. hello
9. one
10. letter
11. called
12. three

13. boys
14. who
15. box
16. after
17. where
18. penny
19. there
20. balloons

MAJOR CATEGORY: COMPREHENSION

8. (The child should read a selection of about 100 to 150 words from a basal reader, primer level. You should develop a set of questions to go along with the story. In order for the child to satisfactorily complete this part of the test, he should get about 80% of the questions correct.

You should include in your directions to the child a motivating sentence, such as:

In this story a very valuable item is lost. Do you think it will be found?

The child should read the selection. You should develop questions to deal with several aspects of comprehension. Samples are included to help guide your thinking as you prepare questions. You should insert your paragraph and questions into this part of the test as you will use them many times. These activities should be developed in materials readily available to you but not usually encountered by the children in the ongoing program of instruction.

Some samples of the type of questions to include are:

1. Main idea
   What is this story about?
   Does the story have a moral?
   What would be a good title for the story?

2. Detail
   Who was the main character?
   What year did the story take place?
   How long did the story take?
   How many?

3. Sequence
   What did Bill do after he lost his watch?
   What did Mary do after she talked to Louise?
   What day did the story begin?
   What day did the story end?

4. Inference
   Is there something in the story that is not said directly?
   Does the story teach any kind of a lesson?

Was there something in the story different from things you have heard or read somewhere else?

What was Bill's problem in the story?

5. Value judgments

Can you agree with the story?

How did you feel about Marge in the story?

Would you like everyone to read this story? Why?

Do you believe the things in the story could really happen?

Are there sometimes things you read that you don't quite believe? Was there anything in this story like that?

Is there anything you can do to find out if a story is really true? For example?

6. Author's purpose

What do you feel the author is trying to say in this story?

Do you think he is trying to say something he has not written directly?

What kind of a person do you think he is?

What do you think he believes about the topic of this article?

7. Personality

Why did you like (dislike) this story?

Did anything like this ever happen to you?

How did the story make you feel? Why?

Were there parts of the story that made you feel differently?

Which character in the story, if any, was most like you?

Would you like to have the main character for a friend?

8. Peer group awareness

Who do you know that would possibly enjoy this story?

Who do you think would enjoy hearing about this story?

Do you know anyone that is like the main character in the story?

9. Personality insight

Is there anyone you would ask to help you if you had a problem like the main character in the story?

Does the story make you feel like doing anything? What?

Was there anyone in the story who acted in a way you didn't like?

10. Vocabulary

In the sentence, "Will you please look after your sister?" what do the words "look after" mean?

In the sentence, "Some people have big feet and some people have small feet," what two words have opposite meanings?

Be sure to try to keep the level of difficulty of the questions consistent with the level of the reading selection you are using.)

EVALUATION INSTRUMENT—LEVEL 3

MAJOR CATEGORY: PHONIC ANALYSIS

1. Given the following list of words read orally, student names or writes the consonant blend heard in the initial position:

a.	snag	l.	smear
b.	spike	m.	frisk
c.	track	n.	glum
d.	cream	o.	gripe
e.	blithe	p.	plush
f.	stint	q.	quest
g.	bray	r.	skit
h.	swap	s.	prance
i.	clog	t.	scare
j.	dredge	u.	slump
k.	flounce		

2. Given the following digraphs and rhyming parts student constructs and states new
words made.

sh	_ake	_ot	_un
th	_an	_at	_en
ch	_at	_ill	_in
wh	_en	_ack	_ite

3. Given the following blends and rhyming parts student constructs and states the
new words made:

br	_ight	_ing	_own
sm	_ack	_ell	_all
bl	_ot	_ight	_ack
sc	_old	_an	_at
dr	_ill	_own	_ake
pl	_ay	_ight	_ot

4. Given the following list of words read orally, student writes or states the final
digraph or blend heard at the end of each word:

a.	bush	e.	wasp	i.	bent
b.	tack	f.	bunk	j.	best
c.	desk	g.	kind	k.	hung
d.	march	h.	cloth		

5. Given the following words, and final consonants, consonant blends, and consonant digraphs, student constructs and names the new words he has made:

man	had	bat	eat
_sh	_ng	_nk	_ch
_d	_nd	_ck	_st
_sk	_s	_th	_r

MAJOR CATEGORY: STRUCTURAL ANALYSIS

6. Given the following list of words stated orally, student states the number of
syllables heard in each word.

    a.   people
    b.   policeman
    c.   sleep
    d.   officer
    e.   almost

7. Given the following sentences containing compound words, student reads the
sentence pronouncing the compound word correctly:

a. He put wood in the fireplace.
b. We have a dog that is a good watchdog.
c. I cry when I am upset.

8. Given the following list of root words with variant endings, student draws a ring
around each root word and underlines the ending:

a.	fishing	d.	named
b.	tells	e.	thinking
c.	painted	f.	walked

9. Given the following lists, student matches each contraction with the two words
from which it was made.

I'm	is not
didn't	I am
isn't	it is
don't	do not
it's	did not

283

10. Given the following sentences, student draws a line under the correct word:

   a.   The girls put the money in_____ bag.
               Mothers   Mother's

   b.   The _____ were happy to play.
             boys   boy's

   c.   The _____ milk is in the dish.
             cats   cat's

MAJOR CATEGORY: STRUCTURE OF LANGUAGE

11. Given the following statements, student responds orally or in writing.
    a.   Name or write 5 consonants.
    b.   Name or write 5 vowels.

12. Given the following exercise, student writes the missing letters:

    b _ d _ f   _ fgh _ _   _ o _ q _ _   s _ u _ _

MAJOR CATEGORY: VOCABULARY DEVELOPMENT

13. Given Level 3 of the Informal Word Recognition Inventory, student names 85% of the words correctly.

    1.   garden
    2.   flowers
    3.   off
    4.   paint
    5.   rain
    6.   way
    7.   stand
    8.   just
    9.   how
   10.   rabbit
   11.   barn
   12.   book
   13.   country

14. truck
15. took
16. shall
17. began
18. chimney
19. snow
20. arms

MAJOR CATEGORY: COMPREHENSION

14. (The child should read a selection of about 100 to 150 words from a basal reader, first reader level. You should develop a set of questions to go along with the story. In order for the child to satisfactorily complete this part of the test, he should get about 80% of the questions correct.

You should include in your directions to the child a motivating sentence, such as:

In this story a very valuable item is lost. Do you think it will be found?

The child should read the selection. You should develop questions to deal with several aspects of comprehension. Samples are included to help guide your thinking as you prepare questions. You should insert your paragraph and questions into this part of the test as you will use them many times. These activities should be developed in materials readily available to you but not usually encountered by the children in the ongoing program of instruction.

Some samples of the type of questions to include are as follows:

1. Main idea

   What is this story about?
   Does the story have a moral?
   What would be a good title for the story?

2. Detail

   Who was the main character?
   What year did the story take place?
   How long did the story take?
   How many?

3. Sequence

   What did Bill do after he lost his watch?
   What did Mary do after she talked to Louise?
   What day did the story begin?
   What day did the story end?

4. Inference

   Is there something in the story that is not said directly?
   Does the story teach any kind of a lesson?

285

Was there something in the story different from things you
   have heard or read somewhere else?
What was Bill's problem in the story?

5. Value judgments
   Can you agree with the story?
   How did you feel about Marge in the story?
   Would you like everyone to read this story? Why?
   Do you believe the things in the story could really happen?
   Are there sometimes things you read that you don't quite
      believe? Was there anything in this story like that?
   Is there anything you can do to find out if a story is really
      true? For example?

6. Author's purpose
   What do you feel the author is trying to say in this story?
   Do you think he is trying to say something he has not written
      directly?
   What kind of a person do you think he is?
   What do you think he believes about the topic of this article?

7. Personality
   Why did you like (dislike) this story?
   Did anything like this ever happen to you?
   How did the story make you feel? Why?
   Were there parts of the story that made you feel differently?
   Which character in the story, if any, was most like you?
   Would you like to have the main character for a friend?

8. Peer group awareness
   Who do you know that would possibly enjoy this story?
   Who do you think would enjoy hearing about this story?
   Do you know anyone that is like the main character in the
      story?

9. Personality insight
   Is there anyone you would ask to help you if you had a problem
      like the main character in the story?
   Does the story make you feel like doing anything? What?
   Was there anyone in the story who acted in a way you didn't
      like?

10. Vocabulary
    In the sentence, "Will you please look after your sister?"
       what do the words "look after" mean?
    In the sentence, "Some people have big feet and some people
       have small feet," what are two words with opposite
       meanings?

Be sure to try to keep the level of difficulty of the questions consistent with the level of the reading selection you are using.)

MAJOR CATEGORY: HANDWRITING

15. Given a copy of the following items in manuscript form, student makes them meeting manuscript standards:

> Upper case alphabet
> Lower case alphabet
> Numerals 1-10
> Symbols $(+, -, <, >)$
> $(., ?, !, "\ ",$ and $,)$

16. Given the following sentence to copy:

> We love our flag, red, white, and blue.

Student scores in "Good" or "Medium" category according to Manuscript Evaluation Scale for First Grade.

EVALUATION INSTRUMENT—LEVEL 4

MAJOR CATEGORY: PHONIC ANALYSIS

1. Given the following list of words stated orally by the teacher, student writes the letter that stands for the vowel sound of each word and indicates whether it is a short or long sound by writing the letter *L* or *S* after the vowel letter.

    a.   white _____

    b.   deck _____

    c.   flap _____

    d.   joke _____

    e.   mumps _____

    f.   cute _____

    g.   waste _____

    h.   hint _____

    i.   shot _____

    j.   cede _____

MAJOR CATEGORY: STRUCTURAL ANALYSIS

2. Given the following exercise on inflection changes, student reads the written directions and completes the assignment:

Read the words and questions. Draw a line under the right answer to each question:

        run   running

How do you make running from run?
1.   Put on n and then ing.
2.   Just put on ing.

        stop   stopped
How do you make stopped from stop?
1.   Put on p and then ed.
2.   Just put on ed.

        want   wanting

How do you make wanting from want?
1.   Put on t then ing.
2.   Just put on ing.

come   coming

How do you make coming from come?
1.   Take off the e and put on ing.
2.   Just put on ing.

MAJOR CATEGORY: STRUCTURE OF LANGUAGE

3. Given the following list of written words, student numbers them in alphabetical sequence.

____ five   ____ hand   ____ sing
____ under   ____ milk   ____ room
____ just   ____ bus   ____ door

4. Given the following sentence, student identifies word or words that answer the questions who, what, when, where, why, and how?

Read the following sentence and answer the questions with a word or phrase from the sentence.

Mary walked slowly to the store this morning because she was tired.
                    Who?
                    What?
                    How?
                    Where?
                    When?
                    Why?

5. Given the following sentences, student reads the sentences and writes or names the antecedent for each pronoun underlined.

1.   Nancy and Susan went to their room.
            their - _____   289

2. Bob and Betty went to the store.
   <u>They</u> bought candy.

   They - _____

3. Spotty has <u>her</u> family on the bed.

   her - _____

4. Sally said "This is <u>my</u> ball."

   my - _____

5. Look at Mary. <u>She</u> is a pretty girl.

   She - _____

MAJOR CATEGORY: VOCABULARY DEVELOPMENT

6. Given Level 4 of the Informal Word Recognition Inventory, student names 85% of the words correctly.

   1. boat
   2. rocky
   3. wife
   4. warm
   5. fields
   6. aunt
   7. never
   8. building
   9. traveled
   10. goat's
   11. evening
   12. foot
   13. keeper
   14. reading
   15. roof
   16. any
   17. think
   18. pictures

19. Christmas
20. closed
21. hope
22. shortest
23. felt
24. fixed
25. almost

7. Given the following exercise, student underlines the word that is opposite or nearly the opposite of the underlined word.

Directions: Choose a word in each line which means the opposite or nearly the opposite of the first word in each row. Draw a line under it.

1.	white	yellow	black	back
2.	work	funny	happy	play
3.	day	play	red	night
4.	old	mother	on	new
5.	run	walk	fast	look
6.	little	every	big	hungry
7.	off	out	high	on
8.	found	lost	good	top
9.	near	far	in	laugh
10.	last	run	fast	first

8. Given the following exercise, student writes the word that means the same or almost the same as the underlined word or words in the sentences.

Directions: Write the word that means the same or almost the same as the underlined word or words in the sentences. Choose from the words listed below:

class - children - hoped - soft - gay

1. Danny wished that he would be able to go. _____

2. The children in our room were in a parade. _____

3. The bears were very <u>happy</u> playing together.

_____

4. I like to hear <u>quiet,</u> pretty music. _____

5. The <u>boys</u> <u>and</u> <u>girls</u> had fun at the zoo. _____

9. Given the following lists of words, student matches the homonyms:

Directions: Draw a line between two words which sound alike.

know	their
hear	no
there	would
by	here
road	buy
wood	rode

MAJOR CATEGORY: COMPREHENSION

10. (The child should read a selection of about 100 to 150 words from a basal reader, second grade level. You should develop a set of questions to go along with the story. In order for the child to satisfactorily complete this part of the test, he should get about 80% of the questions correct.

You should include in your directions to the child a motivating sentence, such as:

In this story a very valuable item is lost. Do you think it will be found?

The child should read the selection. You should develop questions to deal with several aspects of comprehension. Samples are included to help guide your thinking as you prepare questions. You should insert your paragraph and questions into this part of the test as you will use them many times. These activities should be developed in materials readily available to you but not usually encountered by the children in the ongoing program of instruction.

Some samples of the type of questions to include are:

1. Main idea

What is this story about?
Does the story have a moral?
What would be a good title for the story?

2. Detail

Who was the main character?
What year did the story take place?

How long did the story take?

How many?

3. Sequence

What did Bill do after he lost his watch?

What did Mary do after she talked to Louise?

What day did the story begin?

What day did the story end?

4. Inference

Is there something in the story that is not said directly?

Does the story teach any kind of a lesson?

Was there something in the story different from things you have
heard or read somewhere else?

What was Bill's problem in the story

5. Value judgments

Can you agree with the story?

How did you feel about Marge in the story?

Would you like everyone to read this story? Why?

Do you believe the things in the story could really happen?

Are there sometimes things you read that you don't quite
believe? Was there anything in this story like that?

Is there anything you can do to find out if a story is really
true? For example?

6. Author's purpose

What do you feel the author is trying to say in this story?

Do you think he is trying to say something he has not written
directly?

What kind of a person do you think he is?

What do you think he believes about the topic of this article?

7. Personality

Why did you like (dislike) this story?

Did anything like this ever happen to you?

How did the story make you feel? Why?

Were there parts of the story that made you feel differently?

Which character in the story, if any, was most like you?

Would you like to have the main character for a friend?

8. Peer group awareness

Who do you know that would possibly enjoy this story?

Who do you think would enjoy hearing about this story?

Do you know anyone that is like the main character in the story?

9. Personality insight

Is there anyone you would ask to help you if you had a problem
like the main character in the story?

Does the story make you feel like doing anything? What?

Was there anyone in the story who acted in a way you didn't like? 293

10. Vocabulary

> In the sentence, "Will you please look after your sister?"
> what do the words "look after" mean?
> In the sentence, "Some people have big feet and some people
> have small feet," what two words have opposite meanings?

Be sure to try to keep the level of difficulty of the questions consistent with the level of the reading selection you are using.)

MAJOR CATEGORY: STUDY SKILLS

11. Given the following Table of Contents, student answers the questions which follow it:

Thinking of Others

1. What is the title of the first story in this unit?

   _____

2. On what page does the first story begin?

   _____

3. On what page will the second story end?

   _____

4. Who wrote the poem, *Friends?*

   _____

5. Find and write the name of a subtitle.

   _____

6. Find and write the name of the unit title.

   _____

EVALUATION INSTRUMENT—LEVEL 5

MAJOR CATEGORY: PHONIC ANALYSIS

1. Given the following list of words stated orally by the teacher, student names or writes the letters that stand for the initial three-letter blend of the following words:

   a. split   d. scream
   b. spruce   e. thresh
   c. strum   f. squeal

2. Given the following list of words containing vowel digraphs and diphthongs to read orally, student decodes the words accurately:

   a. groan   g. choice
   b. meal   h. plow
   c. speed   i. haul
   d. paid   j. oyster
   e. claw   k. blew
   f. blouse

MAJOR CATEGORY: STRUCTURAL ANALYSIS

3. Given the following written exercise, student reads the directions and completes the assignment independently:

   Write the plural for each of the following words:

   1. gas_____   5. robin_____
   2. truck_____   6. brush_____
   3. class_____   7. ax _____
   4. couch_____   8. family_____

4. Given the following written exercise, student reads the directions and completes the assignment independently:

   Add the suffixes -ed and -ing to the following root words.

	-ed	-ing
1. carry	_____	_____

2. jump _____ _____
3. hate _____ _____

MAJOR CATEGORY: WRITTEN LANGUAGE DEVELOPMENT

5. Given the following sentences in written form, student underlines the correct word for each blank:

Underline the correct word that should be used in each of the following sentences:

1. Guess what I _____ last week.
   (saw - seen)
2. One of the cowboys _____ doing rope tricks.
   (was - were)
3. Have you ever _____ to an airport?
   (gone - went)
4. I don't have _____ crayons.
   (no - any)
5. My sister and _____ knew what was in the box.
   (me - I)
6. Have they _____ you the tickets for the fair?
   (gave - given)
7. Has John _____ his jacket out of the closet?
   (took - taken)
8. Has she _____ her lunch?
   (ate - eaten)
9. _____ the cakes and pies for sale?
   (Is - Are)
10. The monkey has _____ up the flagpole.
    (run - ran)

6. Given the following address, student writes it in correct form:

mr carl woods
45 pine street
frederick maryland 21701

7. Given the following letter, student inserts the correct punctuation marks and draws a ring around all words that should be capitalized.

may 4 1970

dear bill

    i want you to come to my birthday party on monday. mrs brown is going to read my new book to us It is called the happy egg. Can you come

your friend
jack

MAJOR CATEGORY: VOCABULARY DEVELOPMENT

8. Given level 5 of the Informal Word Recognition Inventory, student names 85% of the words correctly.

1. gray
2. round
3. tallest
4. cage
5. because
6. library
7. hardly
8. bunches
9. elves
10. sign
11. reindeer
12. or
13. same
14. joke
15. hit
16. strange
17. hearing
18. noon
19. air

20. hunter
21. plates
22. seemed
23. east
24. myself
25. goose

MAJOR CATEGORY: COMPREHENSION

9. (The child should read a selection of about 100 to 150 words from a basal reader, second grade level. You should develop a set of questions to go along with the story. In order for the child to satisfactorily complete this part of the test, he should get about 80% of the questions correct.

You should include in your directions to the child a motivating sentence, such as:

In this story a very valuable item is lost. Do you think it will be found?

The child should read the selection. You should develop questions to deal with several aspects of comprehension. Samples are included to help guide your thinking as you prepare questions. You should insert your paragraph and questions into this part of the test as you will use them many times. These activities should be developed in materials readily available to you but not usually encountered by the children in the ongoing program of instruction.

Some samples of the type of questions to include are:

1. Main idea
   What is this story about?
   Does the story have a moral?
   What would be a good title for the story?

2. Detail
   Who was the main character?
   What year did the story take place?
   How long did the story take?
   How many?

3. Sequence
   What did Bill do after he lost his watch?
   What did Mary do after she talked to Louise?
   What day did the story begin?
   What day did the story end?

4. Inference
   Is there something in the story that is not said directly?
   Does the story teach any kind of a lesson?
   Was there something in the story different from things you have
      heard or read somewhere else?
   What was Bill's problem in the story?

5. Value judgments

   Can you agree with the story?

   How did you feel about Marge in the story?

   Would you like everyone to read this story? Why?

   Do you believe the things in the story could really happen?

   Are there sometimes things you read that you don't quite believe?
      Was there anything in this story like that?

   Is there anything you can do to find out if a story is really true?
      For example?

6. Author's purpose

   What do you feel the author is trying to say in this story?

   Do you think he is trying to say something he has not written
      directly?

   What kind of a person do you think he is?

   What do you think he believes about the topic of this article?

7. Personality

   Why did you like (dislike) this story?

   Did anything like this ever happen to you?

   How did the story make you feel? Why?

   Were there parts of the story that made you feel differently?

   Which character in the story, if any, was most like you?

   Would you like to have the main character for a friend?

8. Peer group awareness

   Who do you know that would possibly enjoy this story?

   Who do you think would enjoy hearing about this story?

   Do you know anyone that is like the main character in the story?

9. Personality insight

   Is there anyone you would ask to help you if you had a problem
      like the main character in the story?

   Does the story make you feel like doing anything? What?

   Was there anyone in the story who acted in a way you didn't
      like?

10. Vocabulary

   In the sentence, "Will you please look after your sister?"
      what do the words "look after" mean?

   In the sentence, "Some people have big feet and some people
      have small feet," what two words have opposite meanings?

Be sure to try to keep the level of difficulty of the questions consistent with the
level of the reading selection you are using.)

MAJOR CATEGORY: SPELLING

10. Given the following list of words to write from dictation, student achieves an
85% or better score.

1. after	11. hen
2. apple	12. house
3. back	13. little
4. bears	14. men
5. book	15. other
6. came	16. rabbit
7. dear	17. schools
8. eggs	18. thank
9. funny	19. white
10. going	20. add

(Do *not* retain a child in Level 5 if he fails to meet this competency level in spelling. Move him to Level 6 if he meets the 85% criterion on the other items in the test, but continue instruction in spelling at his present level.)

EVALUATION INSTRUMENT–LEVEL 6

MAJOR CATEGORY: PHONIC ANALYSIS

1. Given the following list of words containing phonetically irregular words, student orally decodes the words correctly:

a.	cent	k.	throw
b.	gem	l.	broom
c.	scold	m.	stood
d.	blind	n.	try
e.	mild	o.	foggy
f.	spark	p.	knight
g.	berth	q.	wring
h.	short	r.	listen
i.	halt	s.	comb
j.	crown	t.	thick

MAJOR CATEGORY: STRUCTURAL ANALYSIS

2. Given the following list of written words and sentences, student identifies the root word and selects the correct word to fit the meaning of the sentence.

In the Column A, draw a ring around the root word. Then match the words in Column A with the sentences in Column B by drawing a line between the two that go together.

A

a. treeless

b. unpainted

c. thankful

B

1. The house looked old because it was _____.

2. The train came _____ to a stop.

3. If the forest is burned, it will be _____°

d.   returning   4.   I am _____ for my nice home.

e.   slowly   5.   I will be _____ my library book tomorrow.

MAJOR CATEGORY: WRITTEN LANGUAGE DEVELOPMENT

3.   Given the following evaluation in written language development, student reads the directions and completes the assignment independently:

Written Language Review

I.   Write the groups of words that are sentences. Put periods at the end.

    a.   Like a big book
    b.   The box was very heavy
    c.   On the desk in the room
    d.   In the story yesterday
    e.   Mary put the cat outside

II.   Copy the following sentences. Put the correct punctuation marks at the ends. After each sentence, write whether the sentence is a telling sentence, an asking sentence, or an exclamatory sentence.

    A.   We had a good time at the party

    _____

    B.   Did you have fun

    _____

    C.   What did you do

    _____

    D.   We ate cake and ice cream

    _____

    E.   My, it was good

    _____

III. Underline the right word for each blank.

a. run, ran   John had never ___ in a race before.

b. are, is   The boys ___ in the yard.

c. was, were   Jane and Sally ___ playing with their dolls.

d. no, any   We don't have ___ new work to do today.

e. aren't, isn't   Mother and I ___ going to the store today.

f. went, gone   Dick has ___ to a ballgame.

g. John and I., I and John   ___ are going to watch TV.

h. gave give   I ___ Mary my book to read.

i. did, done   Tom has ___ his best work.

j. me and Jean, Jean and me   Bill saw ___ at the park yesterday.

k. Those, Them   ___ books are yours.

l. wasn't, weren't   The boys ___ at home last night.

m. came, come   Bob has ___ to school with me every morning.

n. saw, seen   They ___ a big dog running down the street.

IV. Write the following words correctly:

a. halloween   _____

b. thanksgiving   _____

c. sunday   _____

d. friday   _____

e. june   _____

f. september   _____

303

V. Write these greetings, closings, and signatures correctly. Be sure to put in the right punctuation marks.

dear mr jones   _____

dear susan   _____

your friend   _____

your son   _____

james h white   _____

sally m brown   _____

VI. Copy the following letter correctly putting in capital letters and punctuation marks where needed.

> 53 pine avenue
> easton ohio 21701
> may 25 1971

dear bob

  our class is going on a field trip to washington d c on june 3 1971 can you go with us please let me know soon

> your friend
> bill smith

VII. Write the following sentences correctly.

a. jane and i live in baltimore maryland

b. we live on park avenue

c. his name is mr tom s jones

d. tomorrow will be tuesday

e. the date will be april 14

VIII. Underline the correct word for each of the following sentences.

    1.   _____ house is painted white. (Hour – Our)
    2.   Did you _____ what I said? (here – hear)
    3.   I have ____ many books to read. (two – too)
    4.   Mother wants to ___ me. (sea – see)
    5.   I went ____ your house today. (by – buy)

IX. Write in sequence the following sentences in paragraph form. Use your best handwriting.
    1.   Then she cut the apples into small pieces.
    2.   She reached in the silver box for her knife.
    3.   She put them on the kitchen table.
    4.   Mother got some apples from a bag.

MAJOR CATEGORY: VOCABULARY DEVELOPMENT

4.   Given Level 6 of the informal Word Recognition Inventory, student names 85% of the words correctly.

1.   treasure
2.   mailed
3.   cabins
4.   done
5.   worth
6.   beautiful
7.   skating
8.   television
9.   logs
10.   forth
11.   held
12.   prairies
13.   steaming
14.   bang

15. quietly
16. neck
17. lazy
18. pilot's
19. wings
20. pony
21. describe
22. donkey
23. turtles
24. straw
25. coast

MAJOR CATEGORY: COMPREHENSION

5. (The child should read a selection of about 100 to 150 words from a basal reader, third grade level. You should develop a set of questions to go along with the story. In order for the child to satisfactorily complete this part of the test, he should get about 80% of the questions correct.

You should include in your directions to the child a motivating sentence, such as:

In this story a very valuable item is lost. Do you think it will be found?

The child should read the selection. You should develop questions to deal with several aspects of comprehension. Samples are included to help guide your thinking as you prepare questions. You should insert your paragraph and questions into this part of the test as you will use them many times. These activities should be developed in materials readily available to you but not usually encountered by the children in the ongoing program of instruction.

Some samples of the type of questions to include are:

1. Main idea
What is this story about?
Does the story have a moral?
What would be a good title for the story?

2. Detail
Who was the main character?
What year did the story take place?
How long did the story take?
How many?

3. Sequence

What did Bill do after he lost his watch?

What did Mary do after she talked to Louise?

What day did the story begin?

What day did the story end?

4. Inference

Is there something in the story that is not said directly?

Does the story teach any kind of a lesson?

Was there something in the story different from things you have heard or read somewhere else?

What was Bill's problem in the story?

5. Value judgments

Can you agree with the story?

How did you feel about Marge in the story?

Would you like everyone to read this story? Why?

Do you believe the things in the story could really happen?

Are there sometimes things you read that you don't quite believe? Was there anything in this story like that?

Is there anything you can do to find out if a story is really true? For example?

6. Author's Purpose

What do you feel the author is trying to say in this story?

Do you think he is trying to say something he has not written directly?

What kind of a person do you think he is?

What do you think he believes about the topic of this article?

7. Personality

Why did you like (dislike) this story?

Did anything like this ever happen to you?

How did the story make you feel? Why?

Were there parts of the story that made you feel differently?

Which character in the story, if any, was most like you?

Would you like to have the main character for a friend?

8. Peer group awareness

Who do you know that would possibly enjoy this story?

Who do you think would enjoy hearing about this story?

Do you know anyone that is like the main character in the story?

9. Personality insight

Is there anyone you would ask to help you if you had a problem like the main character in the story?

Does the story make you feel like doing anything? What?

Was there anyone in the story who acted in a way you didn't like?

10. Vocabulary

      In the sentence, "Will you please look after your sister?"
      what do the words "look after" mean?

      In the sentence, "Some people have big feet and some people
      have small feet," what two words have opposite meanings?

Be sure to try to keep the level of difficulty of the questions consistent with the level of the reading selection you are using.)

MAJOR CATEGORY: STUDY SKILLS

6.   Given the following list of words, student numbers them in alphabetical order:

        body
        begin
        bunch
        brook
        block
        bank
        bicycle

EVALUATION INSTRUMENT–LEVEL 7

MAJOR CATEGORY: PHONIC ANALYSIS

1. Given the following list of written words, student places the correct diacritical mark over the underlined vowels:

    a. age   c. bite   e. broke
    b. bit   d. dust   f. deck

MAJOR CATEGORY: STRUCTURAL ANALYSIS

2. Given the following words stated orally, student states the syllable which receives the most emphasis.

    a. people   c. contraction   e. correct
    b. policeman   d. officer

3. Given the following columns of words, student reads them orally applying principles of syllabication and vowel generalizations:

    a. picnic   g. maple   m. agree
    b. member   h. sparkle   n. begin
    c. trigger   i. jingle   o. beyond
    d. locate   j. secret   p. reloaded
    e. flavor   k. country   q. unlikely
    f. pilot   l. preacher   r. distasteful

MAJOR CATEGORY: WRITTEN LANGUAGE DEVELOPMENT

4. Given the following phrases, student marks the contractions with a C and the possessives with a P:

    a. dogs' bones _____   d. hasn't any   _____
    b. won't go   _____   e. donkey's cart _____
    c. colt's mother _____   f. bees' nest   _____ 309

5. Given the following book titles, student writes them correctly:

   a.   we live in the city

   b.   green eggs and ham

   c.   my box and string

6. Given the following sentences, student underlines the correct word for each blank.

   1.   bring, brought   Did Tom ____ the horses some hay?
   2.   feed, fed   He has ____ the horses every day.
   3.   to, too   I like to feed animals, ____.
   4.   get, got   My cousin ____ a bicycle for his birthday.
   5.   wrote, written   I have ____ a letter to my uncle.

MAJOR CATEGORY: STRUCTURE OF LANGUAGE

7. Given the following sentences, student classifies the underlined word according to Nouns, Verbs, and Adjectives:

   1. John caught a big fish.
   2. The red book is on the table.
   3. The little boy dropped his new toy.
   4. Mother shopped at the large store.

8. Given the following written exercise, student underlines the correct analagous word:

   a.   Calf is to cow as kid is to _____.
             lamb – child – goat
   b.   Trunk is to tree as stem is to _____.
             thickness – flower – root

c.　Sour is to lemon as sweet is to _____.
　　　　salt – pickles – candy
d.　Clock is to time as thermometer is to _____.
　　　　rain – temperature – wind
e.　Scissors are to cut as ax is to _____.
　　　　sharp – tree – chop

MAJOR CATEGORY: VOCABULARY DEVELOPMENT

9.　Given Level 7 of the Informal Word Recognition Inventory, student names 85% of the words correctly.

1.	pirates	14.	lend
2.	insisted	15.	holidays
3.	turkeys	16.	hoofs
4.	matter	17.	mischief
5.	women	18.	cousins
6.	fort	19.	clay
7.	unload	20.	smoothly
8.	biting	21.	descended
9.	thousand	22.	suggest
10.	breakfast	23.	engineer
11.	spinning	24.	grand
12.	press	25.	steel
13.	proved		

MAJOR CATEGORY: COMPREHENSION

10.　(The child should read a selection of about 100 to 150 words from a basal reader, third grade level. You should develop a set of questions to go along with the story. In order for the child to satisfactorily complete this part of the test, he should get about 80% of the questions correct.

You should include in your directions to the child a motivating sentence, such as:

　　In this story a very valuable item is lost. Do you think it will be found?

The child should read the selection. You should develop questions to deal with several aspects of comprehension. Samples are included to help guide your thinking as you prepare questions. You should insert your paragraph and questions into this part of the test as you will use them many times. These activities should be developed in materials readily available to you but not usually encountered by the children in the ongoing program of instruction.

Some samples of the type of questions to include are:

1. Main idea
   What is this story about?
   Does the story have a moral?
   What would be a good title for the story?

2. Detail
   Who was the main character?
   What year did the story take place?
   How long did the story take?
   How many?

3. Sequence
   What did Bill do after he lost his watch?
   What did Mary do after she talked to Louise?
   What day did the story begin?
   What day did the story end?

4. Inference
   Is there something in the story that is not said directly?
   Does the story teach any kind of a lesson?
   Was there something in the story different from things you
       have heard or read somewhere else?
   What was Bill's problem in the story?

5. Value judgments
   Can you agree with the story?
   How did you feel about Marge in the story?
   Would you like everyone to read this story? Why?
   Do you believe the things in the story could really happen?
   Are there sometimes things you read that you don't quite believe?
       Was there anything in this story like that?
   Is there anything you can do to find out if a story is really true?
       For example?

6. Author's purpose
   What do you feel the author is trying to say in this story?
   Do you think he is trying to say something he has not written
       directly?
   What kind of a person do you think he is?
   What do you think he believes about the topic of this article?

7. Personality
   Why did you like (dislike) this story?
   Did anything like this ever happen to you?
   How did the story make you feel? Why?

Were there parts of the story that made you feel differently?

Which character in the story, if any, was most like you?

Would you like to have the main character for a friend?

8. Peer group awareness

Who do you know that would possibly enjoy this story?

Who do you think would enjoy hearing about this story?

Do you know anyone that is like the main character in the story?

9. Personality insight

Is there anyone you would ask to help you if you had a problem like the main character in the story?

Does the story make you feel like doing anything? What?

Was there anyone in the story who acted in a way you didn't like?

10. Vocabulary

In the sentence, "Will you please look after your sister?" what do the words "look after" mean?

In the sentence, "Some people have big feet and some people have small feet," what two words have opposite meanings?

Be sure to try to keep the level of difficulty of the questions consistent with the level of the reading selection you are using.)

MAJOR CATEGORY: STUDY SKILLS

11. Given the following lists of words, student numbers each column in alphabetical order:

bag	clock	fat
bath	clever	far
ball	cling	fairly
band	clay	fall

MAJOR CATEGORY: HANDWRITING

12. Given a copy of the following items in cursive form, student makes them meeting cursive standards:

Upper case cursive alphabet
Lower case cursive alphabet
Numerals (with cursive slant)

13. Given the following sentences to copy, student meets the evaluative criteria for cursive writing.

My name stands for me. I want to write it well.

MAJOR CATEGORY: SPELLING

14. Given the following list of words to write from dictation, student achieves an 85% or better score.

1.	about	10.	hood	18.	second
2.	anything	11.	jumped	19.	sky
3.	bank	12.	lot	20.	snowman
4.	bright	13.	morning	21.	started
5.	clean	14.	next	22.	street
6.	dress	15.	pencil	23.	these
7.	faster	16.	poor	24.	tonight
8.	food	17.	rose	25.	while
9.	ground				

EVALUATION INSTRUMENT–LEVEL 8

MAJOR CATEGORY: VOCABULARY DEVELOPMENT

1. Given an Informal Word Recognition Inventory at Level 8, student names 85% of the words correctly.

1.	barrel	10.	dash	19.	bars
2.	afire	11.	kite	20.	supplies
3.	spy	12.	peeked	21.	fingers
4.	crouch	13.	tremendous	22.	paddled
5.	vest	14.	pretending	23.	courage
6.	rug	15.	certain	24.	package
7.	strength	16.	awoke	25.	sports
8.	wobble	17.	freight		
9.	drooping	18.	wrote		

MAJOR CATEGORY: COMPREHENSION

2. (The child should read a selection of about 100 to 150 words from a basal reader, fourth grade level. You should develop a set of questions to go along with the story. In order for the child to satisfactorily complete this part of the test, he should get about 80% of the questions correct.

    You should include in your directions to the child a motivating sentence, such as:

    > In this story a very valuable item is lost. Do you think it will be found?

    The child should read the selection. You should develop questions to deal with several aspects of comprehension. Samples are included to help guide your thinking as you prepare questions. You should insert your paragraph and questions into this part of the test as you will use them many times. These activities should be developed in materials readily available to you but not usually encountered by the children in the ongoing program of instruction.

    Some samples of the type of questions to include are:

    1. Main idea
        What is this story about?
        Does the story have a moral?
        What would be a good title for the story?

    2. Detail
        Who was the main character?

What year did the story take place?

How long did the story take?

How many?

3. Sequence

What did Bill do after he lost his watch?

What did Mary do after she talked to Louise?

What day did the story begin?

What day did the story end?

4. Inference

Is there something in the story that is not said directly?

Does the story teach any kind of a lesson?

Was there something in the story different from things you have
heard or read somewhere else?

What was Bill's problem in the story?

5. Value judgments

Can you agree with the story?

How did you feel about Marge in the story?

Would you like everyone to read this story? Why?

Do you believe the things in the story could really happen?

Are there sometimes things you read that you don't quite believe?
Was there anything in this story like that?

Is there anything you can do to find out if a story is really true?
For example?

6. Author's purpose

What do you feel the author is trying to say in this story?

Do you think he is trying to say something he has not written
directly?

What kind of a person do you think he is?

What do you think he believes about the topic of this article?

7. Personality

Why did you like (dislike) this story?

Did anything like this ever happen to you?

How did the story make you feel? Why?

Were there parts of the story that made you feel differently?

Which character in the story, if any, was most like you?

Would you like to have the main character for a friend?

8. Peer group awareness

Who do you know that would possibly enjoy this story?

Who do you think would enjoy hearing about this story?

Do you know anyone that is like the main character in the story?

9. Personality insight

Is there anyone you would ask to help you if you had a problem
like the main character in the story?

Does the story make you feel like doing anything? What?

Was there anyone in the story who acted in a way you didn't like?

10. Vocabulary

In the sentence, "Will you please look after your sister?" what do the words "look after" mean?

In the sentence, "Some people have big feet and some people have small feet," what are two words with opposite meanings?

Be sure to try to keep the level of difficulty of the questions consistent with the level of the reading selection you are using.)

EVALUATION INSTRUMENT—LEVEL 9

MAJOR CATEGORY: STRUCTURAL ANALYSIS

Given the following exercises, student reads the directions and completes the assignment without assistance:

1. Underline the base word in each of the words below. Draw a vertical line between the base word and each prefix or suffix.
   Example: dis/<u>trust</u>

mistake	displease	return
hopeless	nonprofit	inland
childlike	likeable	mislead
unhappy	disappear	cupful
clownish	selfishness	worked

2. Write each pair of words below as a contraction.

1.	I am _____	7.	had not_____
2.	does not _____	8.	she will _____
3.	you have _____	9.	was not_____
4.	has not _____	10.	it is _____
5.	they will _____	11.	we are _____
6.	you are _____	12.	is not _____

MAJOR CATEGORY: WRITTEN LANGUAGE DEVELOPMENT

Given the following exercises, student reads the directions and completes the assignment without assistance:

3. Write each of the sentences below. Choose the correct word to replace the xxxx's.

   1. blue, blew   The warm breezes xxxx.
   2. their, there   They sold xxxx house.
   3. write, right   My brother can xxxx his name.
   4. to, two, too   The teacher read xxxx poems.
   5. new, knew   I xxxx both answers.
   6. beet, beat   He xxxx the drum loudly.
   7. there, their   Please sit over xxxx.
   8. some, sum   I bought xxxx popcorn.
   9. by, buy   Did you xxxx the candy?
   10. to, two, too   He ran xxxx the store.
   11. hear, here   Can you xxxx the music?
   12. sea, see   I can xxxx the mouse.
   13. to, two, too   The coat is xxxx large.

4. Write the following friendly letter elements correctly in the proper position on a sheet of paper.

   dear bob

   507 young place
   millersville pennsylvania 17551
   november 5 1972

   steve

   sincerely yours

   we are going to the football game

5. Given an envelope, student writes correctly the following address and indicates himself as the sender in the return address:

   > bob smith
   > 118 north market street
   > millersville pennsylvania 17551

6. Write these sentences. Make the nouns that are underlined show possession.

   1. My *brothers* names are Paul and Frederick.   _____

   2. My *sisters* name is Nancy.   _____

   3. *Jeans* books are on the table.   _____

   4. The *rabbits* nose is pink.   _____

   5. The *pioneers* wagons rolled along.   _____

7. Choose the correct verb to use in each sentence. Then write the sentence.

   1. come, came   My aunt xxx yesterday.

      _____

   2. is, are   The two teams xxxx tied.

      _____

   3. gave, given   Has he xxxx the prize?

      _____

   4. went, gone   They xxxx skiing last weekend.

      _____

   5. saw, seen   I xxxx a strange object!

      _____

   6. took, taken   The jewels were xxxx.

      _____

   7. was, were   We xxxx to cold to swim.

      _____

   8. did, done   Gail xxxx her homework.

      _____

8. Circle the letters in the following sentences that should be capitalized.

1. on friday i received a gift from mrs. bennett.

2. mrs. bennett was my teacher at central avenue school in tennessee.

3. she sent me a funny book called henry huggins by beverly cleary.

4. i moved to new jersey last november.

5. i can see the george washington bridge from the window of my apartment building.

6. sometimes my parents and i drive over the bridge into new york city.

7. i miss tennessee, but i have made many new friends at the elm street school.

MAJOR CATEGORY: STRUCTURE OF LANGUAGE

Given the following exercises, student reads the directions and completes the assignment without assistance:

9. Write a sentence for each group of words below that is not a sentence.

1. Walking through the park

2. The path was very crowded

3. A boathouse near the lake

4. Some children playing near the lake

5. It was warm and sunny near the lake

10. Copy the sentences. Put the right punctuation mark at the end of each. Then tell what kind of sentence each one is.

1. Here comes a snake___   _____

2. Did you see it___   _____

3. I'm going home now___   _____

4. Please stay a few more minutes___   _____

5. My mother is waiting for me___   _____

6. When can you visit us again___   _____

7. I hope I can come tomorrow___   _____

8. What excitement that snake caused___   _____

11. Find and write the eight common nouns and five proper nouns in the sentences below.

1. Pauline is eating a sandwich.

2. My brother has gone to school.

3. Mr. Lang is on a trip around the world.

4. Snow covered the streets on Christmas.

5. Frank and his father visited England.

12. Choose the correct form of the adjective to complete each sentence. Write the word.

    1. faster, fastest   Ron is a xxxx runner than I am.   _____

    2. faster, fastest   He is the xxxx runner on the track team.   _____

    3. new, newer   This is the xxxx of my two coats.   _____

    4. better, best   Of the two cars, this is the xxxx.   _____

    5. better, best   It is the xxxx car of all.   _____

MAJOR CATEGORY: VOCABULARY DEVELOPMENT

13. Given an Informal Word Recognition Inventory at Level 9, student names 85% of the words correctly.

1. hood	8. swallow	14. scarcely	20. rout
2. loft	9. vibration	15. thread	21. grain
3. duty	10. iodine	16. weight	22. tropical
4. report	11. except	17. carnival	23. disappointment
5. swept	12. arrested	18. beneath	24. pleasant
6. salt	13. strike	19. equator	25. cinders
7. herbs			

MAJOR CATEGORY: COMPREHENSION

14. (The child should read a selection of about 100 to 150 words from a basal reader, fourth grade level. You should develop a set of questions to go along with the story. In order for the child to satisfactorily complete this part of the test, he should get about 80% of the questions correct.

You should include in your directions to the child a motivating sentence, such as:

> In this story a very valuable item is lost. Do you think it will be found?

The child should read the selection. You should develop questions to deal with several aspects of comprehension. Samples are included to help guide your thinking as you prepare questions. You should insert your paragraph and questions into this part of the test as you will use them many times. These activities should be developed in materials readily available to you but not usually encountered by the children in the ongoing program of instruction.

Some samples of the type of questions to include are as follows:

    1. Main idea
        What is this story about?
        Does the story have a moral?
        What would be a good title for the story?

    2. Detail
        Who was the main character?

What year did the story take place?

How long did the story take?

How many?

3. Sequence

What did Bill do after he lost his watch?

What did Mary do after she talked to Louise?

What day did the story begin?

What day did the story end?

4. Inference

Is there something in the story that is not said directly?

Does the story teach any kind of a lesson?

Was there something in the story different from things you have
heard or read somewhere else?

What was Bill's problem in the story?

5. Value judgments

Can you agree with the story?

How did you feel about Marge in the story?

Would you like everyone to read this story? Why?

Do you believe the things in the story could really happen?

Are there sometimes things you read that you don't quite believe?
Was there anything in this story like that?

Is there anything you can do to find out if a story is really true?
For example?

6. Author's purpose

What do you feel the author is trying to say in this story?

Do you think he is trying to say something he has not written
directly?

What kind of a person do you think he is?

What do you think he believes about the topic of this article?

7. Personality

Why did you like (dislike) this story?

Did anything like this ever happen to you?

How did the story make you feel? Why?

Were there parts of the story that made you feel differently?

Which character in the story, if any, was most like you?

Would you like to have the main character for a friend?

8. Peer group awareness

Who do you know that would possibly enjoy this story?

Who do you think would enjoy hearing about this story?

Do you know anyone that is like the main character in the story?

9. Personality insight

Is there anyone you would ask to help you if you had a problem
like the main character in the story?

Does the story make you feel like doing anything? What?

Was there anyone in the story who acted in a way you didn't like?

10. Vocabulary

In the sentence, "Will you please look after your sister?" what do the words "look after" mean?

In the sentence, "Some people have big feet and some people have small feet," what two words have opposite meanings?)

MAJOR CATEGORY: STUDY SKILLS

15. Given the following exercise, student reads the directions and completes the assignment without assistance.

Which of the following parts of a book would help you find the information below? Write the answer for each one.

Table of Contents   Index   Glossary

1. The title of the unit in which "The Father of the Northman" and "Two Chests of Treasure" are to be found in a basal reader _____

_____

2. Information about Fort Vancouver in a history book _____

_____

3. The meaning of the word *plaid* as used in a basal reader _____

_____

4. The correct pronunciation of the French name, Henri Le Grande, from a story in a basal reader _____

5. The following topics in a geography book: fur trading, lumbering _____

_____

6. The chapter on the earth's atmosphere in a science book _____

_____

16. Given the following exercise, student reads the directions and completes the assignment without assistance:

The following words all begin with the prefix *trans.* Write the numbers 1 to 9 and list the words in alphabetical order

transfer	transport	translucent
transfusion	transmit	transmute
transition	transgress	transform

17. Given the following exercise, student reads the directions and completes the assignment without assistance:

Here are the guide words on page 471 and on page 472 of your glossary. Write the number of the page on which each word of the list appears.

Guide Words

Page 471   abyss   carbon
Page 472   Canate   Egypt

_____ bazaar   _____ dense

_____ anaconda   _____ custom

_____ chariot   _____ eager

_____ bridle   _____ Cabot

MAJOR CATEGORY: HANDWRITING

18. Given the following paragraph to copy in both cursive and manuscript form, student meets the evaluative criteria:

Seeing America is like seeing the world.
We have many kinds of farms and industries.
Our people do many kinds of work.

MAJOR CATEGORY: SPELLING

19. Given the following list of words to write from dictation, student achieves an 85% or better score.

1. able	10. forgot	18. pond
2. arithmetic	11. harder	19. putting
3. block	12. hundred	20. robin
4. build	13. jelly	21. seat
5. cloth	14. learned	22. silk
6. crossed	15. march	23. stopped
7. died	16. moving	24. trick
8. enough	17. orange	25. Wednesday
9. finding		

EVALUATION INSTRUMENT—LEVEL 10

MAJOR CATEGORY: VOCABULARY DEVELOPMENT

1. Given an Informal Word Recognition Inventory at Level 10, student names 85% of the words correctly.

1.	jewelry	14.	partner
2.	director	15.	flint
3.	oats	16.	embroider
4.	forty	17.	revolution
5.	ankle	18.	framework
6.	pitchers	19.	courageous
7.	single	20.	giggle
8.	sweep	21.	view
9.	battery	22.	weakening
10.	performers	23.	level
11.	rising	24.	laughable
12.	glory	25.	support
13.	sixpence		

MAJOR CATEGORY: COMPREHENSION

2. (The child should read a selection of about 100 to 150 words from a basal reader, fifth grade level. You should develop a set of questions to go along with the story. In order for the child to satisfactorily complete this part of the test, he should get about 80% of the questions correct.

You should include in your directions to the child a motivating sentence, such as:

In this story a very valuable item is lost. Do you think it will be found?

The child should read the selection. You should develop questions to deal with several aspects of comprehension. Samples are included to help guide your thinking as you prepare questions. You should insert your paragraph and questions into this part of the test as you will use them many times. These activities should be developed in materials readily available to you but not usually encountered by the children in the ongoing program of instruction.

Some samples of the type of questions to include are:

1. Main idea
    What is this story about?

Does the story have a moral?
What would be a good title for the story?

2. Detail

Who was the main character?
What year did the story take place?
How long did the story take?
How many?

3. Sequence

What did Bill do after he lost his watch?
What did Mary do after she talked to Louise?
What day did the story begin?
What day did the story end?

4. Inference

Is there something in the story that is not said directly?
Does the story teach any kind of a lesson?
Was there something in the story different from things you have
   heard or read somewhere else?
What was Bill's problem in the story?

5. Value judgments

Can you agree with the story?
How did you feel about Marge in the story?
Would you like everyone to read this story? Why?
Do you believe the things in the story could really happen?
Are there sometimes things you read that you don't quite believe?
   Was there anything in this story like that?
Is there anything you can do to find out if a story is really true?
   For example?

6. Author's purpose

What do you feel the author is trying to say in this story?
Do you think he is trying to say something he has not written
   directly?
What kind of a person do you think he is?
What do you think he believes about the topic of this article?

7. Personality

Why did you like (dislike) this story?
Did anything like this ever happen to you?
How did the story make you feel? Why?
Were there parts of the story that made you feel differently?
Which character in the story, if any, was most like you?
Would you like to have the main character for a friend?

8. Peer group awareness

Who do you know that would possibly enjoy this story?
Who do you think would enjoy hearing about this story?
Do you know anyone that is like the main character in the story?

9. Personality insight

    Is there anyone you would ask to help you if you had a problem like the main character in the story?

    Does the story make you feel like doing anything? What?

    Was there anyone in the story who acted in a way you didn't like?

10. Vocabulary

    In the sentence, "Will you please look after your sister?" what do the words "look after" mean?

    In the sentence, "Some people have big feet and some people have small feet," what two words have opposite meanings?

Be sure to try to keep the level of difficulty of the questions consistent with the level of the reading selection you are using.)

EVALUATION INSTRUMENT—LEVEL 11

MAJOR CATEGORY: STRUCTURAL ANALYSIS

Given the following exercises, student reads the directions and completes the assignment without assistance:

1. Copy the prefixes and suffixes in each of the following words. Next to each prefix or suffix write its meaning.

    a.   monogram   _____ — _____

                                _____ — _____

    b.   distrustful   _____ — _____

                                _____ — _____

    c.   photographer   _____ — _____

                                _____ — _____

    d.   telescope   _____ — _____

                                _____ — _____

    e.   biology   _____ — _____

                                _____ — _____

    f.   hydrophobia   _____ — _____

                                _____ — _____

    g.   unladylike   _____ — _____

                                _____ — _____

    h.   supervisor   _____ — _____

                                _____ — _____

    i.   automotive   _____ — _____

                                _____ — _____

    j.   nonconformist   _____ — _____

2. Copy the following sentences. Make the nouns underlined show possession.

      (1)   *Sam* books were in the *doctor* car.   _____   _____

      (2)   The *women* names were in the paper.   _____   _____

      (3)   The *children* swimming class starts tomorrow. _____   _____

      (4)   The *girls* spelling team won.   _____   _____

      (5)   The *brothers* names are Dan and Don.   _____   _____

      (6)   There is a sale of *ladies* dresses.   _____   _____

3. Make contractions from the words below:

   (1) have not _____ (6) did not _____

   (2) will not _____ (7) you are _____

   (3) we are _____ (8) he is _____

   (4) I have _____ (9) I would _____

   (5) we would _____

MAJOR CATEGORY: WRITTEN LANGUAGE DEVELOPMENT

Given the following exercises, student reads the directions and completes the assignment without assistance:

4. Number the paper 1 to 7. If the group of words is a complete sentence, write *Sentence* and copy it. If it is not, add words to form a complete sentence. Use the necessary capital letters and punctuation marks.

   1. early one summer morning

   2. the boys set off on their hike

   3. after an hour of walking

   4. everyone was tired and thirsty

   5. their campsite at noon

   6. when they had unpacked their gear

   7. they began to prepare lunch

5. Read these sentences and add the correct punctuation marks. Write the kind of sentence each one is. Then underline each complete subject once and each complete predicate twice.

   1. Down the street came a band _____
   2. Have you seen the new library _____
   3. Here comes the tornado _____
   4. There stood the policeman _____
   5. Please be quiet in the library _____
   6. The smell of burning leaves filled the air _____
   7. Isn't autumn your favorite season _____

6. There are four common nouns and five proper nouns below. Make a list of each kind of noun. Capitalize the proper nouns.

   1. hat   4. town   7. friday

   2. dentist   5. america   8. july

   3. kansas   6. river   9. emily

   Common   *Proper*

7. Write each sentence below correctly.

   (1)   broke, broken   The goat has xxxx the fence.

   (2)   Was, Were   xxxx Jane and Bob late for school?

   (3)   is, are   Here xxxx the papers you wanted.

   (4)   grew, grown   The corn has xxxx tall this year.

   (5)   spoke, spoken   Have you xxxx to the new girl yet?

   (6)   begun, began   We xxxx to go as the bell rang.

   (7)   fell, fallen   The skater had xxxx on the ice.

   (8)   drank, drunk   Have you xxxx all the milk?

   (9)   wrote, written   Bill has not xxxx the invitations.

 (10)   brung, brought   Have you xxxx the cups?

8. Write the correct word to complete each sentence.

   1.   them, those   Does Ed have one of xxxx guns?

  _____

   2.   Those, That   xxxx kind of toy is dangerous.

  _____

   3.   bad, badly   The team played xxxx.

  _____

   4.   good, well   This pump works very xxxx.

  _____

   5.   quick, quickly   Al looked up xxxx.

  _____

   6.   hopeful, hopefully Herman's dog looked xxxx at our liverwurst sandwiches.

  _____

   7.   taller, tallest   Which of the two girls is the xxxx?

  _____

   8.   more harder, harder Diamonds are xxxx than glass.

  _____

   9.   anybody, nobody   Wasn't there xxxx at the store?

  _____

 10.   anything, nothing We haven't heard xxxx strange.

  _____

9. Copy these sentences, capitalizing words correctly.

   1.   last sunday the reverend james brown visited us.

   2.   we knew him when we lived on river road.

3. his brother is senator e. l. brown of ohio.

4. senator brown wrote a book called our atomic future.

5. i read the book when i was in the emerson school.

10. Copy these sentences. Use quotation marks, capital letters, and other punctuation marks where they are needed.

(1) may I go to the movies tonight I asked

(2) mother said you haven't done your english homework

(3) there is a wonderful show tonight I said

(4) Mother replied I'm sorry ann

(5) You'll have to wait until saturday she continued

11. Copy these sentences. Put in commas where needed.

(1) We left for Topeka Kansas on June 21 1967.

(2) I took my camera books and bike with me.

(3) Yes the car was crowded

(4) You should see the picture I took Stan!

(5) We got to St. Louis Missouri in three days.

MAJOR CATEGORY: STRUCTURE OF LANGUAGE

Given the following exercises, student reads the directions and completes the assignment without assistance:

12. The verbs in these sentences need helping verbs. Write the sentences, adding a helping verb.

(1) Two men xxxx standing on the bridge yesterday.

(2) The river xxxx covered with ice.

(3) One man xxxx had seen something exciting.

(4) He xxxx pointing it out to the other.

(5) I xxxx never found out what it was.

(6) I xxxx not think of it again.

13. Find and write the verb in each sentence.

(1) The fire alarm has sounded. _____

(2) We could not see the fire. _____

(3) We ran after the fire truck. _____

(4) An old barn was burning. _____

(5) A crowd had soon gathered. _____

(6) Everyone should help the fireman. _____

14. There are four adjectives and three adverbs in these sentences. Write each one and tell which part of speech it is. Then write the word each describes.

(1) Six men were in the little boat.
(2) The wind rose suddenly.
(3) The boat tossed dangerously.
(4) Two frightened men jumped into the water.
(5) They swam expertly toward shore.

Adjectives	Word they describe

Adverbs	Word they describe

MAJOR CATEGORY: VOCABULARY DEVELOPMENT

15. Given an Informal Word Recognition Inventory at Level 11, student names 85% of the words correctly.

1. inform	8. screen	14. you'd	20. foreign
2. quarrel	9. prow	15. twilight	21. dignity
3. sorrow	10. gas	16. grave	22. leisure
4. cable	11. glide	17. regarding	23. swaying
5. problem	12. thorns	18. koala	24. space
6. wilderness	13. vanished	19. notes	25. laughter
7. who's			

MAJOR CATEGORY: COMPREHENSION

16. (The child should read a selection of about 100 to 150 words from a basal reader, fifth grade level. You should develop a set of questions to go along with the story. In order for the child to satisfactorily complete this part of the test, he should get about 80% of the questions correct.

You should include in your directions to the child a motivating sentence, such as:

In this story a very valuable item is lost. Do you think it will be found?

The child should read the selection. You should develop questions to deal with several aspects of comprehension. Samples are included to help guide your thinking as you prepare questions. You should insert your paragraph and questions into this part of the test as you will use them many times. These activities should be developed in materials readily available to you but not usually encountered by the children in the ongoing program of instruction.

Some samples of the type of questions to include are:

1. Main idea

   What is this story about?
   Does the story have a moral?
   What would be a good title for the story?

2. Detail

   Who was the main character?
   What year did the story take place?
   How long did the story take?
   How many?

3. Sequence

   What did Bill do after he lost his watch?
   What did Mary do after she talked to Louise?
   What day did the story begin?
   What day did the story end?

4. Inference

   Is there something in the story that is not said directly?
   Does the story teach any kind of a lesson?
   Was there something in the story different from things you have
       heard or read somewhere else?
   What was Bill's problem in the story?

5. Value judgments

   Can you agree with the story?
   How did you feel about Marge in the story?
   Would you like everyone to read this story? Why?
   Do you believe the things in the story could really happen?
   Are there sometimes things you read that you don't quite believe?
       Was there anything in this story like that?
   Is there anything you can do to find out if a story is really true?
       For example?

6. Author's purpose

   What do you feel the author is trying to say in this story?
   Do you think he is trying to say something he has not written
       directly?
   What kind of a person do you think he is?
   What do you think he believes about the topic of this article?

7. Personality

   Why did you like (dislike) this story?
   Did anything like this ever happen to you?
   How did the story make you feel? Why?
   Were there parts of the story that made you feel differently?

333

Which character in the story, if any, was most like you?
Would you like to have the main character for a friend?

8. Peer group awareness

Who do you know that would possibly enjoy this story?
Who do you think would enjoy hearing about this story?
Do you know anyone that is like the main character in the story?

9. Personality insight

Is there anyone you would ask to help you if you had a problem like the main character in the story?
Does the story make you feel like doing anything? What?
Was there anyone in the story who acted in a way you didn't like?

10. Vocabulary

In the sentence, "Will you please look after your sister?" what do the words "look after" mean?
In the sentence, "Some people have big feet and some people have small feet," what two words have opposite meanings?

Be sure to try to keep the level of difficulty of the questions consistent with the level of the reading selection you are using.)

MAJOR CATEGORY: STUDY SKILLS

Given the following exercises, student reads the directions and completes the assignment without assistance:

17. Below are a *subject card,* an *author card,* and a *title card.* Study each one carefully and answer the questions which follow.

114	Jackson, C. Paul
J	Little leaguer's first uniform
	New York, Crowell, 1952

1.

114	BASEBALL
J	Jackson, C. Paul
	Little leaguer's first uniform
	New York, Crowell, 1952

2.

114	Little leaguer's first uniform.	1952
J	Jackson, C. Paul	

3.

(1) Write the number of the card above which is: the author card_____;
    the title card _____; the subject card_____ .

(2) What does the number in the upper left-hand corner tell you?

_____

(3) When was this book on baseball published?

_____

(4) What is the name of the company that published this book?

_____

(5) In what city was the book published?

_____

18. Here are parts of an index which might be found in a science book. Use it to help
you answer the questions below.

A

Astronomy
    calendar, 157, 160-163
    history of, 152-159
    Newton's law, 165
    solar system, 170-188
    See also Newton, Sir Isaac
Atmosphere, 149, 217, 220

B

Braun, Wernher, von (1912-   )
    life of, 250-253
    space flights, 225

J

Jet
    construction of, 189-191
    engine, 202-210, 256
    fuel for, 212
    performance of, 206-209
    thrust, 193, 195-200
    uses of, 210
Jet propulsion, 256

N

Newton, Sir Isaac, (1642-1727)
    law of motion, 165
    life of, 164-165

P

Planet, 180-186

R

Range stations, 241-245
Rocket
    engine, 212
    four-stage, 222-224
    fuel for, 213-216
    gravity, 219-220
    history of, 165, 231-240
    oxygen for, 217-218
    safety measures, 224, 230
    space flights of, 225-231
    See also Jet propulsion

S

Satellite, 173, 245, 247, 305-309

(1) What pages would you read to learn how the jet engine works? _____

(2) What pages would you read to learn when Sir Isaac Newton lived?_____

(3) On what page can you learn about Newton's law of motion? _____

335

(4) How many pages tell of satellites? _____

(5) What other heading will give you more information about rockets?

_____

(6) What pages would you read to learn about our solar system? _____

(7) What pages might tell you the names of the planets? _____

(8) What pages should you read to learn who Wernher von Braun is? _____

(9) What subtopic will tell you of flights made by rockets?_____

(10) What pages might tell you when rockets were first used?_____

MAJOR CATEGORY: HANDWRITING

19. Given the following paragraph to copy in both cursive and manuscript form, student meets the evaluative criteria.

> I live in America. It is good to live where you have freedom to work and play. As an American, I support my country and what it stands for.

MAJOR CATEGORY: SPELLING

20. Given the following list of words to write from dictation, student achieves an 85% or better score:

1. address _____		14. marbles _____
2. baseball _____		15. nor _____
3. blossoms _____		16. Pilgrims _____
4. camel _____		17. popcorn _____
5. chimney _____		18. quarter _____
6. countries _____		19. ripe _____
7. dirty _____		20. sleepy _____
8. everywhere _____		21. sugar _____
9. fixed _____		22. swimming _____
10. geography _____		23. twelve _____
11. handkerchief _____		24. welcome _____
12. history _____		25. worm _____
13. leather _____		

EVALUATION INSTRUMENT—LEVEL 12

MAJOR CATEGORY: VOCABULARY DEVELOPMENT

1. Given an Informal Word Recognition Inventory at Level 12, student names 85% of the words correctly.

1.	victory	14.	bulldozers
2.	license	15.	burden
3.	horror	16.	reflex
4.	perfection	17.	rigging
5.	exercise	18.	conquer
6.	stout	19.	lord
7.	vicious	20.	worn
8.	hind	21.	scorn
9.	instant	22.	mountaineers
10.	tusks	23.	goggles
11.	worm	24.	unbeatable
12.	dinner	25.	museum
13.	swear		

MAJOR CATEGORY: COMPREHENSION

2. (The child should read a selection of about 100 to 150 words from a basal reader, sixth grade level. You should develop a set of questions to go along with the story. In order for the child to satisfactorily complete this part of the test, he should get about 80% of the questions correct.

   You should include in your directions to the child a motivating sentence, such as:

   > In this story a very valuable item is lost. Do you think it will be found?

   The child should read the selection. You should develop questions to deal with several aspects of comprehension. Samples are included to help guide your thinking as you prepare questions. You should insert your paragraph and questions into this part of the test as you will use them many times. These activities should be developed in materials readily available to you but not usually encountered by the children in the ongoing program of instruction.

   Some samples of the type of questions to include are:

   1. Main idea
      What is this story about?

Does the story have a moral?

What would be a good title for the story?

2. Detail

Who was the main character?

What year did the story take place?

How long did the story take?

How many?

3. Sequence

What did Bill do after he lost his watch?

What did Mary do after she talked to Louise?

What day did the story begin?

What day did the story end?

4. Inference

Is there something in the story that is not said directly?

Does the story teach any kind of a lesson?

Was there something in the story different from things you have heard or read somewhere else?

What was Bill's problem in the story?

5. Value judgments

Can you agree with the story?

How did you feel about Marge in the story?

Would you like everyone to read this story? Why?

Do you believe the things in the story could really happen?

Are there sometimes things you read that you don't quite believe? Was there anything in this story like that?

Is there anything you can do to find out if a story is really true? For example?

6. Author's purpose

What do you feel the author is trying to say in this story?

Do you think he is trying to say something he has not written directly?

What kind of a person do you think he is?

What do you think he believes about the topic of this article?

7. Personality

Why did you like (dislike) this story?

Did anything like this ever happen to you?

How did the story make you feel? Why?

Were there parts of the story that made you feel differently?

Which character in the story, if any, was most like you?

Would you like to have the main character for a friend?

8. Peer group awareness

Who do you know that would possibly enjoy this story?

Who do you think would enjoy hearing about this story?

Do you know anyone that is like the main character in the story?

9. Personality insight

        Is there anyone you would ask to help you if you had a problem like the main character in the story?

        Does the story make you feel like doing anything? What?

        Was there anyone in the story who acted in a way you didn't like?

10. Vocabulary

        In the sentence, "Will you please look after your sister?" what do the words "look after" mean?

        In the sentence, "Some people have big feet and some people have small feet," what two words have opposite meanings?

Be sure to try to keep the level of difficulty of the questions consistent with the level of the reading selection you are using.)

EVALUATION INSTRUMENT—LEVEL 13

MAJOR CATEGORY: STRUCTURAL ANALYSIS

1. Given the following exercises, student reads the directions and completes the
    assignment without assistance:

    Match the prefixes in the first column with their correct meaning in second column
    and write a word using each prefix.

1.	ex-	above
2.	super-	before, in advance
3.	anti-	the opposite of
4.	non-	former, previously
5.	mono-	not
6.	dis-	wrong, badly
7.	com, con-	between, among
8.	inter-	with, together
9.	mis-	single
10.	pre-	against

    1. _____
    2. _____
    3. _____
    4. _____
    5. _____
    6. _____
    7. _____
    8. _____
    9. _____
    10. _____

2. Write the suffix of the first word in the first column. Add the suffix to the first
    word in column two. Tell the meaning of the word you have formed. Do the
    same for numbers 2-10. Do this on the next page.

(1)	pointless	meaning-	(6) condemnation	represent-
(2)	governor	deposit-	(7) careful	power-
(3)	roughest	smooth-	(8) lovable	notice-
(4)	columnist	art-	(9) placement	enjoy-
(5)	manifold	ten-	(10) topmost	upper-

    1. _____ _____ _____
    2. _____ _____ _____
    3. _____ _____ _____

4. _____ _____ _____

5. _____ _____ _____

6. _____ _____ _____

7. _____ _____ _____

8. _____ _____ _____

9. _____ _____ _____

10. _____ _____ _____

3. Write the plural form of each of these nouns:

1. beach— _____   6. echo— _____

2. key— _____   7. trout— _____

3. mouse— _____   8. fox— _____

4. leaf— _____   9. goose— _____

5. hobby— _____

4. Copy these sentences. Make the nouns underlined show possession.

(1) This space is reserved for *doctors* cars.

(2) The *twins* bicycles were in the *neighbor* yard.

(3) The *hero* story was quite exciting.

(4) The *baby* picture hung in his *parents* room.

(5) The *elves* new clothes were of spun gold.

MAJOR CATEGORY: WRITTEN LANGUAGE DEVELOPMENT

Given the following exercises, student reads the directions and completes the assignment without assistance:

5. If the word group below is a sentence, write *sentence.* If it is not, add words to form a complete sentence. Add the right punctuation mark.

(1) The ancient Greeks were great athletes

(2) Even while at war with each other

(3) They would lay aside their arms

(4) Just long enough for the Olympic Games

(5) Great crowds shouting and cheering

6. Choose the right verb to complete each sentence. Write the verb.

(1) threw, thrown   Who xxxx the ball?

_____

(2) Known, knew   I hadn't xxxx about it.

_____

(3) drank, drunk   The boys xxxx some water from the clear brook.

_____

(4) grew, grown   Where were those tomatoes xxxx?

_____

(5) stole, stolen   Someone has xxxx our boat!

_____

(6) written, wrote   He should have xxxx sooner.

_____

(7) run, rang   The bell had xxxx.

_____

(8) froze, frozen   At last the pond is xxxx.

_____

(9) saw, seen   We xxxx the Statue of Liberty.

_____

(10) begun, began   I xxxx reading that book last week.

_____

(11) broken, broke   Is your camera xxxx?

_____

(12) taken, took   Have you ever xxxx the short cut?

_____

(13) spoke, spoken   Not a word was xxxx.

_____

(14) rode, ridden   Joyce has xxxx the black stallion several times.

_____

(15) did, done   She xxxx it this morning.

_____

7. Copy these sentences, adding capital letters, quotation marks, and any other punctuation marks that are needed.

    (1) the junior science club will meet on tuesday may 23

    (2) ive bought some colored slides ben in case youre interested

    (3) stans brother henry is a ranger in sequoia national park

    (4) heavy seas severe gales and fog are delaying the queen elizabeths arrival in new york

    (5) thomas jefferson said miss hoffman was the third president of the united states

    (6) the radio cant be broken said tom we bought it just last week

(7) fred said grandmother is in the sixth grade

(8) can anyone direct us to essex memorial hospital alice inquired politely

(9) arent mr and mrs jamison at home

(10) they have gone to paris to see jan novak their niece

MAJOR CATEGORY: STRUCTURE OF LANGUAGE

Given the following exercises, student reads the directions and completes the assignment without assistance:

8. Find the verb or verb phrase in each sentence. Place it in the second column. Find the subject of the verb. Place it in the first column.

(1) There in front of us was a rattlesnake!
(2) Does Linda really have the measles?
(3) Here are your coat and gloves, Dorothy.
(4) In front of our house rumbled a huge truck.
(5) Someone has been playing the piano.
(6) Several of the keys do not strike.
(7) We certainly must call a piano tuner

(1) _____   _____
(2) _____   _____
(3) _____   _____
(4) _____   _____
(5) _____   _____
(6) _____   _____
(7) _____   _____

9. In one column write the common nouns from the list below. In the other, write the proper nouns. Capitalize the proper nouns.

(1) city   (4) canada   (7) avenue
(2) college   (5) halloween   (8) pacific ocean
(3) nashville   (6) doctor   (9) doctor curtis

Proper   Common

_____   _____
_____   _____
_____   _____
_____   _____
_____   _____
_____   _____
_____   _____
_____   _____

10. Fill in the blank with the correct pronoun from column one.

1. I, me   Jane and _____ went shopping.

2. I, me   What did you buy for Jim and_____.

3. He, him   _____ and I caught a fish.

4. they, them   Have you seen Beth and _____.

5. she, her   The boys and _____ran home.

6. they, them   Was it _____ who left first?

7. I, me   Between you and _____, I won't go.

8. we, us   Are you going with Ed and _____ .

9. he, him   Henry and _____ went fishing.

10. we, us   The costumes were made by _____girls.

11. Fill in the blank with the correct verb that agrees with the subject.

1. need, needs   One of my shoes _____ laces.

2. was, were   In which state _____ you born?

3. were, was   Standing in the road _____two young deer and their mother.

4. is, are   Where in the world _____ my skates?

5. was, were   A sandwich and a cookie _____ all I could eat.

6. don't, doesn't   The noise of cars _____ annoy me.

7. play, plays   Each of the bands _____loudly.

8. is, are   There _____three plans from which to choose.

9. has, have   Neither of the teams_____ won.

10. is, are   Under the trees _____a cool spot.

12. Find the adjectives and adverbs in these sentences. Put the adjectives in one column and the adverbs in another. After each adjective and adverb write the word that is modified.

1. The old man signaled frantically, but the crowded bus sped ahead.
2. I can finish this assignment easily in two hours.
3. Outside, the heavy snow drifted.
4. The red leaves are prettier than the yellow ones.
5. Sheila recently brought us this beautiful book from Bookbinder's in London.
6. Does a porcupine really throw quills?
7. The strong wind shook the bare trees violently.
8. Some pleasant people always smile.

         adjective   *adverb*

_____   _____

_____   _____

344   _____   _____

_____ _____
_____ _____
_____ _____
_____ _____
_____ _____

13. Complete each comparison with comparative or superlative form.

    (1)   well   Jess writes _____ than he used to.

    (2)   careful   You must learn to be _____ than before.

    (3)   easy   These are the _____ exercises we have ever had.

    (4)   hard   This test is _____ than the last one.

    (5)   angry   Ed was the _____ of all.

14. Fill in the blank with the adjective or adverb that correctly completes each sentence.

    (1)   bad, badly   We sang the first song _____.

    (2)   good, well   The boys always sing _____.

    (3)   perfect, perfectly They did the song _____.

    (4)   quick, quickly   They left the stage _____.

    (5)   loud, loudly   The audience applauded _____.

MAJOR CATEGORY: VOCABULARY DEVELOPMENT

15. Given an Informal Word Recognition Inventory at Level 13, student names 85% of the words correctly.

1. stroke	8. ramps	14. necessary	20. lungs
2. destined	9. lenses	15. protested	21. cabinets
3. studiously	10. experimental	16. prison	22. devil
4. clasped	11. fantastic	17. lad	23. narrator
5. valuable	12. crude	18. criticize	24. instructions
6. televised	13. physics	19. nudged	25. revolver
7. herald			

MAJOR CATEGORY: COMPREHENSION

16. (The child should read a selection of about 100 to 150 words from a basal reader, seventh grade level. You should develop a set of questions to go along with the story. In order for the child to satisfactorily complete this part of the test, he should get about 80% of the questions correct.

    You should include in your directions to the child a motivating sentence, such as:

        In this story a very valuable item is lost. Do you think it will be found?

The child should read the selection. You should develop questions to deal with several aspects of comprehension. Samples are included to help guide your thinking as you prepare questions. You should insert your paragraph and questions into this part of the test as you will use them many times. These activities should be developed in materials readily available to you but not usually encountered by the children in the ongoing program of instruction.

Some samples of the type of questions to include are:

1. Main idea
    What is this story about?
    Does the story have a moral?
    What would be a good title for the story?

2. Detail
    Who was the main character?
    What year did the story take place?
    How long did the story take?
    How many?

3. Sequence
    What did Bill do after he lost his watch?
    What did Mary do after she talked to Louise?
    What day did the story begin?
    What day did the story end?

4. Inference
    Is there something in the story that is not said directly?
    Does the story teach any kind of a lesson?
    Was there something in the story different from things you have
        heard or read somewhere else?
    What was Bill's problem in the story?

5. Value judgments
    Can you agree with the story?
    How did you feel about Marge in the story?
    Would you like everyone to read this story? Why?
    Do you believe the things in the story could really happen?
    Are there sometimes things you read that you don't quite believe?
        Was there anything in this story like that?
    Is there anything you can do to find out if a story is really true?
        For example?

6. Author's purpose
    What do you feel the author is trying to say in this story?
    Do you think he is trying to say something he has not written
        directly?
    What kind of a person do you think he is?
    What do you think he believes about the topic of this article?

7. Personality
    Why did you like (dislike) this story?

Did anything like this ever happen to you?

How did the story make you feel? Why?

Were there parts of the story that made you feel differently?

Which character in the story, if any, was most like you?

Would you like to have the main character for a friend?

8. Peer group awareness

Who do you know that would possibly enjoy this story?

Who do you think would enjoy hearing about this story?

Do you know anyone that is like the main character in the story?

9. Personality insight

Is there anyone you would ask to help you if you had a problem like the main character in the story?

Does the story make you feel like doing anything? What?

Was there anyone in the story who acted in a way you didn't like?

10. Vocabulary

In the sentence, "Will you please look after your sister?" what do the words "look after" mean?

In the sentence, "Some people have big feet and some people have small feet," what two words have opposite meanings?

Be sure to try to keep the level of difficulty of the questions consistent with the level of the reading selection you are using.)

MAJOR CATEGORY: STUDY SKILLS

Given the following exercises, student reads the directions and completes the assignment without assistance:

17. It is useful to know where different kinds of information can be found. For example, the best place to look for facts about the size of the United States is in an atlas (a book of maps). There are many other sources where information of all kinds can be found. Select the best source of information for each problem below, and underline the correct answer. The first one is done for you.

Where would you look to find:

1. which syllable is accented in a word?

    atlas   encyclopedia   book review   <u>dictionary</u>

2. information about the thirteen American Colonies?

    atlas   encyclopedia   timetable   dictionary

3. the correct spelling of a word?

    card catalogue   dictionary   book review   atlas

4. a map of Brazil?

    telephone directory   atlas   timetable   dictionary

5. the time an airplane will arrive at the airport?

    encyclopedia   timetable   telephone directory   atlas   347

6. the title and author of a book about pets?
encyclopedia   card catalogue   atlas   telephone directory

7. information about the invention of the sewing machine.
atlas   dictionary   encyclopedia   book review

8. the name and address of a doctor near your home?
dictionary   telephone directory   atlas   book review

9. the title, author, publisher, and price of a new book?
book review   encyclopedia   atlas   dictionary

10. the name of the largest city in the United States?
card catalogue   dictionary   atlas   timetable

11. how to pronounce a word?
atlas   timetable   dictionary   book review

12. information about the products of Canada?
dictionary   book review   atlas   encyclopedia

18. Given the following paragraph to copy in both cursive and manuscript form, student meets the evaluative criteria.

I pledge allegiance to the flag of the United States of
America and to the republic for which it stands, one nation
under God, indivisible, with liberty and justice for all.

MAJOR CATEGORY: SPELLING

19. Given the following list of words to write from dictation, student achieves an 85% or better score:

1. absent	14. nature
2. autumn	15. payment
3. branches	16. pour
4. chocolate	17. purse
5. crawled	18. reward
6. dictionary	19. shoulder
7. education	20. southern
8. fasten	21. station
9. gasoline	22. taste
10. holy	23. thunder
11. intended	24. useless
12. length	25. visitor
13. material	

LEVELED MATHEMATICS SKILL SEQUENCE

Readiness Level:

Upon successful completion of the *readiness* level the child will be
  able to do the following:

To count in sequence 1-7

To recognize numerals 1-7

To correctly form numerals 1-7

To make sets equal by adding or taking away

To recognize the four basic shapes in different positions

To recognize a penny, nickel, and a dime

To count items in a set, using one-to-one correspondence

Level One:

To arrange numerals 1-7 in proper sequence

To recognize sets and subsets 1-7

To do cardinal and ordinal counting 1-7

To associate sets, numerals, and number words 1-7

To supply the missing addends for sums 1-7

To solve the addition and subtraction facts through 7, using counters
  if necessary

To solve simple number problems based on a picture sequence or a
  continuous story

Level Two:

To read and write numerals 1-9

To arrange numerals 1-9 in proper sequence

To associate sets, numerals, and number words 1-9

To do cardinal and ordinal counting 1-9

To supply the missing addends for sums 1-9

To solve addition and subtraction facts through 9, using counters if
  necessary

To solve the multiplication and division facts through 9

Level Three:

To use zero as a place-holder for the empty set

To solve vertical addition facts with sums through nine

To tell the value of a penny, a nickel, or a dime

To make equivalent sets using pennies, nickels, and dimes

To add and subtract using money

To add columns of three numerals with sums through 9

To count to 100 by 10's

To count to 50 by 5's

To count to 50 by 2's

To recognize place value of ones and tens

To fold paper to show 1/2 and 1/4

To tell time on the hour

Level Four:

To solve column addition and subtraction facts of numbers through 10 (with counters)

To read number words and write corresponding numerals through 10

To add and subtract sums of money through 10 cents

To tell what comes before and after a number to 100

To determine value of sets of coins through the teens

To tell time to the half hour

To add sums of money in columns of three numerals

Level Five:

To count in sequence 1 to 100

To write in sequence the numerals 1-100

To count by 2's, 5's, and 10's to 100

To use the symbols $>$, $<$, $=$

To write the addition and subtraction facts to 14 in vertical and horizontal form

To identify the basic geometric shapes by name

To add and subtract to 20 by using a number line

To make pictures illustrating the teen numbers

To demonstrate place value to two places using bundles

To match number words and numerals to 20

To use correctly ordinal number words *first* to *tenth*

Level Six:

To add and subtract two and three-digit numbers vertically (without renaming)

To read three digit numerals

To demonstrate place value of three digit numerals with bundles and pictures of bundles

To write the numbers that come before and after three digit numbers

To write equations to solve word problems using addition and subtraction

To find the missing numeral in an equation

To tell time to the quarter-hour and write these times

To show equivalent value of coins to one dollar and to write them in equation form

To recognize 1/2, 1/3, 1/4 of a whole by use of pictures

Level Seven:

To tell the value of a numeral in different positions to three places

To rename three digit numerals as hundreds, tens, and ones; tens and ones; or hundreds and ones

To recognize number words through the teens and —ty words (i.e. twenty)

To give quick recall of addition and subtraction facts

To recognize odd and even number endings

To make pictures showing 1/2, 1/4, 1/8, 1/3

To identify coins and give their value

To solve story problems involving time, length, weight, temperature, and liquid measure (cup, pint, qt., gal.)

To compute using multiplication and division facts for 2's and 3's

To identify these geometric figures in addition to the four basic shapes: line, line segment, end point, angle, ray, closed space figure, open space figure

Level Eight:

To read and write Roman numerals through 39

To add and subtract three digit numerals with renaming in the tens and hundreds places

To recognize place value to thousands

To multiply and divide two- and three-place numerals by any one digit numeral

To use the dollar sign and the decimal point to indicate money

To make change involving amounts of money to $5.00

Level Nine:

To identify the positions held by a digit in a numeral to the ten-thousands place

To separate a five-place numeral into periods

To compute addition and subtraction examples with renaming in the tens, hundreds, and thousands places

To know multiplication and division facts to 9

To compute multiplication and division examples with renaming; division with remainders; using two digit multipliers and divisors

To add and subtract rational numbers with like denominators

To solve story problems involving the standard units of measurement of length, liquid measures, and time

To choose the necessary operation needed to solve a story problem (addition, subtraction, multiplication, or division)

To read and write Roman Numerals to 100 (38, 46, 29, 58, 62, 83, 94)

Level Ten:

To identify the position held by a digit up to and including ten millions place

To read a numeral with eight digits

To compute addition and subtraction, using renaming; using six digit numbers

To find the product using a three digit multiplier

To compute division with two digit divisors leaving the remainder as a fraction

To find the area and perimeter of a square and rectangle

351

To be able to set up a set of decimal numerals so they can be added and subtracted in vertical form

To add and subtract rational numbers, changing terms

To change improper fractions to mixed numbers and mixed numbers to improper fractions

To solve think type story problems using more than one operation to find the solution

Level Eleven:

To read and recognize place value of a numeral to billions place

To multiply by four digit multipliers

To add and subtract decimals to the hundredths' place

To divide decimals by a whole number with dividends to hundredths

To master division with zero as a digit in the quotient

To multiply and divide rational numbers

To find the area and perimeter of a triangle and a parallelogram

To find the surface area of a cylinder and a right prism

To recognize alternate interior and corresponding angles.

TOPICAL COMMUNICATION SKILLS SEQUENCE

PHONIC ANALYSIS

_____ 1. Discriminates between consonant sounds (s, [hard] k,d,f,s [hard] h,j,l,m, n,p,r,s,t,v,w,v,z) and matches sound with the letter.

_____ 2. Identifies words which rhyme and states additional rhyming words.

_____ 3. Discriminates between final (b, hard c or k, d,f,g, [hard] , j,l,m,n,p,r,s,t,v,z) consonant sound and matches sound with the letter.

_____ 4. Matches the sound and letter for consonant digraphs in initial position (ch, sh, th, wh).

_____ 5. Initial digraph
th-voiced
th-unvoiced

_____ 6. Demonstrates ability to substitute consonants in the initial position using rhyming parts.

_____ 7. Demonstrates ability to substitute consonant digraphs in the initial position.

_____ 8. Identifies letters which are vowels.

_____ 9. Discriminates between consonants and vowels and matches the terms _consonant_ and _vowel_ to the appropriate symbols.

_____ 10. Demonstrates ability to substitute consonants in the final position (d,k, l,m,n,p,r,t,x).

_____ 11. Matches the sound and letters for final consonant digraphs (sh, ch, th, nk, ck, st, ll, kn).

_____ 12. Demonstrates ability to substitute consonant digraphs in the final position.

_____ 13. Matches the sound and letters for initial consonant blends (br, cr, dr, fr, gr, pr, tr, bl, cl, fl, gl, pl, sl, sc, sk, sm, sn, sp, st, sw, qu, kw).

_____ 14. Demonstrates ability to substitute consonant blends in the initial position.

_____ 15. Matches the sounds and letters for final consonant blends (ld, lt, nk, mp, sk, sp, st, nt, nd).

353

_____ 16. Matches long vowel sounds with their corresponding symbols.

_____ 17. Matches short vowel sounds with their correspondent symbols (a,e,i,o,u).

_____ 18. Demonstrates ability to apply vowel generalizations in attaching words.
_____   a. o followed by ld (old, cold)
_____   b. i followed by nd (find, kind)
_____   c. i followed by gh (high, right)
_____   d. i followed by ld (wild, child)

_____ 19. Identifies murmur diphthongs ar, er, ir, ur.

_____ 20. Identifies vowel sounds affected by the letter _r_ as in:

car	her	corn	fir	fur
farm	serve	north	bird	turn

_____ 21. Identifies the sound of the vowel _a_ when followed by the letters _l_ and _ll_ as in _talk, salt, call,_ and _ball._

_____ 22. Distinguishes between the dipthong _ow_ as in cow and the long _o_ sound of _ow_ as in snow.

_____ 23. Understands the use of principles:
_____   a. Long vowel before silent e.
_____   b. Long vowel at end of a word or syllable.
_____   c. The first vowel is usually long when two vowels of a word are together.
_____   d. The vowel is usually short when a vowel in a word or syllable is followed by a consonant.

_____ 24. Identifies the two sounds of the letter combination _oo_ and distinguishes between the two sounds when attacking new words.

_____ 25. Identifies the conditions under which the letter _y_ functions as a vowel.

_____ 26. Identifies silent consonants in words.

_____ 27. Matches three-letter consonant blends with their corresponding symbols (scr, spl, spr, squ, str, thr).

_____ 28. Demonstrates ability to substitute three-letter blends in the initial position.

_____ 29. Matches vowel digraphs with their corresponding symbols (ee, oa, ai, ea, oy).

_____ 30. Matches vowel diphthongs with their corresponding sounds (oi, oy, ou, ow, as in cow, au, aw, er).

_____ 31. Distinguishes between the hard and soft sounds for *c* and *g*.

_____ 32. Identifies the common exceptions to the vowel generalization covering the sound of a vowel in the medial or initial position.

_____ 33. Identifies the diacritical marks-breve and macron.

_____ 34. Identifies the schwa sound in unaccented syllables.

STRUCTURAL ANALYSIS

_____ 1. Identifies compound words.

_____ 2. Forms compound words from two known words.

_____ 3. Identifies "s" signaling plurality.

_____ 4. Demonstrates sensitivity to syllables in polysyllabic words.

_____ 5. Identifies the word endings, *s, d, ed,* and *ing.*

_____ 6. Identifies number of syllables heard in a word.

_____ 7. Identifies compound words when made from one known and one unknown word.

_____ 8. Identifies by naming the structural parts-"root" or "base" word and "word endings." (s,d,ed,ing)

_____ 9. Identifies the singular possessive and distinguishes between the plural form and the singular possessive of words.

_____ 10. Identifies and applies meaning to new words formed when the suffix *er* has been added to the root word.

_____ 11. Constructs and identifies the following contractions.

didn't	don't	let's
hadn't	doesn't	haven't
aren't	I'd	can't
I'll	couldn't	I'm
won't	you're	wouldn't
isn't	it's	I've
o'clock	that's	wasn't
you'll		

_____ 12. Demonstrates ability to add endings to root words that necessitate structural changes in the root words:

_____ a. Doubling the final consonant when adding *ed* and *ing.*

355

_____ b. Changing _y_ to _i_ when adding certain endings.

_____ c. Dropping final _e_ when adding _ing._

_____ 13. Identifies number of syllables and the accented syllable in polysyllabic words.

_____ 14. Identifies the conditions under which the plural of a noun is formed by adding _es._

_____ 15. Forms plurals of words ending in _y._

_____ 16. Identifies the structural changes involved when suffixes are added to root words ending in _y_ or silent _e._

_____ 17. Identifies common prefixes affixed to root words: dis, en, in, re, un.

_____ 18. Identifies common suffixes affixed to root words: er, est, ful, ish, less, ly, ness, y.

_____ 19. Forms plurals of words ending in _f_ or _fe._

_____ 20. Identifies the generalizations that a word has as many syllables as it has vowel sounds.

_____ 21. Identifies prefixes and suffixes previously taught as syllabic units.

_____ 22. Identifies the vowel-consonant-consonant-vowel pattern (v-c-c-v) in words and uses it to divide words into syllables.

_____ 23. Identifies the vowel-consonant-vowel pattern (v-c-v) in words and uses it to divide words into syllable.

_____ 24. Understands rules of syllabication:

_____ a. When two different consonants or a consonant and a blend come between two vowels the first consonant usually ends the first syllable.

_____ b. When a consonant comes before _le_ at the end of a word, the consonant usually begins the last syllable.

_____ c. When a single consonant comes between two vowels, the consonant is usually joined to the second vowel, or when the first vowel is followed by one consonant, the consonant usually begins the second syllable.

_____ d. When the suffix _ed_ is preceded by _d_ or _t_ it forms a separate syllable.

_____ 25. Identifies _ed_ as a syllable when added to root words ending in _d_ or _t._

_____ 26. Identifies the common syllable at the end of words made of _le_ and the consonant immediately preceding the _le._

_____ 27. Is aware that, as a general rule, words are not divided between consonant digraphs and consonant blends.

_____ 28. Discriminates between solid and hyphenated compound words and divides them into syllables.

_____ 29. Identifies as prefixes:

mono-	dis-	uni-
mal-	bi-	mid-
tri-	mis-	deca-
un-	omni-	auto-
pan-	bio-	para-
hydro-	circum-	lith-
com-, con-	phono-	extra-
photo-	intra-	tele-
sub-	pro-	em-
out-	ill-	self-
ir-	enter-	col-
cor-	co-	mal-

Suffixes:

-eer	-meter	-ier
-ology	-ster	-phobia
-ist	-scope	-arium
-most	-cide	-ic
-ee	-al	-gram
-ary	-ant	-ure
-ence	-ative	-wise
-let	-fold	-archy
-itis	-ity	-ance
-ible		

_____ 30. Identifies exceptions to syllabic generalizations.

_____ 31. Applies the rule requiring the use of a hyphen when separating a word at the end of a line.

Structure of Language

____ 1. Orders alphabet sequentially.

____ 2. Classifies alphabet by consonants and vowels.

____ 3. Classifies words according to simple parts of speech:
naming words
action words
descriptive words

____ 4. Identifies phrases.

____ 5. Identifies a sentence as a group of words which expresses a complete thought.
____ a. Constructs sentences using the first word.
____ b. Places a period at the end of a sentence.
____ c. Places a question mark at the end of a group of words that ask a question.

____ 6. Identifies the terms "paragraph" and "indent."

____ 7. Identifies antecedents of personal pronouns.

____ 8. Orders sequentially a list of words by noting the first letter.

____ 9. Identifies words or phrases within sentences that tell who, what, when, where, why, how.

____ 10. Writes sentences expressing complete thoughts using naming, action, and descriptive words.

____ 11. Demonstrates ability to transform statements into questions and questions into statements.

____ 12. Identifies a paragraph as a group of sentences that tells about one thing.

____ 13. Identifies multiple pronoun antecedents.

____ 14. Identifies three basic sentence types and their punctuation:
____ a. Telling or declarative
____ b. Asking or interogative
____ c. Exclamatory (uses exclamation point).

_____ 15. Demonstrates ability to identify the structural elements of the English language:
Letters
Words
Phrases
Sentences
Paragraphs

_____ 16. Identifies nouns, verbs, and adjectives as word form classes and classifies words into these categories.

_____ 17. Identifies comparative and superlative degree of adjectives.

_____ 18. Identifies the command as a sentence type (Imperative sentence).

_____ 19. Identifies the two major parts of a sentence.
_____ a. Subject and predicate both a simple and complete (noun phrase and verb phrase).

_____ 20. Identifies the topic sentence of a paragraph.

_____ 21. Writes a good paragraph built around a topic sentence.

_____ 22. Differentiates meanings for words claimed in two subject fields.

_____ 23. Selects the correct meaning for polysemantic words used in different subject contexts.

_____ 24. Identifies a topic sentence regardless of its position in a paragraph.

_____ 25. Discriminates between "it's" as a possessive pronoun and "it's" as a contraction of the pronoun "it" and the verb "is."

_____ 26. Identifies adjectives by position in sentence, differentiating between those coming before a noun and those that follow verbs like am, are, is, was, will be, were, became, grew, looked, felt and seemed.

_____ 27. Demonstrates ability to use the correct form of the verb "to be."

_____ 28. Identifies adverbs and discriminates the meaning they add to verbs by giving time (when), place (where), and manner (how).

_____ 29. Identifies transitional words and phrases in paragraphs by applying the technique of asking "What word or words in this sentence tie it to an earlier sentence?"

____ 30. Identifies common words that signal nouns (Determiners)

Articles
  the
  a
  an

Numbers
  one
  two
  three

Demonstratives
  this
  that
  these
  those

Indefinites
  every
  many
  any
  several

Indefinites
  each
  both
  some

____ 31. Identifies common prepositions.

of	to	at	into	between	over
in	for	on	under	down	across
by	with	from	toward	among	against

____ 32. Identifies pronouns as parts of speech and applies the following rules relative to their usage:

____ a. Pronouns take the place of nouns.

____ b. Pronouns can be either singular or plural.

____ c. These pronouns are used as the subjects of verbs: I, we, he, she, they.

____ d. These pronouns are used as objects of both verbs and prepositions: me, us, him, her, them.

____ e. When a pronoun and a noun are used as a compound subject, use a subject pronoun.

____ f. When a pronoun and noun are used as the subject of a verb, use a subject pronoun.

____ g. Use a subject pronoun after forms of the verb "to be."

____ h. Most pronouns have two possessive forms. *My, you, her, its, ours,* and *theirs* are used only when the possessive is followed by a noun. *Mine, yours, hers, ours,* and *theirs* are used when the possessive pronoun stands alone. *His* is used either before nouns or alone.

____ 33. Identifies the three basic functions of nouns:

____ a. Subject

____ b. Object of verb

____ c. Object of preposition

____ 34. Identifies compound subjects and compound predicates.

___ 35. Identifies a compound sentence as two independent clauses joined by connectives such as *and, but,* and *or.*

___ 36. Identifies dependent clauses through naming signal words used to introduce them

who	that	after
which	when	before
while	where	although
why	how	since
		because

Written Language

___ 1. Constructs lists, records, and memoranda.

___ 2. Constructs news reports.

___ 3. Writes labels.

___ 4. Writes picture captions.

___ 5. Identifies and writes proper nouns.

___ 6. Identifies *I* as a word and writes it with a capital letter.

___ 7. Demonstrates ability to use language creatively through creative and functional writing.

___ 8. Identifies titles and distinguishes words in titles that are to be written with capital letters.

___ 9. Writes names of days and months with a beginning capital letter.

___ 10. Discriminates among Mr., Mrs., Miss and Ms. and writes them correctly.

___ 11. Writes dates demonstrating correct form as to capitalization and punctuation including "comma."

___ 12. Constructs simple friendly letters and identifies the heading, greeting, body, closing, name, and uses indentations and commas.
___ a. Greetings and close of letters.
___ b. Titles of stories and books.

___ 13. Demonstrates ability to transfer mechanics of composition and usage to creative and functional writing activities.

361

____ 14. Avoidance of *he, she, it, we, they,* following a stated subject, i.e., "Mary, *she* went to the store."

____ 15. Avoidance of *here* and *there* following *this, that, these, those.*

____ 16. Demonstrates ability to write personal address in correct form.

____ 17. Writes other addresses in correct form.

____ 18. Demonstrates ability to use the following skills of capitalization and punctuation in written work:

Capital Letters

―― a. To begin the first word in a sentence.
―― b. To begin the names of people and pets.
―― c. To begin the names of streets and roads.
―― d. To begin the name of a school, city, town, and state.
―― e. To begin the first word and all important words in the title of a book, story, or report.
―― f. To write initials.
____ g. To begin titles—Mr., Mrs., Miss.
____ h. To begin the names of days of the week and months of the year and their abbreviations.
____ i. To begin the names of holidays and special events.
____ j. To begin the first word in the greeting and in the closing of a letter.
____ k. Usually to begin the first word in each line of poetry.

Personal Pronoun I
Periods

____ a. At the end of a statement.
____ b. After each initial.
____ c. After an abbreviation (Mr., Mrs.).

Question Mark

____ a. At the end of a question.

Exclamation Mark

____ a. At the end of telling sentence if the sentence shows strong feeling or surprise.

Apostrophes

____ a. In a contraction to show omission of a letter or letters.
____ b. Before or after *s* at the end of a word to show possession.

Commas

____ a. Between the name of a city and a state.
____ b. Between the day and the year when writing a date.
____ c. After the greeting of a letter
____ d. After the closing of a letter

362 ____ 19. Constructs paragraphs identifying indentation and margins.

____ 20. Demonstrates ability to proofread written work.

____ 21. Writes addresses on envelopes using correct capitalization, punctuation, and form.

____ 22. Discriminates between an apostrophe used in a contraction and an apostrophe used to show possession.

____ 23. Demonstrates ability to write answers to comprehension questions.

____ 24. Indicates titles by underlining.

____ 25. Demonstrates ability to write a simple book report.

____ 26. Demonstrates ability to select the correct form of the following words in written work:

a-an	wrote-written
he-him	rode-ridden
I-me	stole-stolen
is-are	are-aren't
she-her	feed-fed
was-were	get-got
sit-set	run-ran
ate-eat-eaten	took-taken
broke-broken	we-us
came-come	went-gone
do-did-done	where is-where are
doesn't-don't	bring-brought
gave-give-given	hasn't any
has gone-have gone	to-too-two
see-saw-seen	then-this-those
good-well	write-wrote-written
let-leave	No-words and Not-words
teach-learn	began-begun
here is-here are	drank-drunk
grew-grown	chose-chosen
knew-known	fell-fallen
rang-rung	nowhere-nothing
sang-sung	they-them
spoke-spoken	good-better-best
threw-thrown	bad-worse-worst

No-words and not-words are never used together in a sentence.

Avoidance of *here* and *there* following *this, that, these* and *those*. Avoidance of *he, she, it, we, they* following a stated subject, i.e., "Mary, *she* went to the store."

_____ 27. Selects closings for friendly letters that are appropriate for the person to whom the letter is written such as:

Sincerely	Your friend
Respectfully	Love
Your loving nephew	Your granddaughter
Affectionately	

_____ 28. Writes correctly a "thank-you" letter.

_____ 29. Writes correctly an invitation.

_____ 30. Constructs a book list.

_____ 31. Writes correctly a business letter applying the following rules:
_____   a. A business letter must have a purpose.
_____   b. It must be brief as well as complete.
_____   c. It must be neat and clearly written.
_____   d. Punctuation and form must be correct.

_____ 32. Identifies written format of a poem.

_____ 33. Writes direct quotations applying rules of capitalization and punctuation.

_____ 34. Identifies proper adjectives formed from proper nouns and capitalizes each one.

_____ 35. Applies the following rules for using commas:
_____   a. to separate the day of the month from the year, and after the year if the date appears in the middle of the sentence.
_____   b. To separate the name of a city from the name of the state and country in which it is located.
_____   c. To set off the name of a person spoken to or about.
_____   d. After the word "yes," "no," or "well," when a pause follows.
_____   e. To set apart words in a series.
_____   f. To separate words like "he said" from a direct quotation.
_____   g. After the greeting of a friendly letter and the closing of any letter.
_____   h. When "and," "but," and "or" are used to combine two sentences into one, place a comma before these connective words.

_____ 36. Identifies and interprets the purpose of varying type style and punctuation in written language.

Ellipsis	Quotation marks
Dash	Comma
Italics	Semi-colon
Period	Apostrophe
Colon	Parenthesis
Question mark	Exclamation point

___ 37. Writes answer to invitations.

___ 38. Writes titles and authors correctly.

___ 39. Identifies meaning, correct spelling, and punctuation of various abbreviations met in a variety of contexts. (Those listed are only suggestive; teach what the pupil meets and needs.)
    ___ Days of the week
    ___ Months of the year
    ___ States
    ___ Titles of people
    ___ Parts of speech
    ___ Measurement
    ___ Common abbreviations used in address (st., blvd., rd.)
    ___ Others such as: a.m., p.m., Co., Inc., Mt., R.R., C.O.D., P.O.

___ 40. Writes first letter of names of races, religions, nationalities, and language with capital letter.

___ 41. Writes the first letter of the names of clubs, organizations, and business firms with capital letters.

___ 42. Demonstrates ability to capitalize and punctuate sentences containing broken quotations.

___ 43. Applies the following rules for using a colon:
    ___ After the salutation of a business letter.
    ___ To separate hours from minutes in telling time.
    ___ To introduce a list except when the last directly follows a verb or preposition.

___ 44. Applies the following rules for using a semicolon:
    ___ In place of a conjunction between two closely related independent clauses.
    ___ Before connecting words like *besides, however, moreover, never the less, then, therefore.*
    ___ Between items in a series if the series contains commas.

Oral Language

___ 1. Demonstrates effective oral interpretation of printed text by achieving intonation and inflection through punctuation clues.

___ 2. Demonstrates emotional over-tones and meaningful expression through oral language.

365

_____ 3. Chooses standard English forms of usage in oral language.

_____ 4. Identifies large thought units and word groups in oral reading.

_____ 5. Demonstrates effective oral interpretation of printed text in identification of quotation marks.

_____ 6. Demonstrates emotional overtones through stress and pitch.

_____ 7. Demonstrates improvement in phrase reading and in interpretation of printed text by using stress and voice pitch.

_____ 8. States directions accurately.

_____ 9. Demonstrates growth in oral language by extending and refining expressional skills through:
_____ a. Discussions
_____ b. Story telling
_____ c. Dramatization
_____ d. Oral reading
_____ e. Dramatic play
_____ f. Oral descriptions
_____ g. Oral planning
_____ h. Sharing experiences
_____ i. Reporting
_____ j. Conversations
_____ k. Summarizing

_____ 10. Demonstrates correct telephone behavior.

_____ 11. Demonstrates ability to make introductions.

_____ 12. Demonstrates ability to give a simple book talk.

_____ 13. Demonstrates ability to state simple oral reports.

_____ 14. Constructs stories from experiences and states them in story form.

_____ 15. States directions accurately.

_____ 16. Demonstrates ability to conduct a personal interview.

_____ 17. Demonstrates ability to initiate, continue, and conclude a conversation.

_____ 18. Demonstrates ability to be involved in a panel discussion as follows:
_____ a. prepares for participation by using all possible sources to develop presentation and questions.

____ b. Sticks to topic; avoids irrelevancies.

____ c. Listens to other members of the panel.

____ d. Generally accepts standards established by the panel.

____ 19. Builds vocabulary through formal and incidental experiences.

____ 20. Identifies relationships in simple analogies.

____ 21. Demonstrates skill in selecting word opposites.

____ 22. Identifies words with multiple meanings.

____ 23. Selects word opposites and identifies them as antonyms. (oral and written).

____ 24. Identifies the concept of synonymous ideas.

____ 25. Identifies homonyms.

____ 26. Demonstrates ability to identify and use words with multiple meanings.

____ 27. Identifies the following language forms:
    ____ Slang
    ____ Euphemism
    ____ Dialect
    ____ Echoic words
    ____ Archaic Expressions
    ____ Recently coined words
    ____ Words borrowed from other languages
    ____ Idioms
    ____ Colloquialisms

COMPREHENSION

____ 1. Develops and applies literal comprehension skills.
____ a. Specific information.
____ b. Sequence.

____ 2. Develops and applies interpretive comprehension skills.
____ a. Main ideas and supporting details.
____ b. Relationships.
____ c. Figurative and special language.
____ d. Inferences.

____ 3. Develops and applies critical evaluative comprehension skills.
____ a. Prediction of outcomes.
____ b. Evaluation of accuracy.
____ c. Literary forms and author techniques.
____ d. Characterization.

____ 4. Applies comprehension skills stated above to listening activities.

____ 5. Demonstrates ability to read increasingly longer units of material and apply comprehension skills.

____ 6. Demonstrates ability to read increasingly longer units of material with accuracy and comprehension and with less guidance.

____ 7. Demonstrates ability to expand literal comprehension skills:
____ a. Specific information.

____ 8. Demonstrates ability to expand interpretive comprehension skills:
____ a. Main idea and supporting details.
____ b. Relationships.
____ c. Figurative and special language.
____ d. Inference.

____ 9. Demonstrates ability to expand critical-evaluative comprehension skills:
____ a. Prediction of outcomes.
____ b. Evaluation of accuracy.
____ c. Literary forms and author techniques.
____ d. Characterization.

____ 10. Demonstrates ability to expand interpretive comprehension skills:
____ a. Main ideas and supporting details.
____ b. Relationships.
____ c. Figurative and special language.
368 ____ d. Inferences.

_____ 11. Identifies major patterns found in science content, adjusts reading rate to the specific pattern, and applies both the comprehension and study skills necessary in working with the pattern.

_____ 12. Identifies major patterns found in social studies content, adjusts reading rate to the specific pattern, and applies both the comprehension and study skills necessary in working with the pattern.

_____ 13. Identifies major patterns found in mathematics content, adjusts reading rate to the specific pattern, and applies both the comprehension and study skills.

_____ 14. Applies comprehension skills to listening activities.

TOPICAL MATHEMATICS SEQUENCE

1. Numeration

1-1	Differentiate same, different; top, bottom; small, large; over, under; in, out; etc.
1-2	One to one correspondence
1-3	Write missing numerals in an incomplete sequence i.e. 1, 2, –, 4, 5
1-4	Facts numbers 1 to 10
1-5	Reads numbers 1 to 10
1-6	Matches numbers of objects 1 - 10
1-7	Uses the number line
1-8	Cardinal numbers to 10
1-9	Writes numbers 1 - 10
1-10	Tells number before and after a given number
1-11	Tells number in between two numbers
1-12	Matches number word with number 1 - 10
1-13	Deals with 10's
1-14	1 - 100 counts
1-15	1 - 100 writes
1-16	1 - 100 Numbers before, after and in-between
1-17	Uses $<$ and $>$ in proper order
1-18	Identify and write 100 - 200
1-19	Cardinal 0 - 100
1-20	Supplies number one more, less or in-between 100 - 200
1-21	Counts by 10 to 200
1-22	Count by 5 to 100
1-24	Counts by 2
1-24	Reads and writes number to 1000
1-25	Counts by 3
1-26	Counts by 4
1-27	Read, write, 4 digit numeral
1-28	5 digit numeral
1-29	Identifies odd and even numerals
1-30	Rounds numerals to 10 and 100
1-31	Expanded notation 2 and 3 place numerals
1-32	Place value to 1,000,000

5-a-5	Make change from purchases to 25¢, 50¢, $1
5-a-6	Add and subtract using decimals
5-a-7	Multiply and divide money amounts using decimals

5b. Distance

5-b-1	Identify and name foot and yard
5-b-2	Identify and name inch, 1/2 inch
5-b-3	Measure using foot and yard
5-b-4	Measure using inch and 1/2 inch
5-b-5	Identify 1/4, one-eighth, and one sixteenth inches
5-b-6	Measure using 1/4, one eighth and one sixteenth inches
5-b-7	Larger measures such as mile
5-b-8	Instruments for measuring longer distance—odometer
5-b-9	Identify and name metric units—meter and centimeter
5-b-10	Relationship between speed and distance

5c. Time

5-c-1	Time to nearest hour
5-c-2	Time to nearest half hour
5-c-3	Time to nearest quarter hour
5-c-4	Time to nearest minute, giving the hour first and number of minutes after the hour
5-c-5	Relationship among hours, minutes, and seconds
5-c-6	Hours in a day, days in week, weeks in year, months in year, etc.
5-c-7	Add and subtract hours, minutes, and seconds
5-c-8	Add and subtract days, weeks, months and years
5-c-9	A. M. and P. M.

5d. Calendar

5-d-1	Days of week
5-d-2	Seasons of year
5-d-3	Months of year
5-d-4	Relationship of year, decade, and century
5-d-5	Compute age to nearest day
5-d-6	Leap year
5-d-7	Add and subtract days, months, and year
5-d-8	Different historical calendars

5e. Liquid

5-e-1   Identify quart and gallon

5-e-2   Smaller units of a quart—pint and 1/2 pint

5-e-3   Quarts in a gallon

5-e-4   Cooking units—cups, tablespoons, teaspoons, etc.

5-e-5   Identify the correct number of smaller units needed to fill or equal a larger unit

5-e-6   Add and subtract common units of measure

5-e-7   Liquid units of the metric system

5f. Temperature

5-f-1   Identify warmer of two objects

5-f-2   Identify colder of two objects

5-f-3   Large fahrenheit thermometer

5-f-4   Compare temperature morning, noon, and evening

5-f-5   Compare fahrenheit and centigrade thermometer

5-f-6   Identify boiling and freezing points on fahrenheit and centigrade thermometer

5-f-7   Compute relationship between fahrenheit and centigrade

i.e. convert from one to another

$$F = 9/5 \ C + 32 \qquad C = 5/9 \ (F - 32)$$

5g. Weight

5-g-1   Balance sets of objects on a balance scale

5-g-2   Ounces and pounds

5-g-3   Add and subtract ounces and pounds

5-g-4   Metric weight units—gram and kilogram

5h. Area

5-h-1   Identify small and large regions

5-h-2   Choose a unit to measure any surface and report the number of units necessary to cover the surface

5-h-3   Length and width—how to compute area

5-h-4   Identify square units

5-h-5   Perimeter

5-h-6   Compute area of square, rectangle, triangle and circle

5i. Volume

5-i-1   Identify difference in size between and among solid figures

5-i-2   Identify relationship of smaller units to larger ones

375

9. Special Topics and Enrichment

TOPICAL SOCIAL STUDIES SKILLS SEQUENCE

Map Skills

I.   Earth as a Globe

    A.   Model of earth is called a globe

    B.   Globe is "round" so we call it a sphere

    C.   Globe is a map as well as a model of our earth—map or drawing on globe shows where things are on the earth

    D.   Globe is more accurate than flat map—e.g. Greenland

    E.   Hemispheres
        1.   Half a sphere is called a hemisphere so half of the earth is called a hemisphere (hemi-half; sphere-ball)
        2.   Two we live in—
            a.   Northern
            b.   Western
        3.   Land and water hemispheres
        4.   Eastern and Southern

    F.   Rotation—day and night concept

    G.   Revolution—of earth around sun
        1.   Causes 4 seasons in the year
        2.   Seasons in Northern Hemisphere are opposite of those in Southern Hemisphere
        3.   Tilt of earth's axis—axis is imaginary rod thru center of earth

    H.   The surface of earth is curved, although appears flat

    I.   Compares a picture of the earth with a picture of a globe

II.   Directions

    A.   North toward North Pole—South toward South Pole on ANT map

    B.   When facing N., east is always to right—west is to left

    C.   Cardinal directions
        1.   North
        2.   South
        3.   East
        4.   West

    D.   Intermediate directions
        1.   N. W.
        2.   S. W.
        3.   N. E.
        4.   S. E.

    E.   Understand use of compass for directions

F. Relative terms of location and direction
   1. Up and down are different from north and south
   2. Near and far

G. Introduce N., S., E., W.

H. Learns the relationship of the sun to the cardinal points

III. Map Representation

A. How to read a map
   1. Read a variety of special purpose maps
   2. Draw inferences on basis of data obtained from them

B. Two basic types of maps
   1. Physical
   2. Political

C. Specialized maps
   1. Product maps
   2. Vegetation
   3. Climate
   4. Color symbols
   5. Airplane view
   6. Community maps
   7. Relief maps
   8. Outline
   9. Population map
   10. Transportation map
   11. Resource centers
   12. Road map
   13. Rainfall
   14. Weather map
   15. Historical
   16. Cultural

D. Noting how symbols may vary on different maps

E. Learns to use a road map using a compass rose to find directions

F. Make a simple, large-scale map of a familiar area, example, classroom

G. Make inferences about directions. (Will the sun shine through the west window in the morning or in the afternoon?)

IV. Interpreting Maps

A. Interpret map symbols and color and visualize what they mean

B. Locate places on maps and globes

C. Draw inferences by comparing different map patterns of same area

D. Note differences in topography

E. Recognize location of major cities of the world with respect to their physical setting

F. Use atlas—all parts

G. Understand the significance of location as it affected national products

H. Interpret elevation of land from the flow of rivers

I. Understand differences in different map projections and recognize distortions involved in representation other than globe

J. Use maps and globes to explain geographical setting of historical and current events

K. Orient large scale maps in proper place on small scale maps

L. Learn to use legends, key, directional arrow (compass rose)

M. Use map vocabulary accurately

N. Study color contour and visualize the nature of area shown

O. Learns to identify certain geographical and political features (natural and manmade) on a map

P. Reads and interprets the map of a community

Q. Recognizes boundary lines and coastlines

R. Recognizes map symbols; building, bridge, mountain, hill, railroad, island, lake, etc.

S. Reads floor plans and compares a simple with a complete one

T. Learns about the geographical factor in the growth of a community

U. Finds the U.S. on the globe

V. Compare relative size, length, height of oceans, rivers, cities, counties, states, countries, continents, mountains

W. Compare natural conditions and distance from the equator

X. Understand that maps of same area may show different kinds of information

Y. Reading captions to help interpret maps

Z. Direction of flow of rivers: upstream, downstream

V. Land and Water Masses

   A. Land Masses—Continents

      1. Seven large masses on earth's surface

         a. North America

         b. South America

         c. Europe

         d. Asia

            1. c & d sometimes referred to as Eurasia because they are one large land mass divided by a mountain range

         e. Africa

         f. Australia

         g. Antarctica

2. Land masses are divided into regions
   a. Polar regions
   b. Desert regions
   c. Wet tropics
   d. High mountain regions
   e. Forest lands
   f. Grasslands
3. Continents are divided into smaller parts called countries. (Australia is the only continent and a country, too.)
   a. Our continent is N.A.
   b. Our country is U.S. of America
   c. Our country is divided into still smaller parts called states—our state is Pennsylvania

B. Water Masses—Oceans
   1. Atlantic Ocean
      a. ocean closest to us
      b. 2nd in size
   2. Pacific Ocean
      a. largest ocean
   3. Indian Ocean
      a. 3rd largest ocean
   4. Arctic Ocean
      a. smallest
      b. coldest
   5. Antarctic Ocean
      a. listed as 5th ocean in some texts

C. Locates land and water features on a variety of globes and maps

D. Understands that various countries have different physical characteristics

E. Composition of the earth's surfaces
   1. Most of the earth is water
   2. The rest of land mass which is inhabited by men

VI. Geographic Terms

basin	highland	river
bay	hill	sea
butte	island	source
canal	isthmus	strait
canyon	lake	swamp
channel	lowland	tide
cliff	land elevation	tributary
continent	latitude-longitude	upstream
delta	mesa	valley
desert	mountain	volcano
divide	mouth	topography
downstream	ocean	global grid

fiord	peninsula	climate
glacier	conterminous states	natural resources
gulf	plain	raw materials
harbor	plateau	

VII. Imaginary Areas of Earth's Surface

   A. North Pole—point farthest north

   B. South Pole—point farthest south

   C. Equator—halfway between the Poles

   D. Arctic Circle—imaginary boundary of the north polar region. It runs parallel to the equator at 66 degrees 30 minutes (66°30') north latitude

   E. Antarctic Circle—imaginary boundary of south polar regions running parallel to the equator at 23 degrees 30 minutes north of the South Pole

   F. Tropic of Cancer—circle around the earth 23.45 degrees north of the equator

   G. Tropic of Capricorn—circle around the earth 23.45 degrees south of the equator

   H. Grid Lines
      1. east-west lines are lines of latitude or parallels (true east-west lines)
         a. guide children in their use of lines of latitude to note places north or south of their city or state. Places on same line of latitude are east or west of each other.
      2. north-south lines are lines of longitude or meridians
         a. true north-south lines
         b. by checking meridians, children can note places east or west of their city or state
         c. places on same meridian are directly N. or S. of each other
      3. latitude and longitude are expressed in degrees noting directions on different map projections and directions to places studied.
      4. Prime Meridian
         a. located on 0° longitude (Greenwich, England) and all other meridians are numbered east or west of prime meridian.
         b. is used to measure time zones for the world

   I. International Date Line
      1. understand reasons for international date line
      2. compute time problems of international travel

   J. Time Zones
      1. Use scale ring to develop this
      2. time in relation to rotation of the earth
      3. time in relation to longitude
      4. time in relation to Prime Meridian and International Date Line
      5. Earth is divided into 24 time zones, each of which is 15° longitude wide—e.g. when clock at Greenwich shows noon, it is one o'clock in afternoon 15° east of Greenwich

VIII. Scale

    A. Always begin teaching scale concept on GLOBE—not on flat map

    B. Each item on map is of right size to match other items

    C. Determine distance on maps by using scale

    D. Compare maps of differing scales; use the scale to compare and to determine distances between places

    E. Compare maps of different areas to note that a smaller scale must be used to map larger areas

    F. Estimate air distances

    G. Check scale on various maps

    H. Use small objects to represent large ones, as a photograph compared to actual size

IX. The State Map

    A. Shape of your state

    B. Relative location of state of Pennsylvania
        1. each state has a location relative to natural features, e.g. (close to or far from oceans)
        2. each state has a location relative to other states
        3. what forms boundaries of your state (is your state a conterminous state?)

    C. Distinguishing features of the state
        1. Find and identify rivers of Pennsylvania map
        2. Find and identify mountains and hills
        3. Find and identify plateau areas
        4. Find and identify various land regions
            a. Coastal plain
            b. Piedmont
            c. Great Valley

    D. Identify major population centers

    E. Highest and lowest points of elevation

    F. Counties
        1. Penna. is divided into 67 counties
        2. Locate (Lebanon Co.) on desk outline map

    G. Locate Harrisburg—capital city of Pennsylvania

    H. Read Pennsylvania road map and be able to plan a trip between cities

COMMUNICATION SKILLS CONTRACT—INTERMEDIATE LEVEL

1. Name_____ 2. Date_____

3a. Weekly_____3b. Daily_____ 4. Checkout Day_____ 5. Time_____

6. a. _____ Reading Titles   Pages
   b. _____   c. _____
      _____   _____
      _____   _____
              Total

7. Group reading with (teacher) _____

   on (day(s), time) _____

8. a. _____Follow-up activities b. Nos. _____

                                          c. Other _____

9. a. _____ SRA Reading
                              b.   Color _____
                              c.   Number _____

10. Imperial Reading Kit
    b. Red_____ c. White_____ d. Lesson Numbers_____

11. Creative writing with (teacher) a._____
    on (days, time)   b._____
    c. Topics _____
    d. Creative writing list (nos.) _____

12. a. SRA Spelling _____
                              b.   Color _____
                              c.   Number _____

13. Spelling with (teacher) a. _____
    on (days, time)   b. _____
    Worksheets   c. _____
    Spelling list   d. _____

386

14. Skills
    a. with (teacher) _____
    b. on (days, time) _____
    c. Worksheets _____

15. Handwriting with (teacher) a.
    b. Where _____
    c. on (days, time) _____
    d. Learning station (activity numbers) _____

16. Learning Stations _____

17. I agree to do the work on this contract

    Signed _____

18. Work completed _____

19. Teacher's signature _____

20. Parent's signature _____

21. Comments:

PRIMARY CONTRACTS

I agree to do this work.   Name _____

ACTIVITIES	LEARNING STATIONS
X	1

GAMES	WORKSHEET OR WORKBOOK PAGES
3	Numbers 3, 6

READING

	Pages
READING BOOK	
Fun With Dick and Jane	5-7
OTHER	
Green Eggs and Ham	10
Total	12

Work Completed_____   Teacher's Name_____

388

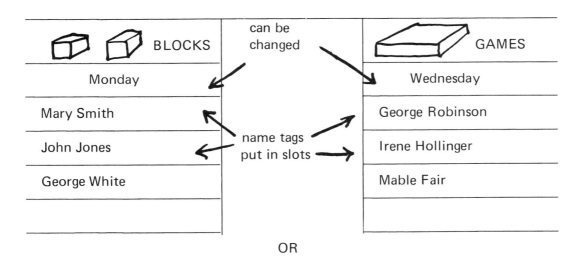

<table>
<tr><td rowspan="2">BLOCKS
Monday</td><td>Mary Smith</td></tr>
</table>

BLOCKS	can be changed	GAMES
Monday		Wednesday
Mary Smith	name tags put in slots	George Robinson
John Jones		Irene Hollinger
George White		Mable Fair

OR

	LEARNING STATIONS				
	Mon.	Tues.	Wed.	Thurs.	Fri.
Number 3	Mary Ann Sue Sal	Ira Bob		Jim Cassie	
Number 4	Ray Dale	Mary Sue Jack		Harry	Arlene
(numbers can be changed) Number 5	Dick Yvonne		Sally Bev Audrey	Elsie	

389

FIGURE 5

MATH CONTRACT

1. Name _____ 2. Date _____

3a. Weekly _____ 3b. Daily _____ 4. Checkout day _____ 5. Time ____

6. Merrill Math Skilltapes

    a. Topic_____

    b. Part _____ c. Steps _____

7. Programmed Math Text or regular Math Text (circle one)

    a. Book _____ b. Units _____ c. Pages _____

8. Group Work with (teacher)_____

    a. on (subject) _____

    b. on (days, time) _____

9. Worksheets in folders _____

10. Learning Stations _____

11. Other _____

    S.R.A. Comp. Skills Kit _____

    Cross Numbers Kit _____

    Math Applications Kit _____

    El. M. Kit _____

    Arithmetic Fact Kit _____

12. Work Completed _____ 14. Parent's signature_____

13. Teacher's Signature _____ 15. Comments _____

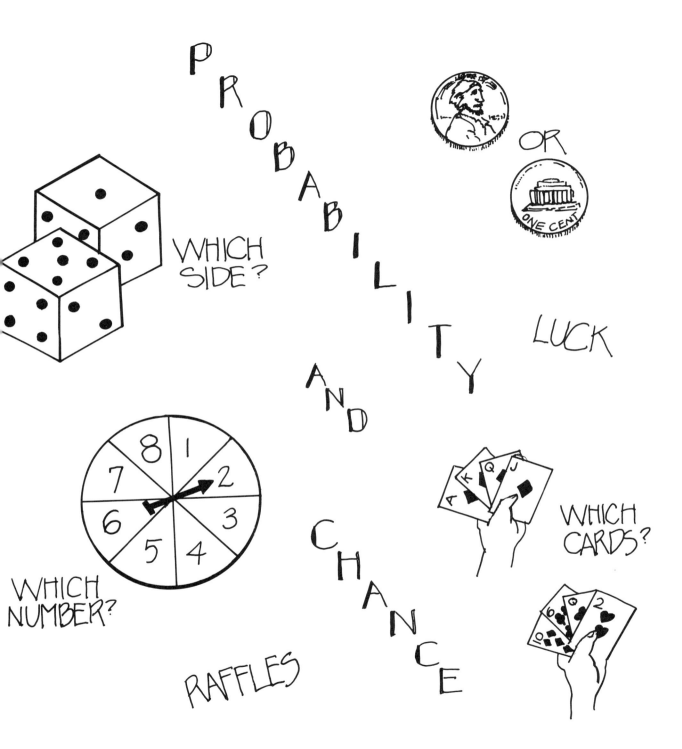

PROBABILITY

OR

WHICH
SIDE?

ONE CENT

LUCK

AND

WHICH
NUMBER?

CHANCE

WHICH
CARDS?

RAFFLES

DIRECTIONS

1. Read this page completely before doing the packet.

2. Read the page entitled "Why Do the Packet?"

3. Take the pre-test and put the answers on the answer sheet.

4. After your pre-test is finished, check your answers on the answer sheet with the pre-test answer key.

5. Each question on the pre-test has a learning activity number in (parentheses) after it. Find the pre-test questions you had incorrect and do the learning activities for those questions. Do those activities to improve your skills.

6. If you had all the pre-test correct, come see me.

7. After you have done the activities, take the post-test. Put the answers on the answer sheet.

8. After your post-test is finished, check your answers with the post-test answer key.

9. Answer the last sheet in the packet honestly. Tell what you thought about the packet.

10. Bring the completed packet to me.

WHY DO THIS PACKET?

This packet offers you the opportunity to learn:

1. the names of men who first worked with probability

2. the ways our government and business use probability to see how much success they will have

3. to define probability and give an example of a probability situation

4. to express the probability of an event happening as a fraction

5. to give the probability of an event occurring or not occurring

PRE—TEST

1. What is probability? (Activity 1)

2. Name an activity you could do that can be tested by probability. (Activity 1)

3. If there are six basketballs in a gym bag and three are brown, two are gold and one is red, white and blue, what is the chance of your *not* picking out a gold one? (Activity 4)

4. Look at this picture.

   Which fraction best describes the probability of someone *not* drinking milk? (Activity 2)

   a) $\frac{1}{1}$ b) $\frac{1}{3}$ c) $\frac{2}{3}$ d) $\frac{1}{4}$

5. Name two men who began working with probability. (Activity 3)

6. In what century did probability start in math? (Activity 3)

7. Jonathan has four pair of pants: two are blue, one is brown and one is grey. What are the chances he will choose a blue pair? a grey pair? a brown pair? (Activity 4)

8. There are four dozen cookies in a jar: two dozen are chocolate chip, one and a half dozen are peanut butter and one-half dozen are oatmeal. What is the probability of your picking out an oatmeal cookie? a chocolate chip cookie? a peanut butter cookie? Express your answers as fractions. (Activity 2)

9. Name three uses of probability in our world today. (Activity 5)

ANSWERS FOR THE PRE-TEST

1. Probability is the chance that something will happen in a certain way.

2. The weather: whether it will rain or not.
   Whether you will go to school or not.
   Whether your teacher will come to school or not.
   Whether you will have pizza for lunch or not.
   Plus many more answers.

3. 4 out of 6

4. c

5. Pascal and Fermi

6. seventeenth century

7. 2 out of 4 ; 1 out of 4 ; 1 out of 4 .

8. $\frac{6}{48}$; $\frac{24}{48}$; $\frac{18}{48}$.

9. taxes   life insurance
   elections   life expectancy
   selling products   card games
   weather   statistics   Any three are fine.

ACTIVITIES

1. Go look up the definition of probability in a dictionary. Write down what you find. Then look up probability in the *World Book Encyclopedia.* Compare the information. With this to help you, write down five things you could do today that have some chance in them. Keep your paper.

2. View a filmloop called "What Are the Chances?" This you will find in the library. When you are finished viewing the film, take a coin and toss it up in the air 100 times. Keep track of the number of times it lands on heads and the number of times it lands on tails. List the results in fraction form.

3. Go to the *World Book Encyclopedia* and look up probability. At the end of the section of probability you will find some names. Go look these up and see what they have to do about probability. Write a paragraph about what you read about each man. Share this information with your friends. You can also check in other encyclopedias for additional information.

4. Do two of the following activities. Compare your results with those of your friends.

    a. Take a coin and toss it up in the air 25 times and record the number of times you get tails and the number of times you get heads. There are only two possibilities: heads or tails.

    b. Then pick a card from a deck of 52 cards and then put it back. Shuffle the cards and then pick out cards 100 times. Keep a record of the cards you pick.

    c. Put your crayons in a bag and pick a crayon. Do this 15 times. What were your chances of pulling out a pink crayon? A silver crayon? Record these results.

    d. Take a thumb tack. Toss it up in the air. Record how many times it turns out "point up," "point down" or on the side.

5. Read the article "Probability" from the *New Book of Knowledge,* p. 470-474. You only need to read the first page and the last four paragraphs on the last page. List ways probability is used today. Do you know any others? Look up probability in a book in the library and see if you find more uses of probability. Try to make one huge list of uses of probability in the world.

POST TEST

1. Mr. Young bought 15 chances on a car raffle. There were 5,721 chances sold. What is the probability of his winning the raffle?

2. In a box, there were four brown marbles, three blue marbles and five red marbles. How many marbles are in the box?
   Does each marble have the same chance of being picked?
   What are the chances of picking a red marble?
   What are the chances of picking a blue marble?
   What are the chances of not picking a brown marble?

3. What is the probability that the arrow will stop on black?
   What is the probability that the arrow will stop on red?

4. Name two men who worked with probability when it first started.

5. What was the century when the theory of probability was started?

6. Define probability.

7. Put an X after each sentence that tells of a situation of chance; it has to deal with probability.
   a. the weather today
   b. the results of a basketball game: winning or loosing
   c. when you were born
   d. what you will have for dinner today

8. There are 6 buttons in a box. The chances of picking out a blue button are 4 out of 6. How many blue buttons are in the box?

9. There are 52 cards in a deck. What are the chances of picking out an ace? a 2? of *not* getting a 9?

10. Name two events in your life that deal with probability?

11. There are 35 boys on a bus trip. Which number best tells the probability of picking a girl to be the leader on the trip?

    a) $\frac{1}{35}$ b) $\frac{1}{20}$ c) $\frac{1}{15}$ d) 0

12. List three modern applications of probability in the world today.

POST TEST ANSWER KEY

1. $\dfrac{15}{5721}$

2. 12 ; yes ; $\dfrac{5}{12}$ or 5 out of 12 ; $\dfrac{3}{12}$ or 3 out of 12 ; $\dfrac{8}{12}$ or 8 out of 12.

3. 2 out of 4 or $\dfrac{2}{4}$; 1 out of 4 or $\dfrac{1}{4}$

4. Pascal and Fermi

5. seventeenth century

6. chance that something will happen in a certain way.

7. a) __X__   b) __X__   c) _____   d) __X__

8. 4 buttons that are blue

9. $\dfrac{4}{52}$ or 4 out of 52 ; $\dfrac{4}{52}$ or 4 out of 52 ; $\dfrac{48}{52}$ or 48 out of 52

10. your own judgment: ask a friend who has already done this packet

11. d

12.
elections	life insurance
weather	business problems
card games	auto accidents
taxes	statistics
life expectancy	

Any three are fine.

FEEDBACK

1. Which activity did you like best?

2. Which activity did you like the least?

3. Which activity did you find the most difficult?

4. Which things didn't you understand?

5. Which face best describes "how you feel" about the packet?

399

The New Stone Age:
What's It All About

Format for a Learning Station
Seventh Grade
Social Studies

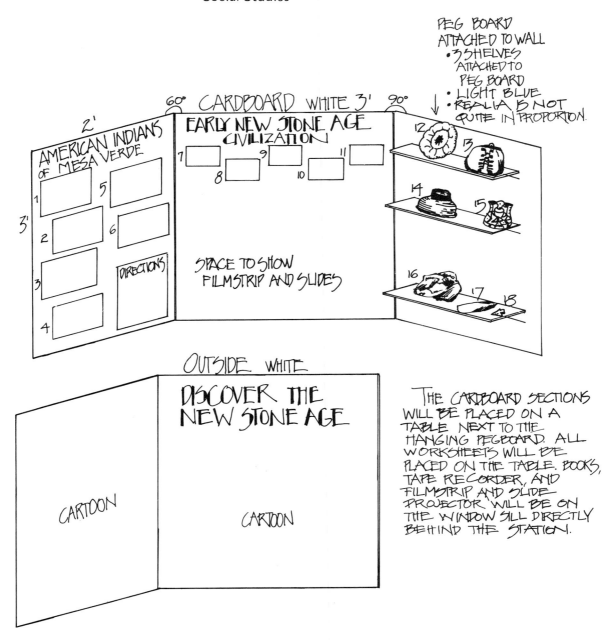

IDENTIFICATION

Large picture cards (6"x9") are pictures of the diaramas at Mesa Verde Museum, Mesa Verde National Park.

1. The Basketmakers

2. The Developmental Pueblo Period

3. The Modified Basketmaker Period

4. Early Man in North America

5. The Great Pueblo Period

6. The Cliff Palace at Mesa Verde (post card)

Small picture cards (3"x5") are post cards of the Indian ruins at Aztec, New Mexico; they have nothing to do with Aztec Indians.

7. Large Kiva

8. Great Kiva

9. Artist's idea of what took place in the Great Kiva.

10. Burial ruins

11. Overall view of the pueblo at Aztec

Realia: these items were mostly obtained in the south-west.

12. Round, woven grass dish

13. Reed basket with lid

14. Black pot

15. Wedding vase

16. Adobe mortar

17. Charred wood

18. Arrow head

DIRECTIONS

1. Read the New Stone Age information in at least one of these books:
   World Background for American History, pp. 28-33.
   Discovering Our World's History, pp. 10-15.
   The Social Studies and Our World, pp. 59-74.
   Building the Modern World, pp. 30-35.
   Long Ago in the Old World, pp. 8-19.
   Out of the Past, pp. 29-40.

2. View filmstrip "Early Man" part I of the Time-Life Series.

3. View videotape "Stone Age Tribes of Mindanao," a *National Geographic* TV special.

4. Do worksheet # 1.

5. Check your answers (in folder tacked on bulletin board).

6. Do worksheet #2.

7. View slides of Mesa Verde and listen to accompanying tape.

8. You may now change answers on worksheet #2 if you want to.

9. Check your answers.

10. Do worksheet #3.

11. Check your answers.

12. Examine the EXTRA ACTIVITY sheet and do one of the suggested activities.

BIBLIOGRAPHY

Eibling, Harold, *et al. World Background for American History.* River Forest, Illinois: Laidlaw Brothers, Publishers, 1968.

Fraser, Dorothy. *Discovering Our World's History.* New York: American Book Company, 1964.

King, Frederick, *et al. The Social Studies and Our World.* River Forest, Illinois: Laidlaw Brothers, Publishers, 1970.

Reich, Jerome, *et al. Building the Modern World.* New York: Harcourt, Brace, and World, Inc., 1969.

Southworth, Gertrude and John Southworth. *Long Ago in the Old World.* Columbus, Ohio: Iroquois Publishing Company, Inc., 1959.

Wilson, Howard, *et al. Out of the Past.* New York: American Book Company, 1959.

ADDITIONAL BIBLIOGRAPHY

Howell, Clark. *Early Man.* New York: Time-Life Books, 1965.

Osborne, Douglas. "Wetherill Mesa Yields Secrets of the Cliff Dwellers," *National Geographic,* CXXV (February, 1964), 155-211.

Shafer, Burr. *Through History with J. Wesley Smith.* New York: Scholastic Book Services, 1953.

MISCELLANEOUS

"Early Man" part I, Time-Life Series Filmstrip.

"Stone Age Tribes of Mindanao" is a videotape of the *National Geographic* TV special, made at Garden Spot High School.

Slides and tape of Mesa Verde prepared by Frank and Karen Herceg (my husband and me) from slides we took in July, 1969.

Pamphlets about Mesa Verde and Aztec National Monument were prepared by the National Park Service and are available from them.

Pictures were obtained at Mesa Verde and were prepared by the National Park Service (cost: $1.25).

Baskets, pottery and adobe were also obtained in the Four Corners area. These are present-day craft items that are made in the same patterns as those of hundreds of years ago.

The charred wood and arrow head are local products. The wood is from my parents' fireplace; the arrow head was found in a field near Bowmansville, Pennsylvania.

Post cards were purchased at the above-mentioned monuments.

WORK SHEET I

1. What are three major differences between the Old and New Stone Ages?

2. What were the geographical features of the areas typically settled by NSA people?

3. What were NSA economic systems based on?

4. Why did NSA people build permanent houses?

5. List as many ways as you can to show how climate affected the way NSA people lived.

6. What did NSA people worship? Why?

7. Who was the religious leader in NSA societies? What were his duties?

8. Why was government needed in NSA societies? How did it develop?

9. Is there any proof that NSA people ever had fun? Explain.

10. List as many jobs as you can that existed in the New Stone Age.

11. Why do you think the NSA was generally very short in comparison with the Old Stone Age?

WORK SHEET II

Study the large pictures in the station.

    1.   Of all of them, which is the only one that could indicate an Old Stone Age society? Why?

    2.   Briefly tell something about each of the other pictures that shows they are of New Stone Age societies.

    3.   Put the pictures into chronological order (use the numbers) starting with the oldest and ending with the most recent.

Study the small pictures in the station.

    1.   Briefly explain what each one is showing.

WORK SHEET III

Study the realia on the shelves in the station.

1. Briefly explain

    A. what each thing is

    B. what each thing is made of

    C. what each thing was used for.

EXTRA ACTIVITIES

1. Make models of NSA tools.

2. Make models of NSA baskets.

3. Make models of NSA pottery.

4. Make models of a NSA house.

5. Develop a play about the NSA, find people to work with you and prepare it for in-class presentation.

6. Make a NSA diarama.

7. Develop a series of cartoons or a comic strip dealing with the NSA.

8. Make a display showing how to make adobe, or thatch, a fish net, canoe, cloth, etc.

9. Pretend you are living in the early days of the NSA. Write a story of your life or keep a diary for a set period of time.

10. Do more research into the Mesa Verde Indians and report on them, or develop some other activities such as these about them.

11. Develop your own Stone Age game that would be a good activity for others to use in reviewing this information.

12. Find an example of a NSA society that still exists. Give a report on it and explain why (you may use your own opinion) those people have not progressed out of the NSA.

GAMES KIDS PLAY TO HELP TEACHERS TEACH

When our school went "open" three years ago, one of our hopes was that the children would learn to cooperate, share, and get along with their peers.

Open Education has helped them do just that. One of the techniques used in open schools and classrooms is learning stations and centers. Our children have been taught by stations for three years, and they have been doing their own stations for 2½ years.

The children in our school do their own stations as a result of independent research. Then they help other children go through them. There have been times when the children helped the teachers teach a unit. For instance, when the intermediate children were studying Pennsylvania, we thought the kids might enjoy making some stations on the Indians of Pennsylvania. So four weeks before the unit started, 8 children were released from their other contract work to study Indians. During the four weeks they researched the topic and set up their learning stations. Then when the unit began, we teachers had each done stations and the eight children had done four so then we had seven stations on Pennsylvania. The children who had worked on the stations became the "teachers" for those stations. Was that good for the station "teachers"? Was that good for the other children? Did it help the teachers?

Here then are some worksheets from stations the children have done:

CHOCOLATE NO. 2

by Kristen Meier
(Student at Elizabeth Jenkins School)

1. How many pounds of cocoa beans grow in Brazil each year?

   _____

2. How many pounds of cocoa beans grow in Ghana each year?

   _____

3. Where do cocoa trees come from? _____

   If you need help, get the book *The History of Chocolate and Cocoa.* Pg. 3.

4. About how many years ago was it before Milton Hershey let visitors come in the chocolate factory? _____

   If you need any help get the pamphlet *Welcome to Hershey.*

   Name _____

CHESS

by Lori Reynolds
(Student at Elizabeth Jenkins School)

What is check?

What is check mate?

How many moves was the shortest game on record?

Who won the first international tournament for the world championship?

How long was the longest chess game on record?

How many moves did it take?

When were the official laws of chess published?

Write a creative writing on the first game of chess you played.

Name_____

Homebase_____

WORLD WAR II

by Tom Wee
(Student at Elizabeth Jenkins School)

Name_____

1. Name three German tanks_____
_____

2. Who was Hitler's girl friend?_____

3. Who started World War II?_____

4. Name one country that was against Germany_____

5. Name one country that was against U.S.A._____

6. Who was in charge of the Africa Corps?_____

"It's a pleasure to read a book that considers the arts as the academic areas, and further, one that suggests how to begin."

Charles Escott, Art Teacher
San Francisco, Cal.

"I student-taught in the situation the authors wrote about, and their freedom with responsibility works. Since I am not now teaching in an open school, I enjoy using their techniques in my 'open' self-contained classroom."

Ms. Alan Valentine, Teacher

"With the kind of atmosphere your people have c one doesn't need magic circles—you are living mag very impressed with the feeling which I felt came youngsters. Everyone seemed to really care. The it was a joyous place."

"John Pflum and Anita Waterman have written a book in the philosophical tradition of the new educators who have not yet witnessed the demise of rigid and highly structured school systems. They are teachers whose message to their colleagues is solidly rooted in the experience of the classroom. Their prose is direct and candid. Their message is clear. Any teacher can open a classroom."

Roy J. Greek, Ed. D.
Director, Falk School
University of Pittsburg

"As a student teacher working for you, and as a teacher working with you, you've encouraged me to provide a classroom atmosphere in which my children can create."

Marianne Dim
Gary, Indiana